Representing East Germany since Unification

Representing East Germany since Unification

From Colonization to Nostalgia

Paul Cooke

Oxford • New York

First published in 2005 by
Berg
Editorial offices:
1st Floor, Angel Court, 81 St Clements Street, Oxford, OX4 1AW, UK
175 Fifth Avenue, New York, NY 10010, USA

Berg is the imprint of Oxford International Publishers Ltd.

Library of Congress Cataloguing-in-Publication Data
Cooke, Paul, 1969-
   Representing East Germany since unification : from colonization to nostalgia / Paul Cooke.
      p. cm.
   Includes bibliographical references and index.
   ISBN 1-84520-188-4 (cloth) — ISBN 1-84520-189-2 (pbk.)
   1. Germany (East)—Civilization. 2. National characteristics, East German.
3. National characteristics, German. 4. Germany—Politics and government—
1990- 5. Germany (East)—In mass media. 6. Civil society—Germany (East)
7. Civil society—Germany. I. Title.

DD289.5.C66 2005
306'.0943'109049—dc22   2005010966

British Library Cataloguing-in-Publication Data
A catalogue record for this book is available from the British Library.

ISBN-13 978 1 84520 188 3 (Cloth)
ISBN-10 1 84520 188 4 (Cloth)
ISBN-13 978 1 84520 189 0 (Paper)
ISBN-10 1 84520 189 2 (Paper)

Typeset by Avocet Typeset, Chilton, Aylesbury, Bucks
Printed in the United Kingdom by Biddles Ltd, King's Lynn

www.bergpublishers.com

Contents

Preface

The picture on the cover of this book, taken in March 2004, is of Aage Langhelle's installation, 'DDR®', which at the time filled the advertising hoardings of one of the many underground platforms at Berlin's Alexanderplatz. It presents the acronym of the old East German communist state in a series of images as if, in the artist's own words, it were simply a 'product logo'.[1] Langhelle's playful re-appropriation of a once vilified political regime highlights an extraordinary shift that has taken place since unification in German society's relationship to this period of history – a shift that is the focus of this volume. On 9 November 1989, in German commonly referred to as the *Wende* or 'turning point', the world witnessed the euphoria of the revellers on top of the Berlin Wall, celebrating the collapse of a structure that had probably been the best-known symbol of the Cold War and with it the beginning of the end of the East German communist dictatorship. 'Now everything [would] grow together that belong[ed] together', the former Chancellor Willy Brandt famously predicted. And, with unification less than a year later, the nation agreed, consigning Germany's failed 'socialist experiment' to the dustbin of history. How was it, then, that some fifteen years later the name of such an unloved regime could become a publicly funded, pop-art exhibit in one of the capital's central stations? How was it, in other words, that by 2004, for some people at least, the GDR had become 'hip'?

In order to answer this question, I trace the changing ways the GDR period has been dealt with since unification, as well as the role played by the east German population within the new Federal state, across a range of cultural discourses produced by both easterners and westerners since 1989.[2] The notion of 'culture' has always played a central role in Germany's self-perception. As early as the eighteenth century, a time when the idea that Germany might one day be a unified political entity was still a distant dream, the concept of the *Kulturnation* (cultural nation) became an important idea around which a German national identity could begin to coalesce. In the unification treaty of 3 October 1990, culture was once again invoked as an important tool in the reconstruction of a national German identity, described in Clause 35 in the following terms:

art and culture were – despite the different development of the two states in Germany – a basis of the continuing unity of the German nation. In the process of state unification of the Germans on the path to European unity, art and culture have an independent and essential contribution to make.[3]

Ironically, however, as Godfrey Carr and Georgina Paul note, 'culture', in the wider sense of the word – that is as a term that not only refers to the aesthetic realm of art, but also to what Wilfried van der Will and Eva Kolinksy define broadly as 'manifestations of political and social organ-ization'[4] – has reflected particularly clearly the tensions within the German national consciousness, as the country continues to negotiate the legacy of forty years of division.[5]

In this study, I understand the concept of culture in a similarly broad sense, looking at the way the GDR past has been represented across a range of phenomena, from society's 'political culture' to that which is traditionally seen as part of either its 'high' or 'popular' aesthetic culture. The aim of this approach is twofold. On the one hand, I examine how far the 'medium is the message', to evoke Marshal McLuhan's oft-quoted but still pertinent maxim,– that is, the extent to which the form and focus of a particular engagement with the past is contingent upon the choice of cultural discourse.[6] On the other, the specific examples I choose allow me to trace developments over time in attitudes across Germany to unifica-tion and the question of dealing with the GDR past. My examination of these examples begins in Chapter 2, where I discuss some of the party-political ramifications of early state-led attempts to come to terms with the legacy of GDR and thus to integrate the eastern population. Focusing on the first Bundestag enquiry, or Enquete Commission into this period of history we see that there was an understandable tendency at the time amongst many of the Federal Republic's political institutions to concen-trate on the GDR's structures of oppression, such as its draconian border regime or the State Security Service, the infamous Stasi. The results of this approach were, however, quite controversial, and provoked a good deal of resentment particularly amongst east Germans. This resentment plays a key role in Chapter 3, where I move on to examine the world of literature and the role played by some of Gemany's key writers in the process of coming to terms with the past. Taking as my example the liter-ary representation of the Stasi, I examine the way some writers sought to question the view of the GDR found in forums such as the *Enquete* Commission, and in so doing find a new public role for themselves in the changing social reality of the unified state. By the end of the decade, while aspects of the GDR such as the role of the Stasi continued to be examined, it was also possible to identify a shift in some spheres towards a view of the past that looked back, at times nostalgically, on the everyday experience of life in the East. It is at this point that the much-debated phenomenon of *Ostalgie* (a conflation of the German for 'east' and 'nostalgia') becomes important. In Chapter 4, I begin my examination of GDR nostalgia by turning to a number of films produced at the turn of the century that first brought the term to the attention of the public at large. The most famous these is Wolfgang Becker's *Good Bye, Lenin!*, a hugely successful film both within Germany and abroad, which critiques some types of *Ostalgie* in a number of interesting ways. Ironically, however, in the wake of its release in 2003 *Good Bye, Lenin!* sparked nothing short of an *Ostalgie* craze, manifest most obviously in a string of popular television shows the following summer, a craze that largely ignored the film's more nuanced engagement with the GDR past, and to which Langhalle's pop-art installation is a somewhat satirical response. It is these television shows that are my focus in Chapter 5, along with the relationship of this *Ostalgie* craze to the broader issue of German consumer culture. Finally, in Chapter 6, I present the findings of two surveys carried out in 2002 and 2004 into the representation of the GDR on the World Wide Web. *Ostalgie* Web sites have, in recent years, attracted a good degree of, at times hysterical, attention in the German press, often being viewed as proof of a dangerous lack of social cohesion, with some Web authors apparently intent upon rebuilding a separate East German state in cyberspace. In this concluding chapter, I question such views, suggesting, instead, that on the Internet we can, in fact, see, more clearly than in many of the other discourses, discussion of some of the more successful aspect of German unification.

The examples chosen are read through the lens of a number of contemporary cultural theorists, most notably Edward Said, Homi Bhabha, and Stuart Hall. All three are connected to the growing field of 'postcolonial studies', an area of enquiry that typically analyses the cultural ramifications of European colonial expansion in the eighteenth and nineteenth centuries. As such, it would initially appear to be wholly inappropriate for an examination of German unification and the legacy of the GDR. However, as I shall discuss in Chapter 1, the language and attitudes of colonization (both from the point of view of the 'colonizer' and of the 'colonized') have pervaded debates about the state of German unity. The use of the colonization metaphor was commonplace, particularly in the early years of unification, but it has not been scrutinized in detail. Clearly the processes of colonization and decolonization addressed by Said, Bhabha and Hall are very different to the situation in east Germany, and one must be careful when applying them in this new context. However, I hope to show how certain aspects of postcolonial theory can shed new light on changing attitudes towards the eastern regions and, specifically, on the way the GDR past has been instrumentalized by both easterners and westerners within cultural debates.

Notes

1. Taken from the artist's description of his installation, Line 2 platform, Alexanderplatz. 'DDR®' was exhibited from December 2003 to April 2004 and was part of the *Kunst statt Werbung* initiative, funded by the *Senatsverwaltung für Wissenschaft, Forschung und Kultur Berlin*, in cooperation with Berlin Transport. For further discussion of the exhibition see Claudia Schwartz, 'Nachgetragene Liebe', *Neue Züricher Zeitung*, 29 December 2003.
2. In this study, I follow the convention of using the lower case 'east' and 'west' for the present German regions, and the uppercase 'East' and 'West' for the pre-1990 states.
3. Quoted in Godfrey Carr and Georgina Paul, 'Unification and its Aftermath: The Challenge of History', in *German Cultural Studies: an introduction*, ed. by Rob Burns, Oxford: OUP, 1995, pp. 325–48 (p. 328).
4. Eva Kolinky and Wilfried van der Will, 'In search of German Culture: an introduction', in *The Cambridge Companion to Modern German Culture*, ed. by Eva Kolinky and Wilfried van der Will, Cambridge: CUP, 1998, pp. 1–19 (p. 2).
5. Carr and Paul, p. 334.
6. See Marshal McLuhan and Quentin Fiore, *The Medium is the Message: An Inventory of Effects*, Harmondsworth: Penguin, 1967.

Acknowledgements

I would like to thank a number of institutions for their support during this project: the Alexander von Humboldt-Stiftung for providing me with funding to study at the University of Potsdam in 2003, along with the Arts and Humanities Research Board and the Deutsche Akademische Austauschdienst for giving generous financial support, as well as the Department of European Languages, University of Wales Aberystwyth and the School of Modern Languages and Cultures at the University of Leeds. At Leeds, I am particularly indebted to the German Department, for time away from teaching and various travel grants. I would also like to thank the staff of the Literary Archive in Marbach and the Hochschule für Film und Fernsehen in Potsdam for their assistance in locating material, as well as Patrick Stevenson for helping me find copies of certain television shows. Thanks also to those individuals who completed my Internet questionnaires, and to Anna and Helen Cooke for helping me collate their responses. Furthermore, I am grateful for the comments and advice of a number of good friends and colleagues who have engaged with my work and have given generously of their time and intellect – in particular Belinda Cooke, Wini Davies, Owen Evans, Frank Finlay, Jonathan Grix, Dan Hough, Bill Niven, Helmut Peitsch, Stuart Taberner and Dennis Tate. Without their support this study would not have been possible. Finally, I would like to thank Alison Fell, who has helped in countless ways in the development of my ideas, who now knows more about east German culture than she perhaps ever would have wanted, and to whom this study is dedicated.

Paul Cooke

–1–

Postcolonial Studies, Colonization and East Germany

Postcolonial Studies began by exploring the relationship between the 'developed' and the 'developing' world, or what was termed during the Cold War the 'First' and 'Third' Worlds, and scrutinized the legacy of eighteenth- and nineteenth-century Western colonization. However, since the late 1970s, postcolonial theory has been used in reference to an ever-broader field of enquiry, appropriated, as Ella Shohat notes, to comment on the experiences of indigenous peoples from Algeria and India to New Zealand and North America.[1] No longer necessarily confined to the study of the legacy of European colonialism, references to postcolonial theory appear in examinations of a wide array of historical moments and inter-cultural encounters. This has laid the field open to the charges of having become so broad as to be of no real analytical use. Russell Jacoby, for example, sees it now as nothing more than an intellectual craze, 'the latest catchall term to dazzle the academic mind'.[2] It is within the context of this recent explosion of interest that German studies has begun to engage with postcolonialism, an engagement that might at first glance appear to confirm Jacoby's fears. Might this recent growth in interest not be viewed simply as a form of intellectual 'me-too-ism', an attempt by Germanists to show that they can also be a part of this fashionable academic discourse? After all, Germany's colonial empire hardly rivalled that of France or Britain, countries whose colonial legacies are more obviously open to interpretation by postcolonial theoretical tools.

However, over the last decade a number of volumes have been produced that argue that, although Germany's colonial history might have been brief, it cannot be ignored. From the early 1990s we begin to find studies using postcolonial theory to examine the effects of German colonial expansion, focusing, for instance, on the consequences of German influence in Togo or Samoa in the late nineteenth century. Moreover, commentators have explored points of correspondence during the colonial period between German attitudes towards the peoples of Central Asia or Africa and those of other European metropolitan cultures. In so doing,

1

they have revealed how German culture, as a product of the Western world, has always been inflected by, and consequently implicated in, the process of colonization.[3]

Yet, even if we accept that postcolonial theory might be useful for assessments of German culture during the colonial period, its application within the context of unification and the representation of east Germany in contemporary culture would appear to be far more problematic. In this introductory chapter I explore the extent to which such theories do, nonetheless, prove useful, pointing to issues that will be dealt with in more depth in the rest of this study. Initially, I outline the way the language of colonization pervaded discussions of German unification and the place of east Germans within this new society in the 1990s. Focusing on economic developments and structural transformation, I show how unification has been presented as a quasi colonial 'subjugation' of the east by the west. However, I also highlight the potential limitations of viewing unification in such terms, arguing that the relationship between the eastern and western regions is in fact far more complex than a colonial paradigm might suggest. I then go on to examine the role postcolonial theory can play in bringing out these complexities. Through an examination of the work of a number of intellectuals, writers, journalists and other commentators, I suggest that while the notion of the west having simply colonized the east may or may not be questionable, *perceptions* of colonization nonetheless have important implications for the way both east and west Germans relate to the unified state and the legacy of the past.

The East as a 'Colony' of the West?

In their study *Kolonialiserung der DDR* (*Colonialization of the GDR*), thus far the most in-depth study to argue that the transformation process in the eastern regions is indeed one of colonization, or of what they term 'colonialization', Wolfgang Dümcke and Fritz Vilmar suggest:

> If one equates colonialization not with the invasion of colonial troops ... with massacres of 'natives' etc., but rather focuses on the fundamental issues: the destruction of an 'indigenous' economic structure, the exploitation of available economic resources, the social liquidation of not only the political elite but also the intellectuals of a country, along with the destruction of ... a population's identity, then one can indeed say that a colonialization process, in the very precise sense of the word, has taken place in the former GDR.[4]

While, Dümcke and Vilmar suggest, the construction of the east as a colony of the west cannot be seen in the same terms as, say, British colonial activities of the eighteenth and nineteenth centuries, it nevertheless remains for them a fitting metaphor to describe what they view as the economic and social subjugation of the former GDR by the FRG. And they are not alone in holding this view. Numerous other commentators provide further evidence that such a process has taken place. For example, in his examination of the transformation of east German intellectual elites, which Dümcke and Vilmar also mention, Thomas Ahbe notes that in the wake of unification three quarters of GDR university academics lost their jobs. The removal of east Germans from this sphere of influence was compounded by the fact that out of the 1878, professors employed in the eastern regions between 1994 and 1998 only 104 came from the east.[5] Similarly, with regard to the other areas of life discussed by Dümcke and Vilmar, several concur that unification did indeed bring about the 'destruction of an "indigenous" economic structure'. The *Treuhandanstalt* (THA), which between 1990 and 1994 was charged with the task of privatizing the industrial and agricultural sectors of the GDR (making it the largest holding company Europe has ever seen) has been accused by many of giving away the 'GDR people's own inheritance' to the west, as Wolfgang Richter puts it, which in turn led to massive levels of unemployment and social instability, the likes of which had never been experienced during GDR times, and which at present still show no signs of abating.[6] This sense of social instability was further aided by the decision to allow property confiscated by the authorities in the GDR to be returned to its original owners (the 'Restitution before Compensation' law), a decision that has left many in the east uncertain about the security of their living arrangements.[7] Daniela Dahn, one of the most strident voices of east German dissatisfaction, claims in her best-selling *Westwärts und nicht vergessen* (*Westwards and Not Forgotten*) that in the wake of unification east Germans lost all independence, and became nothing more than colonial vassals, forced to become 'fatally dependant' on the whims of the former owners of property, this dependency then reflecting the broader state of the east-German economy: 'An economy that was in crisis, but nevertheless still capable of supporting itself, was forced into being kept alive by a drip feed of western money and goods.'[8] For Dahn, east Germans are the defenceless victims of western market forces that have killed off the indigenous economy of the GDR in order to expand their power eastwards. Continuing this trend of criticism, one might also argue that the currency reform of July 1990, in which the Deutschmark was introduced to the east at an exchange rate of 1:1, made east German assets, in Eric Owen Smith's words, 'hopelessly overvalued', and consequently east German products 'highly uncompetitive'.[9] Thus, from this perspective, unification might be seen as the deliberate eradication of eastern economic structures by the west, making under-standable the feeling amongst parts of the eastern population that they are being treated, in Gordon Ross's words, as 'second-class Germans' within the unified state.[10]

However, for others such dissatisfaction has been greeted with a good degree of frustration, not least since it was clear from the outset what unification would mean. Wolfgang Schäuble, former leader of the CDU and in 1989/90, as Minister of the Interior, the man in charge of negoti-ating the unification treaty with the GDR, made this plain in his address to the east German people at the time:

> My dear citizens, what is taking place here is the accession of the GDR to the Federal Republic, and not the other way around. We have a good *Grundgesetz* (Basic Law), which has proved its worth. We will do everything for you. You are very welcome to join us. We do not wish callously to ignore your wishes and interests. However, we are not seeing here the unification of two equal states. We are not starting again from the beginning, from positions that have equal rights. The *Grundgesetz* exists, and the Federal Republic exists.[11]

The German federal government saw it as its place to welcome the new eastern members into its fold, rather than to merge with the GDR. Clearly the East German population was also largely happy with this arrangement because the vast majority voted for unification under these terms.[12] It is beyond doubt that many easterners have suffered, and continue to suffer, very real economic hardships. Nevertheless, unification has also brought huge material advantages. Leaving aside the obvious immense benefits of bringing about the downfall of a corrupt, authoritarian regime that would regularly abuse the human rights of its citizens, 1250 billion euros had been invested in the eastern regions by the German government by 2003.[13] The majority of this money has come via transfers from the west. The burden of 'paying' for the east, as it is often viewed by westerners, has profoundly effected western society, bringing not colonial glory but economic crisis and with it a good deal of resentment.[14] In the east, however, and as Mike Dennis notes, it has provided the population 'with a far higher level of social security and consumer power than in any other post-communist state'. By the end of the century wages were up to 80 per cent of levels in the west, which compares to 55 per cent in 1991.[15] This is, as Dennis also points out, far higher than in any other former Soviet bloc country.

In relation to the transformation of the GDR's infrastructure, too, the eastern regions can in places hardly be seen to be the poor relations of the west. Rather than unification being a process of colonization, the west

German journalist Claus Detjen, for example, argues that 'throughout the east once grey cities, dilapidated villages and stinking industrial areas have become blossoming landscapes'.[16] Evoking here Helmut Kohl's prophesy of the 'blossoming landscapes' that, the former Chancellor claimed, would be found all over the former GDR after unification (a prophesy that has since been much criticized in the east), Detjen points to the great strides that have been made to overcome the structural decay of four decades of neglect, hardly the behaviour of a malign colonial power intent solely on exploitation. These he outlines in detail:

> the extensive protection of the environment, an efficient system of listing buildings, of renovating and building new accommodation ... the replacement of a primitive public transport infrastructure and telecommunications system, along with the development of sports facilities for the general public ... The territory of the GDR has now reached, since the state's demise, that which it had always pretended to achieve, not without success, in its propaganda: a world-class level.[17]

Ironically, he claims, it is only since the demise of the GDR that it has become the world-beater it always put itself forward as in its propaganda. Indeed, with regard to its communications and transport infrastructure, in many cases the east has reached a standard more advanced than anything to be found in the west. Examples often cited are Leipzig's state-of-the-art main station, or the digital telecommunications network in the eastern regions, which any of the world's leading economies might envy.

Furthermore, if we return to some of the evidence cited as proof of the colonization of the east by the west, it is at times possible to use the same evidence to question this thesis. Regarding the issue of the role of the THA and the privatization of the GDR's industry, discussed by Richter and Dahn, Alun Jones suggests that, far from simply selling off the east Germans' 'inheritance' and casting them aside, the organization did its best to protect east German companies and jobs, flying in the face of free-market considerations and forcing the organization to run up huge public debts.[18] Others, such as the FDP politician Günter Rexrodt, argue that there was no other way the government could have faced the mammoth task of dealing with such a decrepit economy. What is noteworthy is *not* that the THA made mistakes – these were unavoidable given the scale of the operation – but that it actually managed to turn *any* of the businesses in its charge into viable concerns.[19] One might also return here to the question of monetary union. This may have turned out to be problematic for east German business, but there is no doubt that the population at large enjoyed the cash windfalls generated by this political decision, which so obviously went against the economic arguments.[20] Indeed, if one compares this monetary union with the postwar currency reform in the western zones, east Germans' savings in 1990 fared much better than those of West Germans in 1948.[21]

For some easterners, too, such widespread disappointment is simply unacceptable. Rainer Eppelmann, the conservative east German politician and the head of the first inquiry commission into the historical appraisal of the GDR (the Enquete Commission, to be discussed in Chapter 2), views many of his fellow citizens as no better than spoilt children:

> The disappointment is as large as the illusions were. Today, the relationship between people from Dresden and Düsseldorf, Rostock and Hamburg is plagued by misunderstandings. The difficulties that we face are, of course, a product of this enormous project 'German Unity'. And we act like children who have asked for ten Christmas presents, but who have only got five, and cannot enjoy the ones they have because they did not get the others.[22]

In Eppelmann's view, east Germans had unrealistic expectations about unification and it is these expectations, not the process of unification itself, which are to be blamed for present levels of dissatisfaction. Here Eppelmann gestures towards what Bill Niven has identified as an east German tendency of 'self-exclusion', whereby the idea of western colonization is used as a means of avoiding taking an active part in dealing with present problems.[23]

For a number of commentators, that many east Germans had unrealistic expectations of what unification would mean is even more worrying than Eppelmann suggests because there is little hope of radical improvement in their lot. Some now argue that, rather than eventually 'catching up' with the affluence of the west, the reality of life in the east is, in fact, the shape of things to come for all Germans. The social scientist Lawrence Mcfalls, for example, suggests that 'the shock therapy of unification' and concomitant rapid implementation of capitalism have left the eastern regions with a social system that has more in common with American *laissez faire* neo-liberalism than with the protective Social Market Economy of West Germany. As such, Mcfalls argues, east Germans can now be seen to be 'ahead of westerners on their common path to a neoliberal global society'.[24] If this is the case, then any perceived colonization of the eastern regions might best be viewed as a microcosm of a broader process, in which the whole of Germany is being subjected to the 'colonizing' forces of globalization. As such, rather than constructing east Germans as victims of unification, might it not be better, in concurrence with the commentator Wolfgang Engler, to see them as the country's 'avant-garde', holding the key, for better or worse, to the necessary restructuring of societal relations and of working patterns in Germany that globalization is setting in train?[25]

Finally, if we turn once again to Dümcke and Vilmar's characterization of unification as a process of colonization, the most curious aspect of their claim would appear to be that the *Wende* brought with it the destruction of an east German identity. After all, many commentators point to what they see as the *creation* of a sense of east German distinctiveness since unification, not so readily found, it is argued, during GDR times. Elisabeth Noelle-Neumann, for example, suggests that in 1990 the majority of former GDR citizens saw themselves as first of all German and then east German, but that by 1994 the inverse was the case, and indeed continues to be so, as more recent polls have identified.[32] East German Protestant pastor, and the man tasked with setting up the agency to investigate the activities of the Stasi, Joachim Gauck, further confirms this development, speaking for many when he claims, 'I never wanted to feel like a GDR citizen. My pride, my understanding of democracy and freedom would not allow it ... But since the division has gone, I feel that I am definitely an east German'.[27] Ironically then, this apparent growth in the relevance of an east German identity would seem to point to another aim of GDR propaganda which was only achieved after the state's demise. For much of its history the ruling party of the GDR, the SED (*Sozialistische Einheitspartei* – Socialist Unity Party) consciously tried to create a sense of a 'GDR people', which would view itself as being distinct from the 'German people'. Consequently, it would appear that, like their claim to be on a 'world-class level' in terms of infrastructure, it was only after the end of the GDR that the party's goal was realized.[28]

Of course, to say that *no* sense of 'east Germanness' existed before 1989 is an oversimplification. As Joanna McKay points out, although there was very little evidence of the kind of 'socialist nationalist consciousness' amongst east Germans that the SED wished to instil into the population, there was a general sense of east Germanness 'based on the everyday experience of day-to-day socialism', and it is this identity that has become more pronounced since the *Wende*.[29] Nevertheless, whether 'east Germanness' as an identity marker existed before 1989 or not, what is indisputable is the level to which it has been viewed as a hindrance to the goal of 'inner unity'. This is the moment that most people still see as some way off, the moment when the chants of the demonstrators on the East German streets in 1989 of 'We are one people' ('Wir sind ein Volk'), as their goal changed from the reform of the GDR to unification,[30] will finally be realized, and when the much lamented 'wall in the head', which still ostensibly divides the German national consciousness will at last be dismantled.[31] For example, in his analysis of the second government enquiry into the historical reappraisal of the GDR period, the SPD delegate and west German academic Bernd Faulenbach echoes commonly held views about expressions of 'east Germanness' when he claims that during the meetings of the commission:

> the east Germans began defiantly (*trotzig*) to defend their identity. However, this tended to lead to the defence of aspects of the GDR past. To distinguish between those parts of GDR history which could be defended and those which were worthy of criticism proved difficult ... leading to a weakening of the critique of the SED-System. This partial nostalgia was not aimed at bringing the GDR back, it did, nevertheless, undermine critical views.[32]

Specifically, Faulenbach points to two concepts that are found throughout discussions of east German self-understanding, both of which are central to the analysis offered in this present study. First, he describes east Germans as 'trotzig' (defiant) in their attempts to assert a sense of being different to westerners. Second, Faulenbach claims that such defiance brings with it a nostalgic re-reading of the GDR. Although he argues such manifestations of nostalgia do not necessarily point to a wish amongst east Germans to have the SED regime back, they do, he claims, nevertheless undermine honest appraisals of the past, and as such are counterproductive to the present process of integration. *Ostalgie*, the word commonly used to describe such phenomena, first coined, according to the east German writer Thomas Brussig, in the early 1990s by the Dresden cabaret artist Uwe Steimle, is presented by Faulenbach as nothing more than a form of selective amnesia.[33] From Faulenbach's point of view, such nostalgia views the former East German regime through rose-tinted spectacles, idealizing it as a land uncontaminated by capitalism's vicious selfishness, and is something, he suggests, that will continue to exist until the economic and social asymmetries between east and west have been overcome.[34]

Faulenbach, like many others, views expressions of east Germanness as a *Trotzidentität* or 'identity of defiance', based on present-day dissatisfaction that manifests itself in a nostalgia for the past.[35] Throughout my examination of the changing representation of the GDR in contemporary German culture, as well as the place of east Germans within the unified state, I explore the tensions between these past and the present elements in east German self-perception.[36] In other words, I am concerned with the manner in which the legacies of the GDR are being both accommodated and inflected by the present-day problems the east German population faces as it comes to terms with the everyday reality of capitalist society. Clearly, it is problematic to see the concept of east and west Germans, or as they are often described in popular discourse *Ossis* and *Wessis*, as singular and homogeneous entities. An individual's sense of his or her identity is the product of a wide range of factors, including age, social class, gender, ethnicity and sexuality. Nevertheless, continuing our focus for the moment on the population of former GDR, while it might be going too far to go to suggest that 'east Germanness' has developed into a new ethnicity, as Marc Howard somewhat provocatively argues,[37] Dennis, for example, notes that within unification debates, 'east Germanness' can, nonetheless, be perceived as a distinctive phenomenon, one 'which transcends ... traditional regional disparities', and which is consequently worthy of specific enquiry.[38]

In this study, I take the notion of 'east Germanness' transcending 'regional disparities' still further, arguing that the east, and particularly the set of values with which east Germanness is often imbued, ultimately provide a discursive space for people in *both* the east and west to explore their relationship to the unified state. For example, I examine how the representation of the east is at times shaped by westerners' fears about their *own* place in society, as the unified state attempts to deal with the problems of integrating its population, of social restructuring in the face of globalization and of its changing role in the world's community of nations. At the same time, as we saw in the comments by Eppelmann, not all east Germans are as dismissive of the trajectory of unification as the notion of an 'identity of defiance' might suggest. Consequently, we can see that unification debates cannot be defined wholly in east/west terms. The geographical boundaries at times blur, or, perhaps more accurately, these boundaries are used as a vehicle for political positions that are not necessarily contingent on where an individual is from.

Postcolonial Theory in an East German Context

It is in connection with our discussion of the east as a discursive space that postcolonial theory becomes a useful analytical device. However, before we can apply the work of postcolonial theorists to cultural representations of east Germany, there are still a number of potential objections to be addressed. The first objection to the use of postcolonial theory in this context that one might have is semantic. What use is *post*colonial theory when east Germany is viewed as currently being *colonized* by the Federal Republic? This criticism can be answered in a number of ways. First, one might adopt the definition of postcolonial studies given by Bill

Ashcroft, Gareth Griffiths and Helen Tiffin, who use the term 'postcolonialism' as shorthand for the entire range of experiences set in train by the process of imperial expansion, of which colonization and decolonization are key elements, because, as they argue, there is 'a continuity of preoccupations throughout'.[39] Second, east Germany appears more obviously 'postcolonial' if we accept David Chioni Moore's contention that the 'post- in postcolonial' is the same as 'the post- in post-Soviet'. East Germany, along with other former Eastern-bloc states, is emerging from a period during which it was subject to Soviet authority, although, as we shall see in the next chapter, the 'post-Soviet' status of the former GDR differs in a number of ways from other Eastern bloc countries due its absorption into a pre-existing western democracy.[40] Indeed, perhaps one might only consider east Germany to be overtly 'post-Soviet', in the way that Poland or Hungary were, in its brief reformist phase, or even perhaps during the GDR's still briefer democratic incarnation, that is from the state's first free elections in March 1990 to unification in October. Nevertheless, it remains the case that if the east is now the victim of a new form of colonization at the hands of the west, as some contend, this would appear to conform to the experience of many former colonies that find themselves to be simultaneously subject to both postcolonial and neo-colonial forces, as their old masters are replaced by 'free markets' and trade agreements which bring with them new, and perhaps equally debilitating, constraints.[41]

A more insurmountable barrier to the use of postcolonial theory in an east German context might be the question of ethnic difference, or rather lack of it, because virtually all of the colonial encounters read through a postcolonial lens involve the domination of one ethnic group by another. While, as I noted above, Howard argues, albeit for polemical purposes, that east German post-unification distinctiveness can be seen as a form of ethnicity, for most this is an argument too far. Ultimately, there is nothing ethnically different between Germans on either side of the Elbe. Yet, how far is ethnicity the defining element of postcolonial studies? One of the key characteristics of east Germany's colonization by the west in Dümcke and Vilmar's view is what they perceive to be the destruction of east Germany's indigenous economic structures. And for some postcolonial theorists it is, indeed, economic rather than ethnic imbalance that is the key common denominator of colonial encounters. In Ania Loomba's examination of European colonization and decolonization, for example, she suggests: 'The essential point is that although European colonialisms involved a variety of techniques and patterns of domination ... all of them produced the economic imbalance that was necessary for the growth of European capitalism and industry'.[42] In a similar fashion to Ashcroft,

Griffiths and Tiffin, implicit in Loomba's analysis is the conflation of the concepts of 'colonial' and 'imperial'. Echoing Lenin's formulation of imperialism as the 'highest stage of capitalism', the question of ethnicity for Loomba is a mask to hide the more fundamental point that imperial expansion and colonization are further forms of capitalist economic exploitation.[43]

Of course, as we have seen, for some it is highly contentious to see the takeover of the east by the west as nothing more than a sinister moment of imperialist expansion. However, the final utility of postcolonialism for my study does not rest upon whether the socio-economic circumstances in east Germany resemble those of other colonial encounters. What matters is the widespread *perception* that a process of colonization has taken place, and how this perception has entered culture, both implicitly and explicitly. Thus, to whatever extent the claim of economic colonization might be refuted, postcolonial theory nonetheless provides a useful framework for tracing developments in cultural attitudes towards the east. In the course of this study we shall see that such theory allows us to identify, for example, what at times might well be viewed as the problematic manipulation of eastern past experience for political purposes, and which perhaps makes understandable the sense of colonization and marginalization some easterners feel. However, it also helps to locate the limits of such perceptions, thereby ultimately offering us a more nuanced image of east-west cultural relations than the metaphor of colonization might at first suggest.

East Germany as the West's 'Orient'

One of the founding texts of Postcolonial Studies is Edward Said's *Orientalism* (1978).[44] A specialist in English literature, Said examines the representation of the Eastern world in Western academic and literary discourses, suggesting that Western images of what he identifies as 'the Orient' have little to do with the actual geographical space they pretend to represent. Instead, they are concerned with propping up colonialist feelings of superiority. 'The Orient', for Said, is 'always in the position of both outsider and of incorporated weak partner for the West'.[45] Central to this asymmetrical power dynamic are the set of values with which the West imbued the East. He argues that 'the Orient', particularly in the eighteenth and nineteenth century, was defined wholly in terms of 'its sensuality, its tendency to despotism, its aberrant mentality, its habits of inaccuracy, its backwardness', values which in turn helped to establish an equally imagined antithesis, 'the Occident', inhabited by the colonizing West.[46]

Although the frame of reference Said uses is very different from that of east Germany, within the economy of stereotyping found in unification debates, one does comes across strong echoes of his 'orientalist' value system. Ingrid Sharp, for example, points to a similar power dynamic to that which Said identifies in his construction of the East as the 'weak partner' of the West. She sees this in the manner that gender-inflected terms permeated discourses surrounding the events of unification. She suggests, 'The union had strong fairy tale elements; star-crossed lovers kept apart by feuding relatives united at last, Cinderella rescued from servitude and exploitation by the handsome Prince.'[47] However, as Sharp goes on to point out, 'assigning the female role to the GDR goes further than simply *describing* the power relations between the two states; it strongly influences the way the GDR is perceived and actually normalizes assumptions which would otherwise appear extremely inequitable.'[48]

As we saw in Schäuble's comments, the inequitable nature of the relationship between the two former states was inscribed into the very unification treaty. It was not a union of equals but an eastern accession to the west. In the next chapter, where I examine some of the judicial and political attempts to deal with the GDR past, this sense of inequality returns as a key factor in the unified state's reading of history. While it is undeniable that the Federal Republic was the more democratic, and in this sense the superior of the two systems, as we shall see, in some of the processes discussed we at times find the problematical equation of the GDR with the Nazi dictatorship in order to underline this superiority and thereby to legitimize the expansion of the West German state. As such, the nation's authoritarian past is constructed as an illegitimate historical trajectory, or in Said's terms, as Germany's evil, 'orientalist' other which stands in stark contrast to the enlightened Federal Republic.

More problematic have been some popular constructions of the east German population itself in orientalist terms. One particularly crass literary example of this is Luise Endlich's bestselling *NeuLand: Ganz einfache Geschichte* (*New Land: Very Simple Stories*), which gives an account of the author's experiences when she moved from Wuppertal to Frankfurt an der Oder.[49] *NeuLand* is packed full of negative orientalist stereotypes about easterners. The inhabitants of Frankfurt, to which she refers by the generic name 'Oststadt' throughout, are seen as primitive, brutal and money-grabbing, with no idea about the benefits of capitalist culture. Instead of embracing what she sees as the opportunities of unification, she finds a population that still worryingly harks back to Germany's authoritarian past, which, to return to Said, apparently provides proof positive of the continued existence of a backward 'aberrant mentality' within the nation that must be educated in the ways of the west's democratic, post-materialist consumer culture, if inner unity is ever to be achieved.[50]

Throughout this study we shall see that this type of orientalism, albeit it in a generally more subtle form, continues to play a role in German representations of the GDR. However, we shall further see that this is not the only version of the east in contemporary culture that draws on what can be viewed as an orientalist value system. For example, another important, and slightly less derogatory trend, is the construction the east, in its 'backwardness', as the preserve of a more authentic German tradition, and specifically one that had not been 'corrupted' by what is often viewed as the postwar Americanization of the Western society, a development that has itself been described as an example of an ideological colonization.[51] Hans Pleschinski's autobiography *Ostsucht* (*Craving the East*), for example, gives an account of growing up in the 1960s and 1970s in a West German village near the border with the GDR, examining the rapidly changing nature of life in the West at the time, due to the US-aided postwar 'economic miracle'. He then contrasts this with his experience of visiting his relations in the East, a place that he constructs explicitly as his 'German Orient', where genuine German values and concepts of family life can continue to exist unchallenged.[52]

Although Pleschinski is far less critical of life in the East than Endlich, it remains for him a more 'primitive' state and, for better or worse, a moment of continuity with Germany's pre-war past, through which comparison is made with post-unification Westernized society. In other orientalist cultural representations of the East, however, the relationship between the East and the West is more complex. In the years since unification, it has gradually become clearer that 3 October 1990 did not simply mean the expansion of the old FRG, but that both former German states, to a lesser or greater extent, have had to change. While the east has undergone a rapid and fundamental metamorphosis, in the west there has been a more gradual realization that the old FRG's special status within the world's community is no longer tenable. The intellectual left-liberal consensus that dominated West German society since the student movement of the late 1960s has been increasingly eroded, as Germany becomes involved in international military operations and its Social Market Economy is dismantled in the face of globalization. As I shall explore further in my discussion of film in Chapter 4, in works such as Osker Roehler's Die *Unberührbare* (*No Place to Go*, (2000), or Wolfgang Becker's international hit *Good Bye, Lenin!* (2003), one finds a response to such economic and cultural change in the use of what commentators are now beginning to call *Westalgie*, or a nostalgia for aspects of the old FRG, a counter impulse to the much-more often discussed phenomenon of *Ostalgie*.[53] Yet, what is particularly curious about the cultural examples I examine is that this *Westalgie* paradoxically finds expression in an eastern setting. Consequently, rather than seeing the east as a remnant of a dangerous and primitive German past, the version of the 'Orient' we find in these films is one where artists can nostalgically rediscover what is for them a more ethical value system, which they feel was part of *West* German culture before 1989, and which they then use to critique the late-capitalist, consumer-driven post-unification state. Thus, in such cultural phenomena we begin to see the markers 'east' and 'west' used to represent not geographical positions but a socio-political value system.

'Writing Back': 'Eastern' Values and the Trajectory of Modernity

Not surprisingly, it is not only within western cultural discourses but also those produced by easterners that we find the eastern regions and their history used as a discursive space to reflect upon tensions within post-unification society. Throughout such eastern cultural representations of the GDR, and the process of unification, a postcolonial theoretical framework also often proves illuminating. Returning for a moment to Said, as important as his work was, he received a good deal of criticism for what has been seen as his Eurocentric perspective. Aijaz Ahmad, for example, suggests 'There had been ... no evidence until after the publication of [*Orientalism*] that Said had read any considerable number of non-Western writers.' He suggests that even those he had read had not 'yet been treated with the hermeneutic engagement and informed reading that Said offers so often for scores of Western canonical figures'.[54] This criticism has led in more recent years to the increased investigation and representation of the experiences of the population of the developing world. With the arrival of anthologies such as Ashcroft, Griffiths and Tiffin's, *The Empire Writes Back*,[55] commentators began to explore what they saw as the 'interaction between imperial culture and the complex of indigenous cultural practices'.[56] The focus here is no longer on the 'Orient' as an imagined space to prop up an image of the west. Rather, the voices of the colonized themselves are given a platform.

From an east German point of view, the explicit construction of unification as a moment of economic colonization, such as we see in the work of Daniela Dahn, is, of course, by its very nature an act of 'writing back'. That is, it is always a result of an impulse not only to expose what figures such as Dahn perceives to be the hierarchical relationship between the east and west, but also to give 'authentic' expression to easterners' feelings of alienation which they feel are excluded from, or misrepresented in, mainstream discourse. In Chapter 3 and my discussion of literature, the notion of 'writing back' takes centre stage, as I examine responses by authors to the type of orientalist instrumentalization of the GDR found in many of the public representations of history examined in Chapter 2. Specifically, I look at the role of the Stasi in historical debates, a key institution in the construction of the GDR as the Federal Republic's illegitimate other, the legacy of which has had a profound effect on literary, as well as more broadly intellectual, life in post-unification Germany. Here, I point to the variety of methods writers have used to counter what is often seen as an obsession with the role of this organization, in order to find what for them is a more balanced expression of their past experience as east Germans.

Interestingly, in such 'writing back', as well as in some manifestations of *Westalgie* discussed above, we at times see the return of some Cold War ideological debates on the trajectory of modernity. This is an issue that in recent years has become an important topic for postcolonial theorists and that once again points to connections between postcolonialism and a broader tradition of Marxist critique, such as we find in the work of Ania Loomba. Thus, theorists have begun to question the view of modernity as part of an enlightenment project driven by a set of universal values. They explore the extent to which these values are in actuality the product of a very specific Western intellectual tradition, in order to decentre this tradition's hegemonic position. Couze Venn, for example, points to how 'the becoming-modern of the world and the becoming-West of Europe', meant 'that Western modernity gradually became established as the privileged, if not hegemonic, form of sociality, tied to a universalizing and totalizing ambition'. This, he argues, points to 'a genealogy of the present which reconstructs a particular trajectory of modernity, inflected by the fact of colonialism and of capitalism'.[57] Colonization, in this analysis, is part of a broader process in which a particular version of western European modernity becomes a universal vision of progress, inflected by capitalism.

The obvious influence of Marx on Veen takes us beyond a specifically postcolonial context and provides us with a further point of contact with the legacy of the GDR in contemporary society. Modernity, for Veen, is synonymous with the development of capitalism. The citizens of the GDR, although themselves part of a European tradition, were members of a state that was on the front line of the Marxist-Leninist Eastern bloc during the Cold War. This was a world that, officially at least, had a differing view on the trajectory of modernity to that of the West, one that claimed to provide a bulwark against capitalist expansion. Since unification, particularly amongst the GDR's intellectual elite, one continues to find a belief in the value of the GDR's ideology as a means of countering the western path of modernity. For example, Christa Wolf, probably the most famous of the GDR's intellectuals, although highly critical of the SED regime, has never lost faith in the value of the state's socialist project. Since the GDR's demise, she has continued to engage with its ideas. As Stuart Taberner notes, in Wolf's first post-unification work *Medea*, a reworking of the Greek myth, we are presented with 'a fantasy projection of the realization of the socialist project untainted by the compromises that, in the event, accompanied the transformation of ideals into deeds.' As such, the book 'has less to do with coming-to-terms with the "real" GDR past than with the desire to confront a clearly imperfect post-unification present with a vision of what socialism in the east *could* have been.'[58] It is not only those who were part of the state-sanctioned intellectual elite that now find value in the GDR's ideals. Wolfgang Hilbig, a GDR writer who had no truck with the view of figures such as Wolf that there was much to be salvaged from the East German state while it existed, has latterly held up aspects of its socialist project as a useful corrective to western consumer culture, that is, within the theoretical framework of this volume, as a means of 'writing back' against this culture's dominant position. In his 'Kamenzer Rede' ('Kamenz speech') he echoes the words of Joachim Gauck, claiming that 'Perhaps one day we'll realize that it was by joining the FRG that we became the GDR citizens that we never were before, at least not as long as we were forced to be.'[59] The GDR only made sense once it had been swallowed up by western capitalism. Its authoritarian power having now been destroyed, all that remains are those ideals the SED pretended to hold so dear and to instil in the population. Echoing Wolf's position, in Hilbig's recent work the attempt to assert a defiant sense of east German authenticity is similarly built on an idealized image of the GDR's socialist project. As such, the view of some east German intellectuals and artists in fact comes close to the left-liberal *Westalgie* of certain western figures, an issue to which we shall return. It should be noted here that this apparent idealization of the GDR's socialist project has not been without controversy, particularly within political discourse where it has been central to the survival of the SED's successor party, the PDS (*Partei des Demoktratischen Sozialismus* – Party of Democratic Socialism). As I shall discuss in the following chapter, while other parties have attempted to paint the PDS as an undemocratic legacy of the past in the political landscape of unified Germany, and proof of the dangers of *Ostalgie*, the PDS presents itself, conversely, both as the only authentic voice of east Germans and the embodiment of the GDR's original socialist ideals.

Hybridity and East Germanness

So far, I have examined east German attempts to counter what is perceived to be the takeover of the east by the west. Here we find some east Germans intent upon 'writing back' against the current path of western modernity, thereby trying to locate what they feel to be a more authentic sense of their own identity that predates capitalist 'colonization'. However, in certain aspects of east German culture, and indeed even during moments of such defiant 'writing back', we also find a more ambiguous relationship amongst easterners both to the west and to their own past experience of living in the GDR. Indeed, at times we find this ambiguity problematizes the very metaphor of colonization itself.

In order to discuss such ambiguity the postcolonial notion of 'hybridity' proves useful, a term used to highlight the degree to which colonial culture, as well as colonial subjects themselves, are always constructed both by and through the colonial master culture, as well as in defiant reaction to it. One of the main theorists of hybridity is Homi Bhabha. Bhabha explores the extent to which the colonized are forced to inhabit the space allocated them by the colonizer: that is, in Bhabha's words, how far the colonized is made to 'mimic' the colonial master. Of particular interest for my study is Bhabha's suggestion that, although this forced mimicry is always oppressive in nature, the relationship between the colonizer and colonized is unstable, ultimately affording the colonized the *potential* opportunity to resist their oppression. Describing in this case the colonization of India by the British, Bhabha suggest that the copy of the 'master' the colonized produces was always imperfect, 'almost the same but not white.'[60] For Bhabha, the incongruity between the colonizer and his/her mirror image is central to the inscription of colonizer's authority, bringing the colonized into line with the colonizer's cultural traditions, while at the same time maintaining the inferiority of the colonized 'copy' vis à vis the colonizer's 'authentic' version. However, paradoxically, the process of hybridization described by Bhabha can also lead to the colonizer becoming disconcerted. As Bart Moore-Gilbert puts it in his discussion of Bhabha, 'mimicry produces subjects whose "not-quite sameness" acts like a distorting mirror which fractures the identity of the colonizing subject'.[61] This distortion can, therefore, potentially empower the colonial subject, the imperfect mirror image becoming a means of provocatively returning the gaze of the colonizer: 'the look of surveillance returns as the displacing gaze of the disciplined', implicitly questioning their authority and making the colonizer aware of the non-natural, non-permanent status of their superiority.[62] As we shall see in Chapter 3 and my more detailed discussion of literature, within examples of 'writing back', the notions of hybridity and mimicry, which for Bhaba are unavoidable consequences of the colonization process, find a particular resonance, as authors ironically, if at times problematically, actively inhabit what they see as the colonizer's view of their history in order to subvert this view, and in so doing find a more authentic sense of self.

More broadly applicable to my examination of east German culture, particularly to that produced from the end of the 1990s, is Stuart Hall's development of the type of ideas we find in Bhabha. In his examination of the postcolonial Caribbean, Hall locates two central strands in the politics of identity construction. On the one hand, he argues that one can identify an identity formation 'grounded in archaeology'. This notion of identity attempts to unearth a lost, in Hall's case precolonial, 'true self',[63] in order to discover 'stable, unchanging and continuous frames of reference and meaning, beneath the shifting divisions and vicissitudes of our actual history'.[64] Hall contrasts this idea of an 'archaeology' of identity with what he views as one of 'production', which in turn can be seen as a potentially more dynamic, if more consolatory, form of Bhabha's hybridity:

> Cultural identity, in this second sense, is a matter of 'becoming' as well as of 'being'. It belongs to the future as much as to the past. It is not something which already exists, transcending place, time, history and culture. Cultural identities come from somewhere, have histories. But, like everything which is historical, they undergo constant transformation.[65]

Throughout my examination of east German culture, I examine the relationship between Hall's poles of identity formation, showing how his concepts of 'archaeology' and 'production' provide a useful means of exploring the changing ways in which east, and at times west, Germans have negotiated their place in post-unification society. However, Hall's concept of 'production' proves particularly useful because it also allows us to take into consideration an important issue raised by Chioni Moore in his application of a postcolonial paradigm to examine the relationship between western Europe and the former Eastern bloc. Chioni Moore reiterates the point, already discussed in connection with other theoreticians, that one must be careful when attempting to equate the experience of Central and Eastern Europe with that of other cultures more 'traditionally' demarcated as postcolonial. In this European context, he suggests, rather than always looking to mark their difference from the west, many such cultures are concerned with 'a return to westernness that once was theirs'. For Chioni Moore:

Any traveller to the region quickly learns that what for forty years was called the 'East Bloc' is rather 'Central Europe'. One hears that Prague lies West of Vienna and that the Hungarians stopped the Turk, and one witnesses an increasingly odd competition to be at Europe's 'geographical centre' – the claimants raging from Skopje, Macedonia, to a stone plinth twenty miles East of Vilnius, in Lithuania.[66]

This urge to reclaim ownership of the west was more obviously confirmed in 2003 by the successful referenda in Poland, Hungary the Czech Republic on joining the European Union, as well as the courting of US favour by such countries in their support of the American invasion of Iraq, through which they attempted to align themselves firmly with a Western hegemony.[67]

In many of the cultural phenomena discussed in later chapters, there is a clear trend towards marking difference from the west, manifesting what is often viewed as a reactive east German 'identity of defiance'. In Hall's terms, this can be viewed as an 'archaeological' impulse, with the colonized subject seeking to preserve, or rediscover, an authentic, lost sense of self. However, elsewhere it is possible to find points of correspondence with Chioni Moore's analysis of the post-Soviet world, where he identifies an urge to insist upon the ownership of a Western identity, an identity that nonetheless still allows the individual to express a sense of east German difference, but from within, rather than in reaction to the unified state. Consequently, we can also find examples of Hall's 'productive' pole of hybrid identity formation, in which the individual's past experience becomes a dynamic element in an ever-developing understanding of his or her present-day identity.

On the 'productive' pole it is also possible to locate the limits of the colonial paradigm, with the continuing representation of an East German heritage being merely one factor amongst many within a heterogeneous understanding of German national identity, which may well have implications, as we shall see in our discussion of film, for both east *and* west Germans. As such, some types of 'productive' hybridity finally begs the question how far east German, or indeed west German, distinctiveness need necessarily be seen as a bar to the goal of inner unity, as it is so often presented to be. Indeed, as scholars such as Hans-Joachim Veen and Martin and Sylvia Greiffenhagen contend, might the continuing focus on the question of 'inner unity', found throughout discussions of the state of contemporary Germany, in fact be artificially skewing debates?[68] Veen, for example, argues that the question of 'inner unity' has largely been resolved, given the fact that the vast majority of the population fully accept the democratic structures and institutions of the Federal

Republic.[69] More agreement is not required. For Veen, to continue to worry about the state of national unity is a waste of time, distracting public attention away from more important issues, such as the question of economic restructuring, the continuing problem of unemployment or eastern mass migration to the west. This sense of a broad consensus having been achieved is particularly pronounced in popular culture, most obviously in the use of the World Wide Web observed during my two surveys and discussed in my final chapter. Here we find a continued engagement with the legacy of the GDR, as well as the statement of east German distinctiveness within the unified state. However, unlike the more 'ideological' construction of east Germanness that we find, for example, amongst intellectuals such as Hilbig and Wolf, there is often no suggestion that the values of Western capitalist society are in question. Instead, authors have a more visceral understanding of an east German cultural heritage, which engages with what it means to have grown up with the GDR as an everyday reality. Crucially, however, this is often presented as an experience that can happily coexist with the individual's experience of post-unification capitalist society. Thus, while one can not ignore the continuing problems facing German society as it deals with the legacies of the past, not least of which is the continuing economic crisis that often continues to be presented as a result of economic 'colonization' by the west, nevertheless, on a cultural level can we, perhaps, see east Germans emerging from any ostensible 'colonized', 'second-class' status, into a truly post-'colonial' phase, one where the language of colonization simply no longer has a role to play?

Notes

1. Ella Shohat, 'Notes on the "Post-Colonial"', *Social Text*, 10(2–3) (1992), 99–113.
2. Russel Jacoby, quoted in Ania Loomba, *Colonialism/Post-colonialism*, London: Routledge, 1998, p. xi.
3. Key texts include Sara Friedrichmeyer, Sara Lennox and Susanne Zantop (eds), *The Imperialist Imagination: German Colonialism and its Legacy*, Michigan: University of Michigan, 1998, along with a number of other books cited by them including Arlene Teraoka, *East, West and Others: The Third World in Postwar German Literature* (1996), Nina Berman, *Orientalismus, Kolonialismus und Moderne: Zum Blid des Orients in der deutschen Kultur um 1900* (1997), and Susanne Zantop, *Colonial Fantasies: Conquest, Family, and Nation in Precolonial Germany* (1997).

4. Wolfgang Dümcke and Fritz Vilmar, 'Was heißt Kolonialisierung: Eine theoretische Vorklärung', in *Kolonialisierung der DDR: Kritische Analysen und Alternativen des Einigungsprozesses*, ed. by Wolfgang Dümcke and Fritz Vilmar, Münster: Agenda Verlag, 1996, pp. 12–21 (p. 13). Unless otherwise stated, all translations are by the author.

5. Thomas Ahbe, 'Deutsche Eliten und deutsche Umbrüche: Erfolg und Verschwinden verschiedener deutscher Elite-Gruppen und deren Wertepositionen', *Deutschland Archiv* 2 (2003), 191–206. (p. 202–4).

6. Wolfgang Richter, 'Kolonialisierung der DDR', in *Mut zur Utopie*, ed. by Fritz Vilmar, Klaus-Jürgen Scherer and Ulike C. Wasmuht, Münster: Agenda Verlag, 1994, pp. 98–100 (p. 98). For further discussion of the continuing economic crisis see Stefan Berg et al., 'Tabuzone Ost', *Der Spiegel*, 15 (2004), 24–41.

7. For further discussion of this law see A. James McAdams, *Judging the Past in Unified Germany*, Cambridge: CUP, 2001, p. 124–56.

8. Daniela Dahn, *Westwärts und nicht vergessen: vom Unbehagen in der Einheit*, Berlin: Rowohlt, 1996, p. 12.

9. Eric Owen Smith, *The German Economy*, London: Routledge, 1994, p. 180, for further discussion see Jens Hölscher and Anja Hochberg (eds), *East Germany's Economic Development since Unification*, London: Macmillan, 1998.

10. Gordon Charles Ross, 'Second-class Germans? National Identity in East Germany', in *East German Distinctiveness in a Unified Germany*, ed. by Jonathan Grix and Paul Cooke, Birmingham: University of Birmingham Press, 2002, pp. 55–67.

11. Quoted in Peter Bender, 'Willkommen in Deutschland', in *Zehn Jahre Deutsche Einheit: Eine Bilanz* ed. by Wolfgang Thierse, Ilse Spittmann-Rühle, Johannes L. Kuppe, Opladen: Leske & Budrich, 2000, pp. 13–21 (p. 13).

12. See Detlev Pollack, 'Ostdeutsche Identität- ein multidimensionales Phänomen', in *Werte und nationale Identität im vereinten Deutschland: Erklärungsansätze der Umfrageforschung*, ed. by Heiner Meulemann, Opladen: Leske & Budrich, 1998, pp. 301–319 (p. 302).

13. For further discussion see Berg et al., 'Tabuzone Ost'. *Bundesbank* figures cited p. 25.

14. Mike Dennis, 'Perceptions of GDR Society and its Transformation: East German Identity Ten Years after Unity', in *The New Germany in the East: Policy Agendas and Social Developments since Unification*, ed. by Chris Flockton, Eva Kolinsky and Rosalind

Pritchard, London: Frank Cass, 2000, pp. 87–105 (p. 90).

15. Dennis, p. 90.
16. Claus Detjen, *Die anderen Deutschen: Wie der Osten die Republik verändert*, Bonn: Bouvier, 1999, p. 10.
17. Detjen, p. 30.
18. See Alun Jones, *The New Germany: A Human Geography*, Chichester: John Wiley, 1994, pp. 121–9. For further discussion of the THA, as well as the privatization process more generally, see Owen Smith, pp. 475–99.
19. Interview with Rexrodt cited in Peter Kirnich and Oliver Lönker, 'Abwickler werden abgewickelt', *Berliner Zeitung*, 20 November 2003.
20. Owen Smith, p. 184.
21. See Owen Smith, p. 178–81.
22. Rainer Eppelmann, *Fremd im eigenen Haus- Mein Leben im anderen Deutschland*, Cologne: Kiepenheuer and Witsch, 1993, p. 417.
23. Bill Niven, 'The *Wende* and Self-Exclusion Theory', in *1949/1989 Cultural Perspectives on Division and Unity in East and West*, ed. by Clare Flanagan and Stuart Taberner, Amerstdam: Rodopi, 2000, pp. 87–99.
24. Lawrence McFalls, 'Eastern Germany Transformed: From Postcommunist to Late Capitalist Political Culture', *German Politics and Society*, 2(17) (1999), 1–24 (pp. 2–3).
25. Wolfgang Engler, *Die Ostdeutschen als Avantgarde*, Berlin: Aufbau, 2002.
26. Elisabeth Noelle-Neumann, 'Eine Nation zu werden ist schwer', *FAZ*, 10 August 1994. In 2000 the Allensbach Institute found that this tendency continued. In response to the question 'Do you feel yourself to be predominantly German or east German', 40 per cent responded 'German' and 53 per cent 'east German'. See Elisabeth Noelle-Neumann and Renate Köcher, *Allensbacher Jahrbuch der Demoskopie*, Munich: K.G. Sauer, 2002, p. 525. For further discussion see Jonathan Grix, 'Introduction to east German political and cultural distinctiveness', in Grix and Cooke, pp. 1–14.
27. Joachim Gauck, 'Von der Würde der Unterdrücktn', in *Aktenkundig*, ed. by Hans Joachim Schädlich, Reinbek: Rowoht 1993, pp. 256–75 (p. 268).
28. See, for example, Mary Fulbrook, *German National Identity after the Holocaust*, Cambridge: Polity, 1999, p. 190; Joanna McKay, 'East German identity in the GDR', in Grix and Cooke, pp. 15–29.
29. McKay, p. 25.
30. This shift is usually shown in the change in the demonstrators' claim

'We are the people' (*Wir sind das Volk*), a call to be listened to by the GDR authorities, to 'We are one people', which claimed ownership of a unified German national identity.

31. The term 'wall in the head' has been much discussed with regard to post-unification society. However it was originally coined in 1982 by the writer Peter Schneider, who famously foretold that 'tearing down the wall in the head will take longer than any attempt to pull down the visible wall'. See Peter Schneider, *Der Mauerspringer*, Reinbek: Rowholt, 1982, p. 102.

32. Bernd Faulenbach, 'Die Enquete-Kommissionen und die Geschichtsdebatte in Deutschland seit 1989', in *The GDR and Its History: Rückblick und Revision Die DDR im Spiegel der Enquete-Kommissionen*, ed. by Peter Barker, Amsterdam: Rodopi, 2000, pp. 21–33 (p. 32). A similar point is made by Ian Wallace, 'German Intellectuals and Unification,' *Germany after Unification*, ed. by Gert-Joachim Glaesser, Amsterdam: Rodopi, 1996, pp. 87–100 (p. 97).

33. See Thomas Brussig, 'Mrux, die deutsche Einheit', *Der Tagesspiegel*, 31 August 2003.

34. Faulenbach, p. 32

35. For a fuller discussion of the notion of *Trotzidentität*, see Patricia Hogwood, 'Identity in the former GDR: statements of "Ostalgia" and "Ossi" Pride in united Germany', *Globalization and National Identities: Crisis or Opportunity?*, ed. by Catherine J. Danks and Paul Kennedy, Basingstoke: Macmillan, 2000, pp. 48–59.

36. For further discussion of these aspects of east Germanness see Hans Joachim Maaz, *Das gestürzte Volk*, Berlin: Argon Press, 1991, C. Lemke, *Die Ursachen des Umbruchs 1989: Politische Sozialization in der ehemaligen DDR*, Darmstadt: Opladen, 1991, M. Minkenberg, 'The Wall after the Wall', *Comparative Politics* 26 (1993) 81–103, Jonathan Grix, 'East German Political Attitudes: Socialist Legacies v. Situational Factors: A False Antithesis', *German Politics*, 2(9) (2000), 109–24.

37. Marc Howard, 'An East German Ethnicity? Understanding the New Division of United Germany', *German Politics and Society*, 4(13) (1995), 49–70. It should be noted here that Howard's use of the term 'ethnic' is as a provocative tool to rethink the lack of emphasis on east German difference he identifies in the early 1990s.

38. Dennis, p. 88.

39. Bill Ashcroft, Gareth Griffiths and Helen Tiffin (eds), *The Empire Writes Back: Theory and Practice in Postcolonial Literatures*, London: Routledge, 1989, p. 2.

40. David Chioni Moore, 'Is the Post- in Postcolonial the Post- in Post-Soviet? Towards a Global Postcolonial Critique', *PMLA*, 1(116) (2001), 111–28 (p. 111). See also Graham Smith, *The Post-Soviet States: Mapping the Politics of Transition*, London: Arnold, 1999, pp. 6–9.

41. Loomba, p. 7.

42. Loomba, p. 4.

43. V.I. Lenin, *Imperialism, the Highest Stage of Capitalism*, Moscow: Foreign Languages Publishing House, 1947, discussed in Loomba, p. 5. For further discussion of the links between colonialism and imperialism see Ania Loomba, *Colonialism/Postcolonialism*, London: Routledge, 1998, pp. 1–57.

44. Edward W. Said, *Orientalism: Western Conceptions of the Orient*, Harmondsworth: Penguin, 1991.

45. Said, p. 208.

46. Said, p. 205.

47. Ingrid Sharp, 'Male Privilege and Female Virtue: Gendered Representations of the Two Germanies', *New German Studies*, 1(18) (1995), 87–106 (p. 90) [Sharp's italics]. See also Ina Merkel, 'Sex and Gender in the Divided Germany: Approaches to History from a Cultural Point of View', in *The Divided Past: Rewriting Post-War German History*, ed. by Christoph Kleßmann, Oxford: Berg, 2001, pp. 91–104 (p. 91).

48. Sharp, pp. 90–1.

49. Luise Endlich, *NeuLand: Ganz einfache Geschichten*, Frankfurt/Main: Fischer, 2001.

50. Said, p. 205.

51. The relationship between the FRG and the USA was, for example, famously summarised by Wim Wenders' *Im Lauf der Zeit* (*Kings of the Road*, 1976), where Robert and Bruno, Wenders' protagonists, agree that 'the Yanks have colonized our subconscious'.

52. Hans Plenschinski, *Ostsucht: eine Jugend im deutsch-deutschen Grenzland*, Munich: C.H. Beck, 1993, p. 58. In this connection one might also mention Friedrich Christian Delius's *Die Birnen von Ribbeck*, Reinbek: Rowohlt, 1991, which also constructs the east as the home of an older German tradition.

53. For a discussion of 'Westalgie' see Andrew Plowman, '"Westalgie" Nostalgia for the "Old" Federal Republic in Recent German Prose', *Seminar Special Issue: Beyond Ostalgie East and West German Identity in Contemporary German Culture*, 40 (2004), 249–61.

54. Aijaz Ahmad, 'Orientalism and After', in *Colonial Discourse and*

Post-Colonial Theory: A Reader, ed. by Patrick Williams and Laura Chrisman, Harlow: Longman, 1993, pp. 162–71 (p. 170).

55. See note 39.
56. Bill Ashcroft, Gareth Griffiths and Helen Tiffin, 'General Introduction', in *The Postcolonial Studies Reader*, London: Routledge, 1995, pp. 1–4 (p. 1).
57. Couze Venn, *Occidentalism Modernity and Subjectivity*, London: Sage, 2000, p. 19. For further discussion of this issue see also Dipesh Chakrabarty, *Provincializing Europe: Postcolonial Thought and Historical Difference*, Princeton: Princeton University Press, 2000.
58. Stuart Taberner, *German Literature of the 1990s and Beyond: Normalization and the Berlin Republic*, Rochester: Camden House, 2005, p. 39. For an overview of Christa Wolf's work since the *Wende* see Peter Graves, 'Christa Wolf in the 1990s', in *Legacies and Identity: East and West German Literary Responses to Unification*, ed. by Martin Kane, Oxford: Peter Lang, 2002, pp. 51–66.
59. Wolfgang Hilbig, 'Kamenzer Rede', *Preis- und Dankreden*, Rheinsberg: Kurt Tucholsky Gedankenstätte, 1996, pp. 13–16 (p. 16). For a discussion of Hilbig's pre-*Wende* position see Paul Cooke, *Speaking the taboo: an examination of the work of Wolfgang Hilbig*, Amsterdam: Rodopi, 2000, pp. 1–54.
60. Homi K. Bhabha, 'Of Mimicry and Man: The Ambivalence of Colonial Discourse', in *The Location of Culture*, London: Routledge, 1994, pp. 85–92 (p. 89). Emphasis in original.
61. Bart Moore-Gilbert, *Postcolonial Theory: Contexts, Practices, Politics,* London: Verso, 1997, p. 121.
62. See, for example, 'Signs Taken for Wonders: Questions of Ambivalence and Authority under a Tree outside Delhi, May 1817', in Bhabha, pp. 102–22.
63. Stuart Hall, 'Cultural Identity and Diaspora', in *Contemporary Postcolonial Theory: a Reader*, ed. Padmini Mongia, London: Arnold, 1997, pp. 110–21, (p. 110).
64. Hall, p. 111.
65. Hall, p. 112.
66. Moore, p. 118. This urge to 'own' the centre of Europe has also recently been amusingly explored further in Stanislaw Mucha's documentary film *Die Mitte* (2004), which sees the film-maker travel across an area of 2000 km in search of Europe's geographical midpoint.
67. Ironically, of course, this policy marked these countries out from the majority of mainland West European states. This was not the case in east Germany, where the population was largely against the war, a

position which, whilst distinct from that of America, nonetheless still aligned them with mainstream Western European views.

68. Hans-Joachim Veen, 'Einheit, Einheit über alles: Das Gerede vom nötigen Zusammenwachsen Ost- und Westdeutschlands führt in die Irre', *Die Zeit*, 13 July 2001; Martin Greiffenhagen and Sylvia Greiffenhagen, 'Zwei politische Kulturen', in *Deutschland Ost-Deutschland West: Eine Bilanz*, ed. by Hans-Georg Wehling, Opladen: Leske & Budrich, 2002, pp. 11–34 (p. 17–18).

69. This is further confirmed in the most recent statistics published by the Allensbach Institute, where only 8 per cent of east Germans asked claimed they would like to undo unification. This compared with 14 per cent of west Germans. Noelle-Neumann and Köcher, *Allensbacher Jahrbuch*, p. 500.

–2–

The Federal Republic's 'Orient'? Dealing Officially with the GDR

It is in the months leading up to unification that Chioni Moore's equation between 'postcolonial' and 'post-Soviet' states, discussed in the previous chapter, would seem most apposite in relation to the eastern regions, as a reform-minded GDR government grappled with the political and legal debates surrounding the legacy of forty years of SED rule. Like other former Eastern-bloc societies, East Germany was faced with the problem of transformation from a satellite state of the 'Soviet empire' into a democratic civil society. Central to this transformation was the need to come to terms with the GDR past.[1] As Jennifer A. Yoder points out, East Germany was very quick in setting about this process.[2] Unlike Eastern-bloc states such as Poland, where the post-communist regime instigated widespread amnesties for the country's Cold War rulers, as early as December 1989 GDR political elites sought to prosecute the highest level of the SED, a process that, after October 1990, was taken over by the FRG.

There are a number of obvious reasons why the communist past in Germany was treated differently from that of many other former Eastern-bloc countries. First, this of course has much to do with German unification, an event that made the GDR unique amongst the post-communist states. As Corey Ross suggests, for example, the Federal Republic had far better resources to fund a public reckoning process than many of its neighbours to the east.[3] Second, and more importantly, this was not the first time in recent history that the Germans had had to deal with the legacy of a dictatorial regime.[4] As we shall see, the shadow of National Socialism and the way the Federal Republic dealt with this period of history loomed large in debates about the GDR. Indeed, the relationship between what was being termed the 'first' and 'second' German dictatorships became increasingly problematic as sections of the east German population started to feel alienated from the post-unification transformation process. Instead of appreciating the benefits available to former citizens of the GDR, who unlike those of other post-Soviet states were able to integrate rapidly into a 'ready-made' Western democracy, many were soon concluding that their newly acquired postcolonial/post-Soviet status was in actuality a takeover by neo-colonial forces, forces that were paying little attention to their pre-unification lives, or to the difficulties they were facing in adjusting to the new social reality. Thus, along with the economic issues discussed in the previous chapter, the instrumentalization of history was viewed by many as a further example of a Western 'colonialist' lack of sensitivity, the central bone of contention in this case being the widespread portrayal of the GDR as a totalitarian state in the mould of the Third Reich. Amongst some academics this raised a number of issues, the most fundamental of which was concerned with the scholarly validity of comparing these two dictatorial regimes. More problematic for others was the view that such a comparative reading of the past was more about casting the East German state as part of Germany's 'illegitimate' historical trajectory than about dealing with the actual nature of life there. In terms of the theoretical paradigm outlined in the previous chapter, in a number of official discourses the GDR seemed to be functioning as a kind of Saidian 'Orient', that is as a historical space through which the FRG could self-reflexively distance itself from the whole of Germany's dictatorial legacy and thereby confirm its democratic credentials. However, in the process, many felt that the everyday experience of the GDR population as a whole was being misrepresented.

The first attempts to deal publicly with the history of the GDR focused on the role of its state security force, the infamous Stasi. In the early 1990s newspapers were regularly full of scandalous rumours 'outing' prominent GDR figures as spies. Once the organization's files were opened these scandals began to subside, and a broader, more regulated process of what has been called the 'destasification' of the east German public sector began.[5] In Chapter 3 I look at the role of the Stasi in post-unification debates more closely, exploring specifically its impact upon intellectual and literary life, areas where the organization's influence had broad-ranging ramifications. In this chapter, I wish to examine two other strands in the state-led process of coming to terms with the past that were intended both to complement, and more importantly to keep in perspective, the focus on the role of the Stasi that so gripped the popular imagination. Initially, I look at the way the courts dealt with former GDR officials. The controversies that surrounded these trials reveal early examples of accusations that GDR history was not being treated fairly, but was subject to a 'neo-colonialist' agenda. The examination of the court cases will then provide the context for a discussion of the first Bundestag inquiry, or Enquete Commission into the GDR.[6] This inquiry, it should be noted, did not have the major immediate impact on the general public that its members might have hoped. However, it was clearly indicative of political views that did have major implications for the way German society viewed its past. In the course of this chapter I hope to show that, as with the description of the process of economic transformation, the claim of colonization in regard to east German history is at times problematic. Nevertheless, it is a view that cannot simply be dismissed, not least due to its impact on the political culture of the unified state. Specifically in this regard, I examine how the official process of dealing with the past, and concomitant perceptions of 'orientalism', helped the survival of the East German communist party's successor, the *Partei des Demokratischen Sozialismus*, in the 1990s.

Putting History on Trial

For Yoder, proof of German thoroughness in dealing with the East German past is readily available in the trials of members of the GDR establishment, which, in her opinion, put the FRG 'far ahead of other post-authoritarian regimes in holding old elites accountable'.[7] Moreover, not only was the treatment of the GDR's communist elites more radical than many other Eastern bloc countries, it was also more thorough, as well as more rapid, than Germany's judicial treatment of the Third Reich. After the Nuremberg trials of the surviving key participants in the Nazi regime, and a brief period of general 'denazification', the Allies, and subsequently the Adenauer government (with Allied encouragement), began playing down the need for (West) Germany to continue dealing with its National Socialist pre-history. This, in turn, allowed many former Nazis to be reintegrated into West German society. Indeed, it was not until the 1960s, and the famous 'Auschwitz trials', that some of the perpetrators of Nazi atrocities were brought to justice, and much of the West German population started to face up to its past.[8] After 1989, those who had suffered under the SED were keen to ensure that this time around there would be no such a delay in bringing the instigators and instruments of GDR oppression to justice. With unification, the FRG authorities were obliged to fulfil this wish, in order both to help east German integration and to underline the decision to build the unified state on the basis of West German institutions and structures. But the task was not to prove easy.

The first problem that faced the courts was the legal status of the GDR. For some East German dissidents and members of the citizen movement (who had been instrumental in the events of 1989–90), as well as those vehement West German anticommunists who had attacked the moral credentials of the GDR throughout its history, the 'Second German Dictatorship', like the First, was an *Unrechtsstaat* ('a state not founded on the rule of law'). If this was indeed the case, then dealing with those in power in the East was clear cut. A. James McAdams, for example, notes that for the proponents of the *Unrechtsstaat* thesis, members of the GDR establishment could be prosecuted on the same terms as former Nazis. Just as the post war authorities rejected the commonly invoked defence that individuals were not guilty because they had simply acted according to the laws of the Third Reich, in the case of the GDR,

> no one – from Honecker down to the lowliest border guards – could be allowed to excuse or to justify manifest violations of human rights by claiming that they had operated within the law of their land. To allow them to hide their crimes behind the elaborate web of legal fictions that had been created to give the GDR its veneer of legitimacy, these critics felt, would be to make a mockery of the idea of law as it was understood in the West.[9]

However, there were a number of problems with this position. First, seeing the GDR as an *Unrechtsstaat* in the mould of the Third Reich re-sparked debate on the thorny issue of the status of National Socialist crimes in the German historical record. As I shall discuss in more detail with regard to the Enquete Commission, for some, such comparisons were construed as a cynical political ploy either to underplay and relativize the crimes of National Socialism, or to overstate those of the SED. Second, others felt that the perception of the GDR as an *Unrechtsstaat* was at best problematical and at worst hypocritical given the fact that since 1972, and the signing of the Basic Treaty between the two states, West Germany had itself recognized the validity of the GDR's 'elaborate web of legal fictions', to quote McAdams once more. Although the political elites in the FRG continued to pay lip service to the question of German unification, it had by this stage accepted the existence of the GDR as a political reality, subsequently even welcoming Honecker on an official 'working visit' to the West in 1987. More difficult still for the *Unrechtsstaat* position was that the recognition of the GDR's legal code was enshrined in the unification treaty. Cornerstones of the Federal Republic's Basic Law are the principles of *nulla poena sine lege* and *nullum crimen sine lege* ('no penalty without legislation' and 'no crime without an offence'), or that laws cannot be applied retrospectively.[10] Thus, by recognizing GDR law in the unification treaty, the FRG also accepted that if an act was not illegal during the GDR period it could not now be prosecuted.

Nevertheless, the fact remained that many Germans were demanding redress for violations of human rights in the East. If the newly enlarged Federal Republic was to prove to its new citizens that it was a *Rechtsstaat*, that is one 'founded on the rule of law', it had to show that its constitution could deal with the legacy of this past. The only way to achieve this, it was decided, was to engage with GDR law, and to examine how far human rights violations could be prosecuted within this context. This principle was first put to the test in the trials of former East German border guards, and the implementation of the 'shoot-to-kill' policy ('Order 101') against individuals committing the 'crime' of *Republikflucht* ('fleeing the Republic'). The first of these trials concerned the death of the last person to be shot attempting to escape over the Berlin Wall – Chris Gueffroy, a twenty-year-old man killed in February 1989. The accused guards, like many Nazis brought to trial, employed the defence of 'obedience to superior orders'.[11] In response to this the judges themselves also appealed to the same period, invoking the famous 1946 pronouncement of the legal philosopher Gustav Radbruch that 'positive law', or the reality of the legal code as it is applied, should be followed, up to the point that the injustice of this legal code becomes so obvious as to be 'intolerable'. As Charles S. Meier points out: 'In the Gueffroy case, argued the judges, the "intolerable disproportionality" (*unerträgliches Mißverhältnis*) between the offence of unauthorized border crossing and the preventive execution of the fugitive voided the legal force of the order to shoot'.[12]

However, in later trials other judges questioned the invocation of Radbruch, claiming that this contravened the principles of the unification treaty. In the second border-guard trial, for example, which concerned the shooting of another twenty year old, Michael-Host Schmidt, in 1984, the judge refused to look to a higher code of ethics, finding instead that the guards had broken GDR 'positive law' in that they had used excessive force, shooting the man fifty-two times and leaving him in no-man's land for two hours without medical aid. Consequently, the guards were in contravention of existing East German law, which insisted that they 'preserve human life if possible'.[13] On appeal, this judgement was overruled. In the appeal court's view, attempting to escape the GDR was a crime that, according to border law, could warrant such an extreme penalty. Here the judges sought to recognize fully GDR 'positive law', namely not only the letter of the legal code, but also how it was actually implemented. Nevertheless, the court also found that the East German recognition of the '1966 International Convention on Civil and Political Rights' actually rendered this law invalid.[14] Thus, rather than applying a higher abstract ethical code, the judges invoked a higher level of international 'positive law', thereby following the principles of the unification treaty but still finding the guards guilty.

The border-guard trials at times posed more questions about culpability for GDR human-rights violations than they answered, highlighting the many legal headaches facing judges. Amongst the east German population, they also provoked a degree of resentment, with some feeling that the effort focused on bringing the border guards to trial was wrong-headed. As Yoder puts it, 'Many easterners wondered how justice could be adequately served if only the trigger-men, and not the actual decision makers responsible for the policy "Order 101", [were] held accountable for past misdeeds.'[15] Soon attention did indeed shift to individuals higher up the chain of command, with the spotlight returning to those in the GDR's highest offices, not least the head of the East German state since 1971, Eric Honecker, as well as his short-term successor Egon Krenz, who were indicted for instigating and maintaining the shoot-to-kill policy. However, this shift in focus brought neither relief to the judges' headaches, nor sufficient legal redress for many of those east German critics looking for justice.

The first attempt to bring Honecker to trial had taken place in the immediate aftermath of his ousting by the SED. In an effort by the Krenz regime to give itself legitimacy with a population demanding reform, it set about investigating abuses of power by the former leader.[16] Shortly after this attempt, Honecker went into exile in Moscow, returning to Germany in 1992, when he was put on trial by the Federal courts. This later trial attracted massive attention from the world media. It was not every day that a head of state was to be seen in a courtroom. Yet, frustratingly for many, this much-awaited trial came to nothing. Like most of the major figures in the GDR government, Honecker was a frail old man by the time of his return to Germany, having been diagnosed with cancer in 1990. Under the Federal Republic's Basic Law, individuals are protected from prosecution if they are not fit to stand trial and, although he was initially deemed capable of standing, it was subsequently decided that his health had deteriorated to such an extent that he had to be released without judgement. Krenz, on the other hand, was convicted and after lengthy appeals started a six-and-a-half year sentence in 2000, being released on parole in December 2003.

Other famous trials of this period included those against the GDR's top 'spymasters'. These were particularly controversial. Erich Mielke, the head of the Stasi and one of the most vilified members of the Politburo, could, initially at least, not be found guilty of any crimes under GDR law. Instead, he was tried and convicted of the murder of two policemen in 1931, a judgement that was partially based on dubious evidence collected by Nazi interrogators and that also saw the Federal authorities stretch to breaking point the statute of limitations. He was sentenced to six years, but released due to ill health after two. Even more problematic was the case of Marcus Wolf, the head of the state security services 'foreign' espionage (a role that included the development of intelligence assets in West Germany). He was, rather bizarrely, convicted of 'treason', a charge that was later overturned when the appeal courts agreed with Wolf himself that he could not have committed treason against the FRG since he had not been a citizen of that state at the time. He was, nevertheless, eventually convicted in 1997 to three-and-a-half years for the false imprisonment of others, a crime punishable under GDR law.[17]

Like the border-guard trials, these later cases, too, caused a good deal of resentment amongst some east Germans. Ironically, amongst their critics were some members of the citizens' movement who had been amongst the first to demand that a judicial reckoning take place. As the GDR dissident Bärbel Bohley famously put it, speaking more broadly of the question of legal redress, 'We expected justice, but instead we got the *Rechtsstaat*'.[18] The legal structures of the FRG, it would seem, were proving inadequate in providing the retributions for past wrongs that many in the east thought they would see. Unsurprisingly, however, the loudest criticisms came from those GDR functionaries who were in the dock. In his only statement during court proceedings, Honecker claimed that his trial was unjust as he could not be held responsible for the set of historical circumstances that brought about the rise of Hitler, the Second World War and the division of Germany. With this trial, Honecker claimed, he and his comrades continued to be the victims of history: 'One would have to be blind or consciously close one's eyes to the events of the past ... to fail to recognize that this trial is a political trial of the victors over the defeated.'[19] Instead of positing continuities between the Third Reich and the GDR, as the proponents of the *Unrechtsstaat* thesis did, Honecker restated the standard SED position that it was the FRG that was the continuation of the German *Unrechsstaat*, a notion that, in a moment of unfortunate irony, also appeared to be symbolized in his being held in the same Berlin-Moabit prison where he had been incarcerated under the Nazis.

There are not many who would defend Honecker's argument. Indeed, far from wishing to make political capital out of Honecker's trial, it was something of an embarrassment to the government, because, whatever the outcome, it was bound to enrage parts of German society. And Helmut Kohl's sigh of relief was almost palpable when Honecker finally took the plane to exile in Chile. However, it is interesting to note that, although the impetus for legal retribution had come to a large extent from east Germans, the fact that the judiciary was dominated by west Germans did, at least for some, now seem to give a degree of credence to Honecker's claim (albeit for fundamentally different reasons) that the east was being subjected to 'victors' justice', which did not offer real restitution for past wrongs and which wrote large their 'colonial', 'second-class' status. It could prosecute border guards, but let the real criminals, such as Honecker, go free. While at times it seemed constrained by the limitations of the Basic Law, at others it was happy to manipulate that same law in order to imprison figures such as Marcus Wolf, who some saw as the 'respectable' side of the GDR intelligence service, equivalent to the CIA or MI6.[20] Indeed, there was even the suggestion that Wolf's prosecution was wholly vindictive, western revenge for the Stasi's effectiveness at infiltrating the FRG's institutions.[21]

From Truth Tribunals to Enquete Commission

Court cases are necessarily concerned with establishing the guilt or innocence of individuals. This fact makes clear the inappropriateness of Honecker's defence, as his statement is based on a wish to evade personal culpability by putting the whole of post-war German history in the dock. That said, and as we also see in Bohley's comment, there was a feeling amongst elements of the wider east German population, in particular, that the judicial process of coming to terms with the past was too limited. As early as 1990 some former East German activists had begun to call for the establishment of a tribunal that could assess the legacy of the GDR more broadly in order to come to a moral judgement on the SED regime's place in history. In so doing, they were not unusual. Many post-dictatorship governments from the mid-1980s onwards, including those of Argentina, Chile, El Salvador, South Africa, Rwanda and the former Yugoslavia adopted a tribunal approach in dealing with their troubled past, the most well-known of these being the South African 'Truth and Reconciliation Committee', which in some cases offered amnesty to criminals in exchange for a full and frank admission of their past acts.[22] In Germany, some former GDR citizens' movement activists were calling for a similar body to promote reconciliation directly between the victims and perpetrators of the former GDR, as well as to help build trust in FRG institutions within the population. Although this can be seen as part of a broader international trend, the immediate reason why there was a call for a tribunal in Germany was closer to home. In the early 1990s there was a real fear amongst some elements of society that democracy was not 'taking' in the east. This was due in particular to a number of well-publicized violent attacks on asylum seekers' homes in eastern towns such as Hoyerswerda and Rostock. Such attacks were bad enough in themselves, but what was more shocking were the images on television of 'ordinary' citizens clapping on the sidelines as the buildings burnt. It seemed to some that these attacks proved the population of the former GDR, unlike that of the FRG, had never fundamentally broken with the Nazi period.[23] For those advocating a tribunal approach to dealing with the GDR, a central aim of any such body should be the prevention of this violence spreading by helping the east finally to make this break and to embed an understanding of democratic structures within eastern society.[24]

Various tribunal suggestions were made, sparking considerable debate, both within the media and amongst politicians.[25] Ultimately, they were all rejected for, among other reasons, the fear that they would undermine the authority of the courts, contravening the principle of the 'separation of powers', enshrined in the Basic Law. Nonetheless, by late 1991 there was a growing consensus that there should be some form of constitutionally legitimate body set up to deal officially with the whole legacy of the GDR. In November of that year the east German SPD politician Markus Meckel drafted a proposal for the Bundestag to set up an Enquete Commission to investigate this period. The Enquete Commission is a mechanism that has been used by the Bundestag since 1969 to investigate particularly complex issues in order to help inform parliamentary decisions. It consists of members of parliament and external experts who can call upon witness statements and commission research, but it does not have any active decision-making powers. For Meckel, the arguments in favour of an Enquete Commission were overwhelming, above all, due to the fact that the task of dealing with the GDR was the responsibility of the whole of German society: 'The history of the Germans in the GDR is … not only their history. It belongs to German post-war history … it is part of the national heritage'.[26] Consequently, as the democratically-elected forum of the entire German nation, the Bundestag was the natural location for any examination of its legacy. Furthermore, and perhaps naively, although Meckel wanted the GDR to be discussed within a political arena, he called for a non-partisan approach to dealing with the issue, for as he later insisted 'the instrumentalization of history by party politics is very short-sighted and hinders the process of dealing with the past, which is necessary to the whole of Germany'.[27] Initially it appeared that Meckel's call for members of parliament to put aside party difference was, to an extent at least, being heeded. In the debate on setting up the Enquete in March 1992, although differing opinions were clearly evident, the concept found broad agreement amongst the main political parties. Even the PDS, the SED's successor organization and the party that, on the face of it, appeared to have the most to lose by a probing inquiry into the GDR and its own prehistory, accepted the principle, albeit with reservations.[28] The Enquete Commission *'Aufarbeitung von Geschichte und Folgen der SED-Diktatur in Deutschland'* ('Working-Through of the

History and Consequences of the SED Dictatorship in Germany') was set up, and asked to report its findings before the next Federal election in 1994.

The Commission consisted of sixteen voting Bundestag members, their deputies and eleven external experts. As is usual with such bodies, its constellation reflected the makeup of parliament. As such, it was dominated by the CDU/CSU, and chaired by CDU representative, Rainer Eppelmann.[29] The members of the Bundestag were largely drawn from those involved in the GDR's citizens' movement. The external experts, on the other hand, came from the west German academy. It held forty-four public hearings, thirty-seven private hearings and more than 150 subgroup meetings, summoning hundreds of witnesses from both former states of Germany to testify. These witnesses ranged from ordinary members of society who had been victimized by the regime to the East and West German ruling elite, such as Günther Schabowski, the member of the GDR politburo who famously read out the declaration that the Berlin Wall was to be opened, as well as Helmut Kohl and the Foreign Minister at the time of the *Wende*, Hans-Dietrich Genscher.

The focus of the Enquete's investigation was the role of institutions within the GDR. These included its mass organizations, education system, military and the Stasi. The Commission was interested in how these institutions maintained control of the state, looking at their physical means of repression as well as their manipulation of the ideological tenets of Marxism-Leninism and antifascism, upon which the GDR was ostensibly founded. The nature of ideology would also play a role in its examination of the GDR's foreign policy and, most importantly, the relationship between the East German state and the FRG. Here the Commission seemed to confirm its intention to examine the GDR within the context of both East and West German history. However, crucially the key question to be addressed was how this relationship impacted upon the GDR's final demise and subsequent unification. Thus, the remit of this contextualization remained narrow. The examination of the state's demise would also lead the Commission to consider the role of dissident groups in the East. A main point of this discussion would be the role of the Church, around which much oppositional activity coalesced, and from where many of the Commission's members came, as well as the role of the 'alternative' cultural scene (a sphere to be discussed further in the next chapter) (E1/I, 189).[30] Over the next two years the Commission amassed a huge amount of information, which was subsequently published in 18 volumes running to over 15,000 pages. These consist of the transcripts of all its meetings, parliamentary debates, responses to questionnaires sent to other bodies engaged in GDR research, along with a very large number of specially commissioned expert reports. As a body of material these volumes constitute a very useful archive for research into this period of history, offering a variety of views on the GDR past. Far more problematic was its final parliamentary report, which put forward a 611–page synthesis of the Commission's findings. Here, we are presented with the unambiguous line the government majority took on the evidence with which it was presented. Any opinion deviating from this line is included in a number of separate minority opinion reports (*Sondervota*), which punctuate the majority findings. Like the Commission itself, its findings cover a wide range of topics. However, here I touch on just a few of these, in order both to suggest the general direction the report took and to highlight areas which subsequently proved problematic for commentators.

Initially, the report strongly echoes Meckel's original proposal in its reiteration of his view that 'the process of coming to terms politically with the history and consequences of the SED-Dictatorship in Germany is the responsibility of all Germans. It is of particular consequence for the process of the inner unification of Germany' (E1/I, 188). For the report's authors, the specific reason why dealing with the GDR is the responsibility of all Germans was that it, along with Hitler's Germany, forms part of the nation's 'totalitarian past' (E1/I, 182). Although, as the report also makes clear, what these two dictatorships did with power varied drastically, making the point that the GDR neither committed mass murder nor started a world war, it insists that the similarities between them are striking:

> Both dictatorships were the enemies of open society and consequently of free democracy ... Both regimes used modern methods to exert mass influence and mass surveillance; they refused to accept the rights to freedom of opinion and association for dissenters; they made taboo or persecuted all opposition. (E1/I, 744)

As I shall discuss below, the characterization of the GDR as a 'totalitarian' system provoked a good deal of debate. For the authors of the report, however, it is a crucially important term because it allows them to demarcate the difference between the whole of Germany's dictatorial legacy and its present democratic system:

> [Dealing with the past] can contribute to the stabilization of democratic self-confidence and to the development of political culture in as far as it brings into focus the superiority of the freely democratic *Rechtsstaat*, through the examination of both the dictatorships founded on German soil, and creates

what the members of the Enquete Committee termed an 'anti-totalitarian consensus', that transcends party boundaries. (E1/I, 745)

This need to build an 'anti-totalitarian consensus' is one which is reiterated time and again in the report, underlining its openly didactic intention of using history to help shape present-day German society, and most importantly to help construct a democratic political culture.

The overt use of the past to influence present attitudes is revealed in a number of areas addressed by the report. For example, it acknowledges the criticisms of those who were frustrated by what they perceived to be the limitations of the justice system in redressing past grievances, seeing it as part of the Committee's remit to address this dissatisfaction. The authors insist that 'the discussion of the illegal nature of the SED regime should see that at least *history* does justice to the regime's victims, for whom only limited legal and material redress is possible' (E1/I, 182, my emphasis). Unlike the court cases examined above, the Enquete did not need to worry about the details of individual cases. It could, therefore, address broader issues, through which a wide variety of victims could be recognized and the crimes against them, for the official record at least, acknowledged. In so doing, the Committee hoped to begin a widespread process of reconciliation that would help these victims to overcome their past and to integrate into unified Germany.

Along with the need to acknowledge the victims, the report also sees a need to apportion blame. The bulk of this blame is, rather unsurprisingly, laid at the door of the SED, although the report acknowledges the role of the Soviet Union (E1/I, 208–15) and also makes it clear that the SED's affiliated organization, including the so-called 'independent' bloc parties (created to provide the illusion that the GDR was a multi-party state) must take their share of responsibility (E1/I, 222–3). Nevertheless, it is the SED that is overwhelmingly to blame, its 'totalitarian power structures' having 'deformed the life of every individual as well as the life of the whole of GDR society' (E1/I, 182).

Over and above looking at the physical structures and institutions of this apparently totalitarian regime, the Commission was also interested in the party's ideological basis, not only of Marxism-Leninism – which dominated the whole of the Eastern bloc – but also the more GDR-specific concept of 'antifascism'. This was an idea, the report suggests, which was 'probably the most effective ideological integration factor for the SED'. The GDR was officially set up to be an 'antifascist' state, the realization of the leftwing legacy of the Weimar Republic and of the resistance to Hitler under the Third Reich, which would protect the population from a resurgence of National Socialism. The report argues that in reality the term was 'misused' to legitimize attacks 'in an undifferentiated fashion [on] all political and social trends that did not support the politics of the Soviet Union'. Consequently, it goes on, 'antifascism' was a very elastic concept in the hands of the Party, used to justify a number of extremely draconian acts of oppression, from the suppression of protest after the workers' uprising of 17 June 1953, to the building of the Berlin Wall, termed in official parlance 'The Antifascist Protection Barrier' (E1/I, 279). Still more disturbing, it was argued, was that the *de facto* declaration of the GDR as an 'antifascist' state meant in practice that it did little to deal fundamentally with its Nazi history:

> Denazification was far less thorough than it is often claimed to be [...]. People guilty of complicity with National Socialism would even deliberately be given key positions, while conversely, those who had been persecuted under National Socialism were in no way safe from persecution in the Soviet Zone of Occupation or the GDR. (E1/I, 278)

For the report's authors, the sham of 'antifascism' was revealed most obviously in the resurgence of rightwing extremism in the 1970s. At a time when the West was still undergoing the seismic social shifts set in train by a youthful post-war generation, who were attempting to address the legacy of the past in the West more directly than ever before, thereby effecting a fundamental break with National Socialism, in the East it seemed that the state's claim to have provided its youth with an 'antifascist education' had had no similar effect. Indeed, the authors claim that the resurgence in rightwing activity at this time 'even begs the question whether the specific character of the SED's antifascism did not in fact have the opposite effect, and help give rise to "fascistic" rightwing phenomena' (E1/I, 281). The GDR's regime had not only failed to deal with the past but its policies were, potentially at least, encouraging the continuing existence of overtly fascistic traits amongst the population.

The central thrust of the majority report is the de-legitimization of the GDR regime. Along with this de-legitimization comes a concomitant legitimization of the FRG. This is shown particularly clearly in its discussion of inter-German relations during the Cold War. Although, as the report is at pains to point out, 'the construction of a consistent "Reunification Policy" from Adenauer to Kohl, which finally led to unification is not born out in the historical record' (E1/I, 470), due to its democratic, capitalist social order, the FRG was, nonetheless, a central factor in unification eventually taking place. In the West, the Allies founded their state on the 'democratic structures of the Social Market Economy'. These principles 'relatively quickly made possible a correspondence of interests between the victorious Western powers and the Germans in their zones of occupation', leading the population to identify with this new state's principles, and thereby endowing it with 'legitimacy [and] inner stability'. On the other hand, 'The SED state, in its entire 40 year history, never managed to achieve stability through inner legitimacy', shown most obviously through the measures the state needed to employ in order to maintain its power – the report again mentions the suppression of the workers' uprising in 1953 and the building of the Berlin Wall in 1961 (E1/I, 492). Throughout its history, the report argues, the population of the GDR remained oriented to the West (E1/I, 477). While the FRG's recognition of the East German state, as well as its dealings with the SED, might have seemed to seal German division, the increasing contact between the populations of both states in the 1970s and 1980s in the wake of the Basic Treaty meant that the GDR population became evermore fixated on West Germany. This, in turn, set in motion what the report paints as an almost organic process of unification, under the auspices of the FRG: 'with the benefit of hindsight it appears as if the divided nation at that time was secretly making its way back to each other in unconscious anticipation of the events to come' (E1/I, 478).

Yet, the West's salvation of the East could not, the report also insists, have been achieved without the active participation of the GDR population. Thus, it points to the achievements of those who were brave enough to challenge the SED's authority from within. These included individuals who were active in dissident organizations, however loosely defined, many of which, as already mentioned, were involved with the Protestant Church.[31] The Church itself came in for a degree of criticism for what the report sees as its ready complicity with the state, and in particular with the Stasi (E1/I, 505–8). Nevertheless, the actions of individual activists are praised. Furthermore, the report also notes that one must not just focus on members of specific groups, because this would not do justice to the mass of citizens who exercised opposition to the regime in their everyday life (E1/I, 606–10). It is this opposition which is ultimately seen as a crucial factor in the state's collapse, erupting into the mass demonstration of 1989, when these same brave citizens took to the streets of Leipzig and Dresden, their chants of 'We are one people' demanding union with the West (E1/I, 745).

In sum, therefore, the report paints the GDR as an aberration of history. Following the proponents of the *Unrechtsstaat* thesis discussed in connection with the court cases, the GDR is constructed as a totalitarian, criminal state, which was organically overcome by the natural superiority of the West German state and the brave heroes of the 'Peaceful Revolution' of 1989. It sees it now as the job of all Germans, from the east and the west, to face history's painful legacy in order to complete the project of unification, so that the population of the former GDR might overcome the torments of the past to become integrated members of a democratic FRG that will never allow the *Unrechtsstaat* to wield power again.

Criticism of the Commission: 'Colonizing' History and the GDR as 'Orient'

Clearly the task the Enquete set itself was immense, and the amount of material it collected together and published in such a short space of time was a major achievement. A good deal of the specific detail of its findings is also beyond historical doubt. However, its broader portrayal of the GDR as a totalitarian state, as well as the relationship of this state to the National Socialist period did provoke criticism. It should be noted that the first place where potential points of criticism are raised is within the report itself. In its final remarks the authors insist that, due to the limitations of time, its findings can only be provisional and that much more detailed research is required into the areas the committee explored. Indeed, it admits, some of the areas originally selected for examination (for example the role of the military) were hardly addressed. However, it also claims that it was never its aim to write an official history of the GDR. This is not the job for the Bundestag but for academics. Rather, the authors stress that their focus is the effect of the past on the present, and the project of securing inner-German unity (E1/I, 739). Nevertheless, the caveats built into the report were not enough to assuage some commentators and public figures in their view that in the Enquete, as in the trials, history was being rewritten by the victors of the Cold War to expedite a process of cultural colonization, to consolidate the economic colonization discussed in the previous chapter. The GDR, it appeared, was being cast as the west's evil 'other', an historical version of Said's 'Orient', through which the FRG sought validation for its own existence as a superior, enlightened German state. Later in the chapter I will examine some of the political repercussions of the report. However, first I would like to look at some of the broader issues raised by adopting a 'totalitarian' model to examine the GDR and how they seemed to promote a view that the past was being instrumentalized for 'colonial' purposes.

The concept of 'totalitarianism' has been used since the 1930s to link fascist and socialist dictatorships, and was made popular in the late 1940s and 1950s during the early days of the Cold War by the work of Hannah

Arendt and Carl J. Friedrich. Totalitarian rule is based, in Arendt's formulation, on a one-party system of 'state terror', the power of which is
absolute, implicating the entire population within its structures and
allowing little or no room for autonomous behaviour.[32] The focus of
comparison for Arendt was Hilter's Germany and Stalin's Soviet Union.
Yet, as Ross notes, over the course of the Cold War it became clear to
many that while her theory might have held true for the Third Reich, 'it
[was] less satisfactory on Stalin's Soviet Union, and certainly bears little
resemblance to the increasingly conservative and sclerotic communist
systems after Stalin's death'.[33] With regard to the GDR, commentators
began to describe its system of governance in the 1970s and 1980s, after
Honecker's assumption of power, as a 'post-totalitarian', or 'authoritarian' regime, concepts which suggest a (slightly) more conciliatory relationship between the state and the population, and which led to more
nuanced images of life in the GDR than the black-and-white one
suggested by a totalitarianism model. A classic example of this shift in
thinking is Günter Gaus's seminal early 1980s study *Wo Deutschland
liegt* (*The State of Germany*), where he describes the GDR as a
'Nischengesellschaft' ('niche society') that allowed for pockets of semi-
autonomous activity (within one's family, or Church group), as long as
the public façade of conformity was maintained, thereby building a
society not based on 'state terror', but rather on what Jonathan Grix has
identified as the 'conditional loyalty' of the citizenry.[34] Indeed, as Mary
Fulbrook remarks, by this time those who continued to see the GDR as
an example of totalitarianism generally came from the right and
'appeared to be arguing from an increasingly embattled corner against the
tendencies of neo-Marxists, leftwingers, and even moderate liberals to
develop a more differentiated picture of the regime and a society'.[35]

In the immediate aftermath of the *Wende*, however, the totalitarian
model once again came to the fore. For some this shift was a welcome
corrective, allowing a broader plurality of critical positions than were
available in the previous two decades, which had been dominated by the
left-liberal consensus identified by Fulbrook above.[36] However, there also
appeared to be a number of reasons why black-and-white images of the
GDR should have replaced the shades of grey found in the latter part of
the Cold War that had far more to do with present political expediency
than coming to a better understanding of history, reasons that continued
to highlight academic splits between the left and the right. Some of these
will be discussed in my examination of the legacy of the Stasi in the
following chapter. However, of importance to the present discussion was
the usefulness of the totalitarian model for the consolidation of a unified
FRG. By constructing an absolutist, totalitarian image of the GDR, such

as we see in the report, a historical narrative is built in which guilt can be unambiguously apportioned, heroes identified, and unification painted as a redemptive moment for the German people. In Fulbrook's words, the more complex model of life in the GDR found in the 1970s and 1980:

> Does not ... lend itself quite so easily to simplistic projects of building a new national identity as do the sensationalist tales of heroes and villains, the heroic overthrow of the unjust yoke of oppression, and the reunification in peace and freedom of the German people under their 'unification chancellor,' Helmut Kohl.[37]

Thus the report distinguishes between what Konrad Jarausch and Michael Geyer identify as 'the abject history of Germany', and 'the paradigmatic success of West Germany', through which it sets in stone the validity of the present unified state.[38]

For critics of the report, the reading of the past it put forward was more about furthering a western political agenda than about exploring the complexity of life in GDR. On a political level this is an understandable project. Clearly, the FRG is a more legitimate German state than either the GDR or its National Socialist predecessor. However, with regard to the investigation of German history, the type of comparison we find in the Enquete's report was found by some to be highly problematic. Of course, as the report makes clear, comparing two things does not necessarily suggest that they are the same. Indeed, Christopher Beckmann makes the obvious but important point that 'without comparison there can be no differentiation'.[39] Nevertheless, for others, the reality of such comparisons, particularly in the popular discourse the report writers ultimately wished to influence, was that differentiation was generally lost. Fritz Klein, for example, suggests

> That comparison does not mean equivalence is always emphasized, and if one looks at it logically, this is self-evident. But this fact is easily lost in everyday discussion amongst people who as a rule do not make judgements according to abstract logic but who are rather influenced by opinions and prejudices.[40]

The question of comparison leading to equivalence could be problematic in either direction. First, such comparisons ran the risk of relativizing the obviously worse crimes of National Socialism. Here the report seemed to be on the verge of re-igniting controversies first sparked during the *Historikerstreit* (historians' dispute) of the mid 1980s, during which conservative academics such as Ernst Nolte provocatively painted

National Socialist atrocities as a defensive response to, as well as a continuation of, those committed by Stalin. In so doing, such academics attempted to alleviate Germany of its guilt for the past, thereby hoping that the country might at last draw a line under its history and become a 'normal' European nation.[41] In similar vein, within the context of debates on the GDR, Nolte argues that

> the GDR was the older German state: older than the Federal Republic, older than the Third Reich, older even than the Weimar Republic. Of course, not as a visible reality. But the GDR was ... the state that Stalin was convinced had to come into existence in 1933 once the short-lived victory of Hitler's fascism had led to the inevitable collapse. But the GDR was also the state that Hitler feared when he continually referred, in his early speeches, to the 'bloody swamp of Bolshevism,' in which millions of people had perished; and it was the state those uncounted 'bourgeois' organizations had in mind when they assured themselves and others that at the last minute, 'People's Chancellor Hitler' had saved Germany from the 'abyss of Bolshevism'.[42]

In a curious manipulation of chronology, Nolte paints the GDR as part of the trajectory of socialist history that led to National Socialism. Paradoxically, the GDR, as Stalin's German proxy state, is not only seen as an 'effect' of the Third Reich, it is also its cause. Both dictatorships thus become inextricably intertwined aspects of Germany's dark historical 'other', for neither of which Germans can ultimately be held responsible.

Second, by drawing a comparison between the GDR and National Socialism, or even to see one as the continuation or the other, as the report's rejection of the state's antifascist credentials implies, it ignored the more differentiated views of GDR society that had begun to develop in the 1970s and 1980s, with leftwing commentators in particular seeing such views of the past as a misrepresentation of the historical record. Rather than the Commission seeking to overcome the feared potential links between the GDR and its Nazi pre-history, it appeared to some that it was more intent upon overstating and confirming these links for present political gain.

Moreover, as I suggested in the introduction to this chapter, it was not just the report that appeared to be intent upon creating an equivalence between National Socialism and the GDR in order to put this whole past to rest, or to over-emphasize the crimes of the latter for current political effect. This tendency was equally evident, some argued, in the official attitude to the GDR in its memorial culture more generally. Critics pointed, for example, to the renaming of streets in the early 1990s, during which the apparent fallacy of the GDR's antifascism appeared to be confirmed in the widespread erasure of those antifascist 'heroes' memorialized on street signs throughout the east of the Republic. Much of this criticism, it must be said, is overstated. To see this renaming process as a product of a western takeover, another example of cultural colonization, ignores the fact Bill Niven points out, that for the most part the changing of streets was a locally decided issue: 'If some towns were over-zealous in eradicating antifascist street names, then this has much to do with an east German wish to make a clean break with the past – rightly or wrongly.'[43] The one exception to this might be the case of Berlin, where a commission charged by the city's western-dominated central senate was given a say in the renaming of streets in the eastern borough of Mitte, and in whose decisions there was, perhaps, more room for criticism.[44] More obviously reminiscent of the report's instrumentalization of the past is the Leipzig 'Forum of Contemporary History', the brainchild of Helmut Kohl, opened in 1999. The museum writes large the findings of the Enquete Commissions, its advisory board of conservative historians presenting an image of postwar Germany that, for Niven, 'perfects the portrayal of the GDR as little more than a continuation of National Socialism', by continually stressing 'equational thinking' between the two German dictatorships.[45] The most obvious example of this is the sculpture that stands outside the exhibition. Wolfgang Mattheuer's *Century Step* shows an abstract figure striding boldly across history, its right hand held outstretched in a Nazi salute, while the left is clenched in a fist, a symbol of socialist solidarity, and decorated with a red stripe. Thus, the impression is created that National Socialism and communism form a single body, dominating the twentieth century. Throughout, the exhibition emphasizes continuities between the two dictatorships, confirming the report's finding that 'denazification [in the GDR] was far less thorough than it is often claimed to be' (E1/I, 278). A further example of this is the museum's focus on members of the Nazi elite who continued to wield power in the GDR. In actuality, high-level continuities were relatively unusual in the GDR. In the FRG, on the other hand, they were a far more common occurrence. Yet the museum makes only cursory reference to this fact.[46]

In postcolonial terms, then, such readings of history constructed an illegitimate, 'orientalist' trajectory of German history from the Third Reich to the GDR. Such orientalism has not only proved controversial amongst historians – it has also fuelled a wider perception that institutions designed to aid the former GDR in moving beyond its 'post-Soviet' status have fed a western colonial takeover, which is not only seeking to delegitimize the SED but also the biographies of the population as a whole. Amelie Kutter suggests, for example: 'this primarily west German "appropriation" of GDR history for the purposes of self-justification, was tantamount to an "expropriation" of GDR history as it was lived, and remembered, by east Germans'.[47] Specifically, she points to certain aspects of GDR society, such as the everyday experience of the world of work, which are often warmly remembered by east Germans, but which are unequivocally dismissed by the report. In regard to the nature of life at work, she quotes the report's rejection of a remembered 'collegiality, harmony and a certain sense of community in the face of impositions by the SED and the state'.[48] Such positive memories are painted, she argues, as 'misjudgements' that must be 'devalued'.[49] Consequently, in Kutter's view, the Enquete's report is an unambiguous example of the west's 'colonialist practice', intent upon nothing less than the 'destruction of indigenous social cultural and historical legacies, the assimilation of the subjugated to the value of the conquerors, the integration of the conquered into the history of the victors'.[50] Indeed, for Kutter, the fact that a number of east Germans were involved in the Commission is simply further evidence of the success of this western colonization and its ability to turn the 'natives' into loyal subjects.[51]

It is, I would suggest, somewhat patronizing to see the east German members of the Committee as having been duped by the west. It must be mentioned, as Bernd Faulenbach notes, that all the official attempts to come to terms with the past can be 'traced back to east German initiatives', to which the Federal government was then forced to respond.[52] Of course, the various processes of coming-to-terms with the GDR past were not happening in a political vacuum and the version of history produced by the Commission and other official forums clearly attempts to validate the political choices made by CDU/CSU-led coalition. That said, this was also a government for which the east German population in 1990 had voted in droves. However, ultimately we must accept the fact that whether east German perceptions of 'colonial' marginalization were justified or not, they were without doubt very real and, as we shall now see, have had widespread political consequences.

Orientalism, the PDS and the Enquete Commission

That the Enquete Commission was not working in a political vacuum is actually admitted in the report itself: 'without doubt, the beginning of the 1994 election campaign did not make the work of the *Enquete* Commission easier; its instrumentalisation for campaign purposes could not be completely prevented' (E1/I, 192). And, just as the majority report is shaped by the political opinion of the ruling coalition, so too are the minority reports presented by the opposition parties. One often-cited example of party politics impinging upon the Commission's work is its handling of the role of the Church. While, as McAdams notes, the discussion of this topic to be found in the Enquete's volumes of material was wide ranging, and showed a variety of positions on the relationship between the organization and the state, the majority report tends to condemn what it sees as the compromises the Church leaders made in order to come to an accommodation with the authorities. This led to a particularly indignant 'minority report' by the SPD, who read these comments as a not-so-veiled attack on Manfred Stolpe, SPD Minister President of Brandenburg, and former Church leader, who since 1992 had been under investigation for collaborating with the Stasi.[53] Yet, party politics aside, in general the majority report claimed that it welcomed the inclusion of dissenting minority opinions, stating that they should be seen as part of the democratic process. As its authors make clear 'cooperation in the Enquete Commission was not always very easy. In spite of all our conflicts, we have learnt from each other: we have told each other our stories' (E1/I, 183). Moreover, it is not just the majority report that claims this. In a similar vein, Faulenbach argues that just as important as the final report was the discussion process it gave rise to – 'the journey itself was the point'.[54]

The one notable divergence from the view that airing political disagreement might be part of the Enquete's brief was the response to the minority report presented by the PDS and its Bundestag partner *Linke Liste* (Left List, LL). This was held by the majority report to be nothing short of an apologia for the SED, and a cynical mechanism by which the party could justify its existence (E1/I, 740). Although the PDS went along with the idea of an Enquete Commission, from the very start the party's relationship with it was, to say the least, fraught. As Peter Barker notes, most of the party was sceptical of its intentions, preferring, unlike any of the other parties, to draw a line under the GDR period. The one exception to this position was that of Dietmar Keller, a former SED minister in the GDR. Keller maintained the party's connection with the Commission's workings, becoming the party's sole delegate.[55] Keller's work with the Enquete did him no favours within his party. His critical evaluation of the structures of power in the SED were highly controversial within the PDS, leading to his effective de-selection for the 1994 General Election.[56] Nevertheless, although Keller was largely sympathetic to the Enquete's work, the minority report he helped to write is highly critical of it, reflecting more strongly mainstream opinion within the party.[57]

Many of the criticisms in the PDS/LL minority report follow those already mentioned. It was indignant that the GDR could be dismissed as a totalitarian *Unrechtsstaat*, and was particularly incensed at the report's equation of fascism with socialism. To make this link, it argues, is nothing short of a 'falsification of history' (E1/I, 708). Recalling Honecker's overblown statement at his trial, the PDS report argues that the aim of any historical commission into this period must be to look at the set of historical circumstances that led to postwar German division, viewing both states in essence as potentially 'legitimate'. The lesson to be learnt from the GDR, it argues, is not that dictatorship in German is a thing of the past, but rather why the obviously admirable idea of building an antifascist, socialist state went so wrong (E1/I, 681). Indeed, even to see the GDR as a dictatorship is too limiting as it ignores the state's obvious achievements: 'The GDR as a state and society was also a state that provided for its population and was to an extent even a caring society with a specific "we feeling" (*Wir-Gefühl*)' (E1/I, 682).

If it is problematic to equate the GDR with Hitler's Germany, the PDS/LL presents a no-less distorted view of history. We see the continuation of the SED's propaganda, which painted the GDR as being built on the 'democratic traditions of the European Labour Movement' (E1/I, 709), and insisting on the peaceful credentials of all the Warsaw Pact countries: 'It was typical for the GDR to campaign for peace and put forward suggestions for disarmament. The Warsaw Pact embraced the suggestion of the independent states, calling for peaceful coexistence, and supported this wholeheartedly' (E1/I, 710). Then, in a rhetorical sleight of hand, this is placed along side the apparent experience of the GDR population as a whole:

> The history of the GDR is the history of victims and perpetrators, of mistakes, failures and crimes; but above all it is the everyday history of millions of people, whose personal happiness and suffering, sense of security and well-being, whose conflicts and protests, daring public acts and private withdrawal into the 'niches' cannot be found in any archival source. If these people do not find their history and their stories, their normality ... in the history that is written and the value judgements of the ruling political class, then the latter has failed. (E1/I, 683)

This is a revealing quotation that highlights a number of the strategies employed by the PDS in the report, strategies that are also exemplary of its wider political agenda, and which are furthermore echoed in other cultural discourses to be discussed in this volume. First, it accepts the limitations of the GDR state. In so doing, the party underlines its claims that it has a 'critical relationship' with its SED predecessor. Later in its report this is stated more overtly: 'As much as the PDS does not deny its origins, it also distances itself in its programme and statutes from Stalinist crimes and structures' (E1/I, 702). Interestingly here, however, while the party accepts responsibility for its history, it also seems to suggest that responsibility for the crimes carried out in the name of the GDR ultimately lay at the door of the Soviet dictator and not the SED. Second, having ostensibly distanced itself from the GDR's dictatorial legacy (a legacy that the PDS in any case sees as being of only limited importance), it shifts its attention away from state structures to the nature of 'everyday life' in the GDR. This is an important change of focus since it potentially provides a far wider point of identification for the former GDR population, accommodating people who do not fit neatly into the black and white totalitarian model seen in the rest of the report. As Peter Christian Segall *et al.* observe 'In the last analysis the PDS profiles itself as the defender of the past of every single eastern German – not just the former members of the SED and the citizens who worked in the public services in the GDR.'[58] The PDS claims here to speak for 'normal' people, not just the heroes or villains Fulbrook identifies and that are central to the report's main story. Thus the party feeds the perception that the report is seeking to de-legitimize not only the SED regime, but also the lived experience of the GDR population.

Third, it is important to see how the PDS presents its view of 'normality'. Part of the 'everyday' experience of the population, it claims, was a 'sense of security and well-being'. Here we see a conflation of two competing aspects of east Germanness, already mentioned in connection with the notion of the 'identity of defiance' and what I have identified as part of a cultural process of 'writing back', both of which are central to the party's policies. On the one hand, we have an ideological view of the GDR as a progressive socialist state. As we saw in the previous chapter in the position of some former GDR intellectuals, the PDS was not alone in attempting to recuperate the SED's ideological agenda. However, the problem the PDS faced was that it was also directly implicated in the corruption of this agenda. For the other members of the Commission, the version of the GDR propagated by the PDS in the report was particularly distasteful, described by the SPD members as a dangerous 'tendency nostalgically to transfigure the GDR past'. This is an early reference to the controversial phenomenon of *Ostalgie* that would come to dominate debates on dealing with the GDR from the mid to late 1990s, and to which we shall return at length in subsequent chapters.

An idealized, 'ideological' image of the GDR is then finally linked in the quotation with a more visceral sense of what it means to be east German, and to have grown up in this region as 'normal' people who need not be ashamed of their biography prior to unification. Here the party identified a widespread fear amongst the citizens of the eastern regions discussed above, that their life during the GDR risked being devalued within, or even elided from, the historical record in an attempt to build a teleology of history culminating in the salvation of Germany by Helmut Kohl. This is an issue that has become particularly central to popular debates on the GDR in recent years. As one of PDS's election slogans declared in 1994: 'My biography does not begin in 1989.'[59]Thus, we have the curious state of affairs in which the party that advocated most loudly drawing a line under the GDR period could now present itself as the only party dealing honestly with this period of history. Even more curious was the fact that a party which – to whatever limited extent – was defending the record of a regime that the vast majority of the population in the east were very glad to see the back of, could now portray itself as the only authentic voice of that same population.

For much of the political mainstream the continued existence of the PDS in the 1990s was an extremely worrying development. A good number of established politicians, particularly from the CDU/CSU, saw it as their job to discredit the party whenever possible. Ironically, however, the more other parties attempted to discredit the PDS by making a connection between it and the SED, the more the party seemed to be able to capitalize on this very point of identification. Dan Hough points, for example, to the 'Red Socks' and 'Red Hands' campaigns of the 1994 and 1998 elections respectively instigated by the CDU, during which the PDS was vilified as being nothing more than the SED reincarnated. In doing this, the CDU actually played into the hands of the PDS, as they allowed, in Hough's view

> PDS politicians ... to take the moral high-ground by depicting CDU and CSU politicians as stooping to populist rhetoric in order to try and increase their profile – principally in the West, where the PDS [was] still a tool with which the conservative parties [could] mobilize support. [60]

Such attacks could, therefore, be instrumentalized as proof that the other parties were wholly western in their outlook, with little understanding of the complexities of east German politics, and particularly of the PDS's apparent attempts to wrestle honestly, and in a differentiated manner, with its past.

The more the other parties tried to cast the PDS as part of Germany's abject past, and thereby, in orientalist fashion, legitimate their own position, the more the party could construct itself as the authentic voice of the eastern outsider. To be sure, in the 1994 and 1998 elections this strategy was successful. In 1994 the PDS nearly doubled its national vote (4.4 per cent), and in the east gained a 20 per cent share, with four directly elected seats, thereby giving it a place in the Bundestag (albeit as *Bundestagsgruppe*, with limited rights). In 1998 it went further to clear the hurdle of 5 per cent of the national vote and to enter the Bundestag as a full *Bundestagsfraktion*. On a regional level it has had even more success, establishing itself as the third most important power in the east, and forming coalition governments with the SPD in Mecklenburg Western-Pomerania in 1998 and Berlin in 2001.

However, just eleven months after its success in Berlin, when one in two east Berliners voted for the party, it failed to achieve the 5 per cent hurdle in the national election and so was not returned to the Bundestag.[61] There are a number of reasons generally cited for this failure that might be mentioned here, because they will also impact upon our discussion on the shifts in both social constructions of the GDR past and, more broadly, of the place of easterners in German society since the early 1990s. Amongst the most important of these is, as Daniel Küchenmeister suggests, the fact that the party could no longer represent itself as either the sole voice of an idealized (GDR) socialist tradition – such as it paints itself in the Enquete – or as the sole defender of eastern-specific social issues, a stance that would normally underline its visceral appreciation of what it means to be an east German. One of the key issues in the run up to the election was the proposed US-led invasion of Iraq. Since coming to power in 1998 the SPD/Green coalition had continued the 'salami-tactic' policy of the previous CDU-CSU/FDP coalition, gradually extending German contributions to multilateral military campaigns, sending, for example, initially Tornados and then troops to join NATO forces in Kosovo in early 1999. Such involvement had always been rigorously opposed by the PDS, which, drawing on its portrayal of the GDR in its minority report, had consistently painted itself as the sole 'party of peace'. In opposing intervention in Iraq in 2002, however, the SPD left no room for the PDS to take up what would have previously been more obviously the latter's ground. Similarly, in acting quickly and decisively in the face of the floods that hit the eastern regions in the run up to the election, Schröder showed that the SPD could put east-specific issues centre stage. Consequently, the PDS could no longer present itself as the 'authentic voice of the east', ignored by the other parties.[62] Ironically, it would seem the party's previous success was ultimately instrumental in its failure in 2002. East German issues, along with aspects of the political legacy of the GDR, now appeared to have been taken up by the political mainstream, thereby undermining the PDS' manipulation of perceived 'orientalist' tendencies in the other parties to legitimize its political position.

More recently, the PDS has once again achieved electoral success, this time in Brandenburg, suggesting that predictions of the party's complete demise might be somewhat premature.[63] Moreover, it should be noted that Schröder's position on Iraq went down well with a substantial proportion of the whole of the German electorate of course. In the west too, as in much of the rest of Europe, there was widespread popular protest against the war. Within a German context, the popularity of Schröder's decision on Iraq reflected, perhaps, a feeling amongst the population at large a wish to return to the more comfortable pre-unification days when West German politicians could follow a policy of avoiding war at all costs. Consequently, we might identify here not only feelings of the type of *Ostalgie* instrumentalized by the PDS, but also a type of political *Westalgie* for the position of the old FRG, mentioned in the previous chapter.

If it is not only the eastern population that will look nostalgically to its past traditions when allowed to do so, we can return briefly to the question of which part of the country is more 'backward looking' – that is, which region lags behind the other. In this connection, it is worth noting that many commentators tend to view the eastern regions as having a more 'modern' political culture than the west, modern here meaning acting more like Britain and the US, states generally viewed as being further along the 'evolutionary scale' of democratic capitalism. Unlike the old FRG, the eastern electorate exhibits a high level of volatility in its voting patterns, acting more in response to short-term societal circumstances than to traditional party affiliations determined by social class or religion.[64] Furthermore, more worryingly the east would seem to be ahead of the west, and thus closer to Britain and the US, in terms of the number of people who fail to vote, with 23 per cent fewer people proportionally turning out in eastern regions.[65] Consequently, it might seem that eastern political culture provides further evidence of this region as Germany's 'avant garde', pointing to the shape of things to come for the whole of the country.

Throughout the state-led processes of dealing with the GDR outlined here orientalist perceptions pervade. The GDR is constructed as part of what Jarausch and Geyer term Germany's 'abject' history, from which the whole nation was liberated with unification. Although it should not be forgotten that the impetus for these state-led processes came mainly from the east, the former GDR population widely felt that they were ultimately highjacked by western-dominated elites that were happy to run roughshod over eastern past experiences, at best manipulating them for present political gain, at worse eliding them from the historical record.

A final problem of the Enquete's work that should again be mentioned was its inability to capture the imagination of the population as a whole. Although its findings were highly revealing of certain political agendas, and sparked heated debate amongst political and intellectual elites, unlike forums such as the South African 'Truth and Reconciliation Committee' its many public meetings were not well attended by the general public.[66] In the following legislative period, a second commission was set up. To a degree, this tried to learn from the mistakes of the first. For example, in the introduction to its thirteen volumes of published findings, Rainer Eppelmann, its chair, quotes the first report, in order to prove that 'the political and moral condemnation of the SED Dictatorship does not mean that the people who were subjugated to it are to be condemned', thereby attempting to dispel the perception we have discussed above that this was ever the case.[67] Nevertheless, the feeling amongst the even smaller number of east Germans who took any notice of the findings of the second Commision was that this was precisely what the condemnation of the GDR's political system in actual fact meant. It is not surprising, then, that the PDS continued to be vocal in its condemnation of the second Commission. However, this criticism could now be largely ignored because the committee of the second Commission was far smaller than the first, and excluded the PDS as a voting member.[68]

With regard to German political culture more generally, in the PDS we see a good example of a political party using perceptions of colonization to mobilize an electorate. While one might be cynical of the motivations of some PDS members, the party clearly hit a nerve amongst elements of the east German population, giving voice to a widespread feeling of marginalization and, as I shall discuss in the following chapter, it was not just political culture that was conditioned in the early 1990s by such reactions to what was deemed by some to be the misrepresentation of East German history.

Notes

1. For further discussion of social transformation in other former Eastern bloc countries see Leslie Holmes, *Post-Communism: an Introduction*, Cambridge: Polity, 1997; Jon Elster, Claus Offe and Ulrich K. Preuss, *Institutional Design in Post-communist Societies*, Cambridge: CUP, 1998; Smith, *The Post-Soviet States*.
2. Jennifer A. Yoder, 'Truth without Reconciliation: An Appraisal of the Enquete Commission on the SED Dictatorship in Germany', *German Politics*, 3(8) (1999), 59–80 (p. 65).
3. Corey Ross, *The East German Dictatorship: Problems and Perspectives in the Interpretation of the GDR*, London: Arnold, 2002, p. 183.

4. The only other partially equivalent cases in this respect are Croatia, Hungary and Romania, which also had for a time semi-autonomous fascist regimes.

5. For a discussion of the obvious echoes the term 'Destasification' has with the postwar process of 'Denazification' by the Allies, see Alexander von Plato, 'Eine zweite "Entnazifizierung": Zur Verarbeitung politischer Umwälzungen in Deutschland 1945 und 1989', in *Wendezeiten- Zeitenwände Zur 'Entnazifizierung' und 'Entstalinisierung'*, ed. by Rainer Eckert, Alexander von Plato and Jörn Schütrumpf, Hamburg: Ergebnisse, 1991, pp. 7–31.

6. The first Commission's material and findings was published in nine volumes, split into eighteen books: Deutscher Bundestag, *Materialien der Enquete-Kommission 'Aufarbeitung von Geschichte und Folgen der SED-Diktatur in Deutschland'*, Baden-Baden: Nomos Verlag; Frankfurt am Main: Suhrkamp, 1995, hereafter (E1). In the following legislative period there was a second commission. This was published in eight volumes, split into thirteen books, Deutscher Bundestag, *Materialien der Enquete-Kommission 'Überwindung der Folgen der SED-Diktatur im Prozeß der deutschen Einheit'*, Baden-Baden: Nomos Verlag; Frankfurt am Main: Suhrkamp, 1999, hereafter (E2). There was also one Commission set up on the *Land* level in Mecklenburg Western Pomerania, *Landtag Mecklenburg-Vorpommern* (ed.), *Leben in der DDR, Leben nach 1989*, ten volumes, Schwerin: Stiller & Balewski, 1995–8.

7. Yoder, pp. 64–5.

8. For further discussion of this period see Jeffrey Herf, *Divided Memory: The Nazi Past in the Two Germanys*, Cambridge: Harvard, 1997, pp. 201–333.

9. A. James McAdams, *Judging the Past in Unified Germany*, Cambridge: CUP, 2001, pp. 26–7.

10. For further discussion see McAdams, p. 29 and Thorsten Lauterbach, 'The Germans Reunified – Challenges to the Legal System', in *East Germany Continuity and Change*, ed. by Paul Cooke and Jonathan Grix, Amsterdam: Rodopi, 2000, pp. 141–7.

11. Quoted in McAdams, p. 31.

12. Charles S. Meier, *Dissolution: The Crisis of Communism and the End of East Germany*, Princeton: Princeton University Press, 1997, pp. 320–1.

13. McAdams, p. 33.

14. Meier, pp. 321–2.

15. Yoder, p. 67.

16. McAdams, p. 28.

17. Pól Ó Dochartaigh, *Germany since 1945*, Basingstoke: Palgrave, 2004, p. 227.

18. Quoted in Andreas Zielcke, 'Die Kälteschock des Rechtsstaates', *FAZ*, 9 November 1991.

19. Quoted in McAdams, p. 37.

20. It is, nonetheless, highly problematic to draw such a clear divide between the Stasi's internal and external activities. Such a division runs the risk of absolving parts of the organization from the culpability of the whole. The Ministry for State Security was a highly structured institution and its various subsections worked closely with one another. For an examination of the level of internal cooperation between the different sections of the MfS and between the MfS and other State organs see Thomas Rudolph, 'Die Bearbeitung von Kirche, Kultur und Opposition durch die Diensteinheiten der Linie XX des MfS – Verantwortung, Funktion, Methodik' in E1/VIII, pp. 19–47.

21. Maier, p. 322. The most famous example of this was the Günther Guillaume affair, which saw the Stasi successfully plant an operative as an advisor to Willy Brandt, the then German Chancellor, whose exposure caused the government's downfall.

22. For a comparative study of a number of various truth commissions see *Truth v. Justice: The Morality of Truth Commissions*, ed. by Robert I. Rotberg and Dennis Thompson, Princeton: Princton University Press, 2000.

23. See, for example, Antonia Grunenberg, *Antifaschismus – ein deutscher Mythos*, Reinbek: Rowohlt, 1993.

24. For fuller discussions of the development of the tribunal ideas see Petra Bock, 'Von der Tribunal-Idee zur Enquete-Kommission des Bundestages "*Aufarbeitung von Geschichte und Folgen der SED-Diktatur in Deutschland*", *Deutschlandarchiv*, 28 (1995), 1171–83; also Dorothee Wilms, 'Begründung, Entstehung und Zielsetzung der Enquete-Kommission 1992–94 im Deutschen Bundestag', in Barker, pp. 9–20.

25. For a collection of views aired during this debate see Albrecht Schönherr, *Ein Volk am Pranger?* Berlin: Aufbau, 1992.

26. Markus Meckel, 'Einander Fragen stellen und zuhören – das ist das ganze Geheimnis', in Barker, pp. 3–8 (p. 7).

27. Markus Meckel, 'Demokratische Selbstbestimmung als Prozeß: Die Aufgabe der Politik bei der Aufarbeitung der DDR-Vergangenheit', in *Die Partei hatte immer recht – Aufarbeitung von Geschichte und Folgen der SED-Diktatur*, ed. by Bernd Faulenbach, Markus Meckel and Hermann Weber, Essen: Klartext, 1994, pp. 250–78 (p. 262).

28. See 'Debatte des Deutschen Bundestages am 12 März 1992', in E1/I, *Enquete Kommission: Anträge Debatten Bericht*, pp. 25–177. One of the most memorable moments of this debate was the speech by Willy Brandt, the architect of the new *Ostpolitik* in the late 1960s, which saw the FRG eventually recognize the GDR in 1972. Brandt's speech also highlighted the limits of the non-partisan approach to the Enquete Commission, during which he offered a seemingly critical appraisal of Honecker's visit to the West, thus implicitly attacking the Kohl government (E1/I, 31–39).

29. The make up of the commission was as follows: CDU/CSU seven politicians and five experts, SPD five politicians and three experts, FDP two politicians and one expert, one Alliance 90/Greens, one politician and one expert, PDS, one politician and one expert. 'Bericht der Enquete-Kommission "Aufarbeitung von Geschichte und Folgen der SED-Diktatur in Deutschland" gemäß Beschluß des Deutschen Bundestages vom 12. März 1992 und vom 20. May 1992– Drucksachen 12/7820, 12/2230, 12/2597', E1/I, pp. 178–778 (p. 186).

30. Defining what constituted oppositional behaviour in the GDR remains a thorny issue for scholars. This problem is clearly reflected in much of the commissioned research for the Enquete. See, for example, Ilko-Sascha Kowalczuk, 'Artikulationsformen und Zielsetzungen von widerständigem Verhalten in verschiedenen Bereichen der Gesellschaft', in E1/VIIii, pp. 1203–85. For further discussion of this point see Jonathan Grix, 'The Enquete-Kommission's Contribution on State-Society Relations in the GDR', in Barker, pp. 55–65 (p. 60–1).

31. For material connected to the Church, see E1/VI; for 'oppositional' activity more generally see E1/VII.

32. Hannah Arendt, *The Origins of Totalitarianism*, London: Allen & Unwin, 1951.

33. Ross, p. 22.

34. Günter Gaus, *Wo Deutschland liegt*, Hamburg: Campe, 1983, pp. 156–227. Grix sees 'conditional loyalty' in the GDR as a multi-layered, unspoken 'agreement' between state and society, whereby the masses tacitly agreed to go through the motions of conformity in exchange for limited freedoms within the private and semi- private spheres, full employment and subsidised food. See Jonathan Grix, *The Role of the Masses in the Collapse of the GDR*, Basingstoke: Macmillan, 2000, pp. 22–6.

35. Mary Fulbrook, *Anatomy of a Dictorship: Inside the GDR 1949– 1989*, Oxford: OUP, 1995, p. 6.

36. For further discussion see Ross, p. 189.
37. Mary Fulbrook, 'Heroes, Victims, and Villains in the History of the German Democratic Republic', in *Rewriting the German Past: History and Identity in the New Germany*, New Jersey: Humanities, 1997, p. 175–96 (p. 190).
38. Konrad H. Jarausch and Michael Geyer, *The Shattered Past*, Princeton: Princeton University Press, 2002, p. 11.
39. Chrstopher Beckmann, 'Die Auseinandersetzung um den Vergleich von "Drittem Reich" und DDR vor dem Hintergrund der Diskussion um Möglichkeiten und Grenzen vergleichender Geschichtsforschung', *Deutsche Studien* 38 (2002), 9–26 (p. 12).
40. Quoted in Beckmann, p. 10.
41. See Ernst Nolte, 'Die Vergangenheit, die nicht vergehen will', in *Historikerstreit: Die Dokumentation der Kontroverse um die Einzigartigkeit der nationalsozialistischen Judenvernichtung*, Piper: Munich, 1987, pp. 39–47.
42. Quoted in Jürgen Habermas, 'What does "Working off the Past" mean today?', in *A Berlin Republic: Writings on Germany*, translated by Steven Rendall, Cambridge: Polity, 1998, pp. 17–40 (p. 23), Habermas was one of Nolte's main opponents in this debate.
43. Bill Niven, *Facing the Nazi Past: United German and the Legacy of the Third Reich*, London: Routledge, 2002, p. 85.
44. For further discussion of the renaming of streets see also Rainer Eckert, 'Straßenumbenennung und Revolution in Deutschland', in *Vergangenheitsbewältigung*, ed. by Eckhard Jesse and Konrad Löw, Berlin: Duncker & Humblot, 1997, pp. 45–52.
45. Niven, p. 58–9. For further discussion of the way the GDR has been memorialized throughout German museum culture see Silke Arnold-de Simine, 'Theme Park GDR? The Aestheticization of Memory in post-*Wende* Museums, Literature and Film', in *Cultural Memory and Historical Consciousness in the German-Speaking World since 1500*, ed. by Christian Emden and David Midgley, Oxford: Peter Lang, 2004, pp. 253–80 (p. 258–65).
46. See also Niven, pp. 58–61. Niven further points out that the use of Mattheuer's statue in this context is very different to the artist's original intention, which was to signify 'the conflict between National Socialism and GDR socialism' (p. 59).
47. Amelie Kutter, 'Geschichtspolitische Ausgrenzungen in der Vereinigungspolitik. Das Beispiel der Enquete-Kommission', in *Die DDR war anders: eine kritische Würdigung ihrer sozialkulturellen Einrichtungen*, ed. by Stefan Bollinger and Fritz Vilmar, Berlin: Verlag Das Neue Berlin, 2002, pp. 25–59 (p. 49).

48. Quoted in Kutter, p. 40, emphasis in Kutter's quotation.
49. Kutter, p. 40.
50. Urs Schoettli, quoted in Kutter, p. 49.
51. Kutter, p. 57.
52. Bernd Faulenbach, 'Die Arbeit der Enquete-Kommissionen und die Geschichtsdebatte in Deutschland seit 1989', in Barker, pp. 21–33 (p. 32).
53. McAdams, p. 100; see also Stephen Brown, '"Angepasste Kirchenleitungen und aufmüpfige Basis?" Die Kirchen im Spiegel der Enquete-Kommission', in Barker, pp. 113–28.
54. Faulenbach, in Barker, p. 25
55. Peter Barker, '"Geschichtsaufarbeitung" within the PDS and the Enquete-Kommissionen', in Barker, pp. 81–95 (p. 86).
56. Keller's evidence, and the debate that ensued is reproduced in Dietmar Keller and Matthias Kirchner (eds), *Zwischen den Stühlen: Pro und Kontra SED*, Berlin: Dietz, 1993.
57. As Barker suggests, the PDS/LL 'Sondervotum' 'represented a compromise between the views of Keller and Heuer'. Uwe-Jens Heuer was a PDS member of the Bundestag who was one of the most vocal in his rejection of cooperation in the official process of the historical appraisal of the GDR. See Barker, p. 84–8. The party's dissatisfaction actually led it to set up an alternative historical 'Commission', complete with its own alternative expert witnesses. See Hans Modrow, Dietmar Keller and Herbert Wolf (eds), *Ansichten zur Geschichte der DDR*, I–IV, Bonn/Berlin: PDS/Linke Liste im Bundestag, 1993–4.
58. Quoted in Dan Hough, *The Fall and Rise of the PDS*, Birmingham: University of Birmingham Press, 2002, p. 132. For an overview of the PDS in the 1990s see, along with Hough, Peter Barker (ed.), *The Party of Democratic Socialism: Modern Post-Communism or Nostalgic Populism?* Amsterdam: Rodopi, 1998.
59. Quoted in McAdams, p. 115.
60. Hough, p. 136.
61. For further discussion of this result see Rita Kuczynski, *Die Rache der Ostdeutschen*, Berlin: Parthas, 2002, pp. 7–16.
62. Daniel Küchenmeister, 'Linkssozialistisch oder ostdeutch? Die PDS am Scheideweg', *Deutschland Archiv*, 6 (2002) 926–930, p. 927–8.
63. In this regional election the PDS achieved 28 per cent of the vote, beating the CDU into third place. See 'SPD kann sich Koalitionspartner aussuchen', *Süddeutsche Zeitung*, 19 September 2004.
64. See, for example, Dieter Roth and Matthias Jung, 'Ablösung der

Regierung vertagt: Eine Analyse der Bundestagswahl 2002', *Aus Politik und Zeitgeschichte*, B 49–50 (2002), 3–17.

65. Kai Arzheimer and Jürgen W. Falter, 'Ist der Osten wirklich rot? Das Wahlverhalten bei der Bundestagswahl 2002 in Ost-West-Perspektive', *Aus Politik und Zeitgeschichte*, B 49–50 (2002), 27–35.

66. For further discussion see Grix, pp. 62–3.

67. Rainer Eppelmann, 'Vorwort', in E2/I, iii – vi (p. iv).

68. One major achievement of the second commission which should be noted, was the setting up of *Foundation for working through the SED-Dictatorship*, which provides invaluable funding for ongoing research projects.

–3–

'Writing Back': Dealing with the Stasi in Literature

In the previous chapter I discussed how the early historical appraisals of the GDR initiated by the state tended to construct it as part of Germany's totalitarian past. In so doing, the political elites sought to legitimize unification as the expansion of the FRG's democratic capitalist system. Here we can view the GDR as a version of Said's 'Orient', an ideological other to the former West German state, through which the new FRG could gain further validation. Amongst some east Germans, this led to a perception that mainstream readings of history were misrepresenting the actual experience of life in the GDR – a perception that had a profound effect on post-unification political culture.

If we move now from political to aesthetic, literary culture, orientalist uses of the past similarly shape responses to the process of unification. Of particular importance to the historical appraisal of the GDR for writers, as indeed it was for much of German society, was the role of the *Ministerium für Staatssicherheit* (Ministry for State Security – the MfS) or Stasi. In this chapter I wish to exame how literary representations of this organization have developed over time. As we shall see, in the first literary texts to deal with the Stasi we find an understandable desire amongst those who were its victims to tell their stories, to condemn the GDR's power structures, and thus to confirm a view of the state that allows the clear apportionment of blame, in turn providing further examples of the 'heroes and villains' view of the past identified by Fulbrook. However, gradually it is possible to locate a shift away from victim narratives to texts that explore the position of those who perpetrated Stasi abuses of civil and human rights.[1]

I argue that in some of these narratives one seems to find evidence of the the type of 'identity of defiance' identified by Bernd Faulenbach in his examination of the Enquete Commissions, where east German self-identification is the product of what can be seen as a negative reaction to the perceived limitations of totalitarian images of the GDR, propagated in official discourses and often viewed to have a western, colonialist

61

agenda.[2] In postcolonial terms, such texts can seen as part of a broad trend of 'writing back'. Yet, what might initially be viewed as a knee-jerk, defiant, reaction to western stereotyping is at times better understood as part of a more sophisticated, reflective trend through which authors endeavour to locate a more authentic representation of east German experience than they find in many mainstream discourses.

In some of the literary texts examined here, the attempt at 'writing back' is then further complicated by the fact that the need to counter western orientalism is also infused with a kind of postcolonial hybridity, identified in a different context by Homi Bhabha, in which authors' narratives themselves also reflect the very 'colonialist' views they wish to counter. That is, we see writers produce texts that mirror the image of the GDR found, for example, in the Enquete Commissions' reports. That said, I argue that for most of the writers examined in this chapter the position of the 'hybrid' is used as a rhetorical stance, through which they seek to question a binary division of the population into 'victims' and 'perpetrators' in order to suggest a more differentiated version of GDR history and of east German experience. So far, I have painted my examination of literary responses wholly in eastern and western terms. As I suggested in Chapter 1, of course, attitudes towards the cultural representation of 'east German experience' cannot always be defined as a geographical issue, and this is particularly clear in the literary representation of the Stasi. Consequently, I also examine here how the type of 'writing back' we find in certain eastern 'perpetrator narratives' plays an important role in western engagements with the topic, as the old left-liberal FRG intelligentsia attempts to find a role for itself in this new society. Finally, I look at the limitations of 'writing back', and more importantly the problem of asserting the validity of the artist's role in society if writers use their status as producers of aesthetic texts to transcend, or even to ignore, the question of actual collaboration with oppressive state structures.

The Stasi and East German Writers

Of all the aspects of the GDR discussed in the early 1990s, it was without doubt the Stasi that grabbed most of the headlines.[3] In the immediate aftermath of the *Wende*, German public life was punctuated by numerous scandals that came to light as the miles of Stasi files accumulated in its forty years of existence were gradually worked through. These scandals mainly concerned the 'outing' of a range of prominent East German figures as Stasi collaborators, from Lothar de Maizière, the first democratically elected premier of the GDR, to Manfred Stolpe, the former

Minister President of Brandenburg. Indeed, the influence of the Stasi on contemporary life did not stop at the borders of the GDR, but was also felt on the political life of West Germany, when surveillance tapes made by the MfS were cited as showing that the former Chancellor Helmut Kohl had received illegal funds for his party.

It was not only the political sphere that was rocked by Stasi scandals. One of the most controversial areas of influence of the MfS was on intellectual life in the East, and in particular the organization's position within the literary scene. That the Stasi should have been so exercised by the activities of writers in the East reflects the special status of the arts within the Eastern bloc. From the early days of the GDR, writers were seen as a crucial weapon in the state's propaganda arsenal. They were to be, as Stalin put it, the 'engineer[s] of the human soul', who would help to educate the masses in the ways of socialism.[4] State-endorsed writers were given special privileges, such as generous financial support and Western travel. However, as time went on, relations between some of the GDR's most important writers and the ruling elite became strained. From the 1960s, rather than simply toeing the party line, writers such as Christa Wolf and Heiner Müller saw it as their duty to provide a forum for public debate absent elsewhere. Never losing faith in the ideals of socialism, such writers nonetheless believed that it was their responsibility to try to reform the GDR from within, in order to turn it into a truly democratic socialist state. In the process, some of these writers, in particular Wolf and Müller gained huge international recognition.[5]

In the 1970s and 1980s, new groups of writers began to emerge, the most well known of which centred around the Prenzlauer Berg area of East Berlin. Poets such as Uwe Kolbe, Jan Faktor, Sascha Anderson and Rainer Schedlinski started to organize an underground literary scene that criticized the SED state far more radically than Christa Wolf's generation had done, ironically by simply refusing to engage in the political life of the state – taking a non-political stance being one of the most effective means of dissidence in a country where political ideology was its very *raison d'être*. Unlike those older writers, who had experienced the Third Reich and had embraced the GDR as their salvation from National Socialism, this new generation, the so-called 'Hineingeborenen' (the 'born into it ones'),[6] had not been party to the decision to build a socialist state, and so therefore did not feel obliged to conform to its limitations. As this group began to publish in the 1980s, it was viewed by the Western media as representing new hope for the GDR. Its work was greeted as a truly autonomous, democratic form of literature that offered a radical challenge to the draconian cultural politics of the SED.

With the collapse of the GDR, attitudes towards its writers and intellectuals changed drastically, a change that, from the start, was due in no small part to the relation of these figures to the MfS. The beginning of this shift in attitude was heralded with the *Literaturstreit* (Literature Debate) of 1990/1991. This initially revolved around the publication of Christa Wolf's *Was bleibt* (*What Remains*), a story based on her victimization at the hands of the Stasi, which she first wrote in 1979 and then revised for publication in 1990.[7] Here, Wolf gives a fictionalized account of the Stasi surveillance operation carried out on her in the 1970s. The publication of the story caused uproar among certain western critics, condemned, for example, by Frank Schirrmacher and Ulrich Greiner who interpreted its delayed publication as an attempt by Wolf, a writer who had enjoyed many privileges under the SED, to redefine herself as a GDR dissident. It should be mentioned, however, that throughout their attacks such critics ignored the fact that, far from being a moment of redefinition, the text was largely a continuation of the exploration of the aesthetic and political positions Wolf had held since the 1960s. *Was bleibt* is a further stage in Wolf's literary 'process of painful self-analysis', as Georgina Paul puts it.[8] Indeed, one of the central ironies of the *Literaturstreit* was that the target of her critical self-analysis in this case was the very same ambiguous relationship with the state that her detractors claimed she was ignoring.[9]

The highly personalized *Was bleibt* controversy subsequently provoked a broader debate on the validity of GDR literature as a whole, with these same critics suggesting that the type of work produced by Wolf had had its day. During the Cold War, it was argued, GDR writers had always been given a special status due to the conditions under which they were writing. Now that these conditions no longer held, their work should be judged according to purely artistic criteria – criteria that, it would seem, many of their texts could not meet. The scope of these attacks was wide ranging, and soon they began to reach beyond the GDR, with Greiner questioning what he saw as the predilection for writers in both the East and the West (particularly in the case of the latter on left-leaning figures such as Günter Grass who had dominated mainstream intellectual life in the FRG) to produce 'Gesinnungskitsch' (kitsch of conviction), or literature more preoccupied with its moral and political message than its artistic value.[10] In a post-Cold War climate, writers should now withdraw from the political sphere and get on with the business of producing aesthetically interesting literature.

The hatchet job that began with the *Literaturstreit* then gained momentum as rumours began to surface about the extent to which the Stasi had infiltrated artistic life in the GDR. As the MfS documents started to be worked through a startling picture of the relationship between writers and the state emerged. The German press regularly reported on the substantial files the MfS had collected on a huge number of GDR writers, both on those who worked within official state structures and on those who wrote and published in the underground cultural scene.[11] More shocking, though, was the fact that certain 'dissident' authors had actively co-operated with the Stasi as *Inoffizielle Mitarbeiter* (unofficial collaborators) (IMs). It was discovered that figures such as Müller and Wolf, and – even worse – Sascha Anderson and Rainer Schedlinski, key figures in the apparently autonomous Prenzlauer Berg Scene, had all worked as IMs for the MfS.[12]

As one looks back on the scandals of the early 1990s, it is in some cases more alarming to reflect upon how information uncovered by the opening of the files was used, rather than upon many of the revelations themselves. The decision to open the files was taken in August 1990 by the GDR's de Maizière government, under pressure from members of the citizens' movement. Like the judicial processes, discussed in the previous chapter, responsibility for the files passed to the Bonn government after unification. This government set up the *Behörde für die Unterlagen des Staatssicherheitsdienstes der ehemaligen Deutschen Demokratischen Republik* (Agency for the Files of the State Security Service of the Former German Democratic Republic), generally referred to at the time as the 'Gauck Agency', after the Protestant minister and political activist Joachim Gauck who was mandated to set it up.[13] The Gauck Agency began to admit members of the public in January 1992. Its aim was primarily to allow the MfS's victims, historians and other academics, to find out the extent of the organization's activities. This decision should be seen within the context of the processes discussed in the previous chapter: a key motivation for the agency's policy was to facilitate a process of reconciliation amongst east Germans in order to aid their integration into democratic society. However, for some, much of the agency's work seemed to undermine to this aim. If we return to Mary Fulbrook's view of post-*Wende* historiography, with regards to archives such as the Stasi files, she suggests that in the east 'there was the very understandable sense of emotional outrage felt by victims of former communist regimes, who wanted to express their anger through the use of an analytic concept emphasizing oppression and injustice'.[14] This, as we have already seen, led to the spread of a black-and-white image of the GDR, where the population could be split neatly into 'heroes and villains'. However, as with the other processes of historical reappraisal, Fulbrook notes that using the newly available information in this manner was ultimately reductive:

Curiously, although the archives were now open, providing rich materials for the construction of a far more differentiated picture than was previously available, they were at first rapidly plundered simply in order to pad out and prop up preconceived views based essentially in a desire to effect a political and moral demolition job.[15]

For some, judging the past through the prism of the Stasi files seemed to be leading to very harsh pronouncements on who precisely the 'villains' in the GDR were. Walter Mittenzwei goes so far as to suggest that 'what was to be a highway to freedom became, in the words of Friedrich Schorlemmer from the citizens' movement, "a noose around our necks"'.[16] On the one hand, in the very early 1990s, the mere hint of collusion with the organization (as was initially the case with de Maizière, for example) was enough to exclude a person from public life. On the other, the influence of the Stasi on oppositional activity (however tentative) was often deemed to undermine completely the validity that such activity may have played in questioning, and ultimately bringing down, the government. The way the Stasi was being reported seemed simply to confirm the view expounded by GDR poet and songwriter Wolf Biermann as well as others, that 'all opposition groups were eaten away by Stasi metastases', and consequently, that their activities were of little real value.[17]

For the cultural sphere, such readings of the past had a particularly profound effect. Slyvia Klötzer, for example, in her commentary on the Prenzlauer Berg scandals, sees the Stasi revelations as confirmation of a view of the scene in which

[the IMs] served as functionaries in the underground with the aim of organizing the alternative art scene to make it controllable and open to manipulation. As a result of this, many of the writers were unwittingly bound back into structures they thought they had freed themselves from.[18]

It became common to talk of the alternative cultural scene as a postmodern 'Simulation', sponsored by the state Security Service, in which well-placed IMs, who could act without fear of State reprisals, guided its activities.[19] In the view of some commentators, such as Mittenzwei, the information released by the Gauck Agency was feeding a media frenzy, the aim of which was nothing less than the 'defamation and liquidation of the socialist intelligentsia'.[20] Within the context of our broader discussion, the use of the word 'liquidation' is revealing, recalling the charge of social colonization made by Dümcke and Vilmar. For the GDR's beleaguered writers these scandals did indeed appear to be fulfilling such an aim, because even the quasi-political function of literature during the GDR period could now ostensibly be rejected by the fact of Stasi involvement.

It is beyond question that the Stasi was a manifestation of an oppressive state system, which had a hugely destructive effect on many individuals, breaking up families, causing untold psychological damage and in some cases even death.[21] Indeed, it would seem somewhat crass to claim, as Mittenzwei does, that the Stasi scandals of the 1990s saw the re-emergence of the same atmosphere of suspicion common place in the East before the *Wende*,[22] or, as in the view of the writer and Stasi victim Jürgen Fuchs, that 'The Gauck Agency [… was] the continuation of the Stasi with other means'.[23] Clearly, such claims must be balanced against the point Alison Lewis makes, that the Stasi legislation that brought about the Gauck Agency can also be said to have 'put a stop to media gossip and speculation about East Germany's intelligensia and the extent of its collaboration with power almost immediately … shifting the burden of proof … from the individual to the files'.[24] While the opening of the files did not bring an end to Stasi scandals, it did mean that they now had to be based on documentary evidence rather than hearsay.

Nevertheless, the fact remains that in the early 1990s the role of the Stasi was the overriding focus of popular readings of GDR history, a focus that moreover appeared to be skewing views of the past. As Stephen Brockmann suggests, 'In the midst of these revelations about its power, the Stasi became a synecdoche for the tyranny of the GDR itself.'[25] For Brockmann, this had two central effects; for those who had grown up in the East, 'the Stasi allowed one simple, straightforward assignation of blame for the past. Questions of individual and collective guilt vanished before the overwhelming and evil divinity of the Stasi.' He continues, 'after the Second World War Germans had used the conveniently dead figure of Hitler as a repository for historical responsibility, thus absolving themselves from individual guilt; after the collapse of the GDR, the Stasi seemed to be serving a similar role'.[26] On the other hand, the 'Stasi equals GDR' constellation could be used as a means of dismissing any call for an inclusive view of the new Germany that would also take into consideration the experience of former GDR citizens.[27] Here Brockmann echoes the views of the psychologist Hans Joachim Maaz, who at this time feared what he saw as a culture of blame in unified Germany, where the Stasi, and in particular the figure of the IM, served as a 'common scapegoat' that was having a profoundly damaging effect on Germany's social psyche.[28] The outing of IMs, he argued, was doing little for the process of reconciliation. It was, rather, simply turning former victims into a new type of perpetrator in a witch hunt for justice that was undermining a more fundamental process of dealing with the past, required if Germany was ever to become a truly unified nation – one that could make a break with its legacy of violence and authoritarianism.[29]

Victim Discourses: Making Stories from Stasi Files

Given the level of influence the Stasi exerted over the literary scene in the East, and the profile its role has been given since the GDR's demise, it is perhaps unsurprising that its workings should have become an important topos for writers. Wolf's *Was bleibt* was only the first of many fictional and non-fictional engagements by writers in both the east and the west with the MfS.[30] What is interesting is how this topos has developed. One of the first responses by a writer to post-*Wende* Stasi revelations was Reiner Kunze's *Deckname »Lyrik«: Eine Dokumentation* (*Codename: 'Poetry': a Documentation*).[31] This is a text that caused a great stir at the time of its publication not least for its confirmation of the fact that Ibrahim Böhme, the leader of the East German SPD during the election of 1990, had worked as a MfS informant, a claim that he himself had always denied.[32] Kunze's text is made up almost entirely of extracts from his Stasi dossier, with the occasional interjection to explain certain MfS abbreviations, and shows in frightening detail the destructive thoroughness of the surveillance operation carried out on him. The text presents the reader with a chilling account of the vicious, somewhat euphemistically termed 'operative Maßnahmen' ('operative measures') (D, 77) undertaken by the Stasi against him and his family in order to undermine his literary activities both inside the GDR and abroad. These measures ranged from the near total surveillance of Kunze and his family, to the organization's physical intervention in his life by the placement of IMs within his circle of family and friends. Clearly the MfS had a profoundly damaging effect on Kunze and his wife, bringing them to the point of 'physical and psychological ruin', as one of the reports suggests (D, 87), eventually forcing them to leave the GDR in 1977. Moreover, it would appear that the Stasi did not intend to stop its operation against Kunze when he left for the West. The book ends with a sinister report outlining the organization's plans to discredit Kunze in the FRG, mentioning a number of measures, including the spreading of rumours that Kunze himself was a Stasi informant (D, 98).

That the Stasi was interested in Kunze was clearly understood by him and his circle of friends at the time. For example, in a moment of disturbing humour in the text, Kunze quotes a report that notes the dry sarcasm of one person writing to him: '... Letter from Sweden (date 15.3.1976)

… On the reverse side of the letter was a comment with two arrows pointing to it: "Here is the best place to open and reseal the letter"' (D, 53). Yet,
it is also clear from the text that Kunze was not aware of the full magni-
tude of the Stasi operation against him until after the *Wende*. As Böhme,
alias 'IMV »Bohkarz«' notes with ominous pride in a report dated 12
May 1976 'K … underestimates the quality of those who work for the
Ministry of State Security' (D, 58).[33]

One of the most frightening revelations of Kunze's text is the apparent
readiness of a wide section of society to cooperate with the Stasi in its
campaign against the writer. The reader learns of a certain 'W.', a professor of German, who is more than willing to produce a damning testimony
to what he sees as the 'pronounced antisocialist tendency' of Kunze's
work, even suggesting that Kunze's simple prose style is specifically
designed to corrupt children (D, 69f.). Elsewhere, a report describes how
one of Kunze's neighbours is happy to bore a hole in his wall in order to
give officers better access to Kunze's flat (D, 73f.). When the neighbour's
wife shows her scruples at her husband's readiness to spy on his neighbour, her husband suggests that 'K has thrown his lot in with the shoddy
forces who oppose our socialist society and is not worth being protected
and respected by her' (D, 74). The GDR is presented as a society in
which, as Kunze suggested in a subsequent interview, 'almost an entire
population proved itself to be as useful to the Stasi as it had previously
been to the Gestapo'.[34] Furthermore, Kunze shows how the organization
tried to sanitize its activities in the Orwellian 'New Speak' of its reports,
which, as Heimo Schwilk notes, replaced the notion of spying with the
term *Aufklärung* (enlightenment) and psychological warfare with the
term *Bearbeitung* (treatment).[35]

Kunze's text tells the story of a vicious example of state-sanctioned
oppression. Yet, it is far from unique and can be seen as typical of many
early post-*Wende* accounts of life in the GDR, such as those discussed in
the previous chapter where we also find a degree continuity between the
Third Reich and the GDR. In terms of Fulbrook's analysis, in *Deckname
»Lyrik«* Kunze gives a, perhaps understandably, black-and-white picture
of life in the GDR, in which it is easy, with the benefit of hindsight, to
define who the victims and who the perpetrators of the Stasi were. Indeed,
whenever a shade of grey enters the narrative it is immediately dispelled.
We are told, for example, of the Stasi's attempt to blackmail one of
Kunze's friends into working as an IM by threatening to prosecute the
man's son for weapon offences if he does not comply with its wishes (D,
61). We then subsequently learn that the man proves himself to be unsuit-
able for use as an informant (D, 65). Similarly, with regard to those who
do cooperate with the organization, such as the professor, there is never

any discussion of the coercive pressures to which they might have been subjected. Thus any sense of moral ambiguity such situations could have given rise to need not be addressed.

In an interview with Wolfgang Kraus, however, Kunze acknowledges the fact that collaboration with the State cannot always be seen in such black-and-white terms, pointing to the existence of what Maaz terms 'victim-perpetrators'.[36] He claims that 'one has to look at the reasons why a person became an IM for the state Security Services'.[37] Furthermore, he suggests that it is crucial to examine the post-*Wende* response by the IMs themselves to their activities, claiming that those who now show remorse should be forgiven, thereby pointing to the role the Stasi files might play in the process of post-unification reconciliation. In fact, Kunze claims that the venom of his attack against Böhme was only provoked by the former IM's denial of his past, and his wish to continue in public life, a stance the author found completely unacceptable, thus forcing him to become a participant in the culture of blame identified by Maaz.

Another potentially problematic area of the text is the status of the Stasi files as a truthful representation of the past. On the one hand, as Timothy Garton Ash declares in his examination of his Stasi file, at first glance, one's Stasi records appears to be a wonderful 'gift to memory',[38] or as Biermann famously claimed in his poem 'Die Stasi-Ballade' ('The Stasi Ballad'), for him 'the Stasi was my Eckermann', equating the organization with the meticulous historian of Goethe's later life.[39] Likewise, Kunze's Stasi file would seem to provide him with a thorough, coherent and reliable representation of his final years in the GDR. Other commentators, such as Joachim Walther, also emphasize the verisimilitude of the files, suggesting that the Stasi insisted on cross-referencing all reports to ensure that their informants did not lie.[40] Clearly, many of the Stasi's records were reliable, the MfS being one of the only conduits for information about the state of the nation that the ruling elite could, to any degree, rely upon. Nevertheless, Kunze himself points elsewhere to the fact that there is also a good deal of unreliable information in the reports. In an interview with Karl Corino he makes the point that it is imperative to distinguish between what he terms 'objective and non-objective' documents, claiming that 'some informants invented material for their reports'. It would appear that, particularly with regard to the files on specific victims, certain informants wrote what they thought their superiors wanted to read. For example, Kunze relates a report that describes his 'connections to a counter-revolutionary circle' in Czechoslovakia, a circle of which Kunze maintains he had no knowledge. 'It is unbelievable how many lies you find in these reports', he claims.[41] In fact, although he claims to have been able to discern between reliable and unreliable documents in his book, he himself was taken to court by Hermann Kant for his inclusion of a report that claimed that Kant was to write a damning article on Kunze for *Neues Deutschland* (D, 72), an allegation Kant consistently denied.[42]

In the course of the 1990s, the 'truth problem of the files', as the east German writer Adolf Endler puts it, became a main focus for writers engaging with Stasi documentation.[43] Valeri Scherstjanoi's radio play *Operative Personenkontrolle »Futurist«* (*Operational Person Check 'Futurist'*),[44] in a similar fashion to Kunze's text, is constructed entirely from extracts of the author's Stasi file. However, the nature of the piece and the picture given of the organization's workings are radically different. As we find in Garton Ash, when Scherstjanoi first received his file he was struck by the thoroughness of the Stasi's work, seeing his dossier as an excellent archive of his past activities, especially of his artistic life as a concrete and sound poet.[45] His experimental texts, many of which consist of nothing that can be recognized as language, clearly baffled the Stasi. Nonetheless, it meticulously made copies of all the poems he sent out of the GDR by post. In the play the thoroughness of the Stasi is held up to ridicule. Kunze's text gives the impression that the MfS was like a frightening 'Big Brother' who allowed no detail of his life, however banal, to go unobserved. In Scherstjanoi's play this idea is turned upside down. The Stasi has nothing of interest to report. As a result, its surveillance officers are forced to give banal details in the desperate attempt to find something to write about. In a report detailing the MfS's first examination of Scherstjanoi's home, for example, we are told:

> On passing through the front door, one enters a hallway, approximately 5 metres long. On the left-hand side are the building's letterboxes. The letter-box of the *object person* is fastened with an iron chain and a simple padlock. On the right-hand side one finds the electricity meters for the whole building. These are visible through a piece of glass. During the process of *enlightenment* the counter of the object person's meter was only moving very slowly. (O, 20, my emphasis)

A perverse comedy is created by such 'surveillance' reports, at the heart of which is a tragedy of wasted energy. The report is full of the Stasi's bureaucratic jargon; it is all form and no content, conveying only trivial information, none of which can be considered a matter of state security. The MfS's bastardized use of the term 'enlightenment', already discussed in connection with Kunze, in this context would seem particularly ridiculous. The information the Stasi receives from its operatives is hardly enlightening.

The irony of the Stasi's use of the concept of 'enlightenment' is one which plays an important role in many literary engagements with the workings of the MfS. Michael Haase notes that the term normally recalls the dynamic, productive and open-ended nature of literary writing encapsulated in the work of figures such as Lessing or Jean Paul, figures who were products of the eighteenth-century philosophical tradition to which the term gives its name. He then contrasts such writing with the static, oppressive and limiting nature of the Stasi's texts.[46] Citing Walther, he argues that the Enlightenment motif in literary engagements with the Stasi tends to throw into stark relief the '"moral demands of literature and art" which can be derived from the Enlightenment's "ethos of literature", and which is irreconcilable with the Enlightenment "ethos" of the Stasi'.[47] This contrast becomes particularly obvious in Scherstjanoi's text. Juxtaposed with the Stasi's surveillance reports are the poetic texts that he also found in his files. Through this juxtaposition, the poet brings into sharp focus the difference between the aesthetic world of his poetry and the banality of the Stasi's language. The play opens with the poet performing one of his 'pure' sound poems, which in this case is a piece consisting of a string of music-like utterances. The poem then fades out to be replaced by the voice of an actor reading one of his Stasi reports, a report that appears far more comprehensible to the listener than the earlier poem. However, as the play develops the very notion of comprehension is itself ironized. It becomes clear that the poet sees his own use of language and sound as a radical counterpoint to the misuse of language in the Stasi's bureaucratic jargon. The actor's voice gives way to another of Scherstjanoi's poems, in which he claims: 'words tie up/ language confines/ sounds liberate' (O, 3). Later he quotes Vladimir Dal, declaring: 'the tongue is the fleshy weapon in your mouth' (O, 10). Deliberately, the poet's language is highly physical in nature. Manifesto-like, he continues, 'think about your speech-tools, you mouth- throat- nose- lip/ cheek/ palate/ tongue-stories' (O, 10). His is a living, bodily language through which he attempts to reflect actual experience. The Stasi's, on the other hand, is the dead language of the pen pusher.

In *Operative Personenkontrolle »Futurist«* one finds a far more abstract appropriation of the Stasi files than in Kunze's text. While Scherstjanoi's work, like that of Kunze, is a critique of a sinister organization, the immediate feeling of shock that one senses in *Deckname »Lyrik«* is absent. There could be several reasons for this. Most importantly, the nature of the surveillance operation carried out on Scherstjanoi was different from that of Kunze. Kunze was the victim of a full-blown *Operativen Vorgang*

(Operational Process), the level at which the Stasi would actively interfere with the subject's life; Scherstjanoi, on the other hand, was the subject of an *Operativen Personenkontrolle* (Operational Person Check), a preliminary stage during which the MfS attempted to assess the level of the individual's 'threat' to society. Furthermore, by 1996, six years after the publication of *Deckname »Lyrik«*, when Scherstjanoi's play was first broadcast, the public was far more aware of the activities of the secret police. Indeed, as Andreas Staab points out, in the mid 1990s there was a sense of 'over-saturation' with regard to Stasi controversies, which perhaps encourages the writer to treat his subject matter with a degree of humour.[48] Nevertheless, that is not to say that Scherstjanoi wishes to trivialize the banal bureaucratic world found in the files. On the contrary, the Stasi is presented as an appallingly sick joke. The only compensation that Scherstjanoi can find for its existence is through the exploitation of the files as a foil for his illustration of the potential of the poet's role in countering such monstrous abuses of language.

'Writing Back'

In many of the literary texts dealing with the Stasi that were produced after the first wave of outings, we similarly find the MfS used as a point of departure for the discussion of aesthetic rather than explicitly historical issues, with the organization employed as a metaphorical landscape for the examination of the nature of artistic production, as it is in Scherstjanoi's work. This in turn led some writers to engage with the broader issue of the changing role of the intellectual in Germany since the GDR's collapse and the ramifications of the *Literaturstreit*. It is at this point that the Stasi, somewhat ironically, begins to function as a vehicle through which writers attempt to 'write back' against, or challenge, popular constructions of the GDR as an all-encompassing, totalitarian dictatorship, in which the MfS had the entire population in its thrall, a view seen by many easterners as largely emanating from the west. However, curiously, the urge to question readings of the GDR that paint it as nothing more than a 'Stasi state' often expresses itself in the construction of narratives that appear to be wholly a product of this very view. That is, we see writers willingly inhabit the space allocated them by what they consider to be the colonizing power of a western hegemony. In Bhabha's terms, they actively take up the position of the 'hybrid'. But, in adopting this stance, such texts ultimately challenge, through parody, what they view as a reductive reading of history, demanding instead a more differentiated approach to the past. Again, if we adopt the language of Bhabha, such writers return the controlling gaze of the colonizer in order to displace its power: 'the look of surveillance returns as the displacing gaze of the disciplined'.[49] For Bhabha, the destabilizing process of returning the colonizer's gaze is an inevitable side-effect of colonization. With regard to the cultural sphere of east German literature, this notion is, at times, radicalized, being provocatively appropriated, within the context of an 'identity of defiance', in order to counter negative western stereotyping. However, the defiant appropriation of a hybrid position can also actually go beyond being a mechanism to question popular views of the GDR as a Stasi state. In the text by Thomas Brussig, discussed below, for example, the writer, whose wrath knows no bounds, uses this position not only as a means of challenging what he sees as limited western views, but also as a self-reflexive mechanism through which he can interrogate the views of his fellow east Germans. In other texts, we find authors adopting a more conciliatory tone. On the one hand, we see writers calling for a process of reconciliation between those who lived on either sides of the power equation in the GDR. On the other, we find these same narratives being used to recuperate the role of the intellectual in the wake of the *Literaturstreit*, focusing on the continued importance of the critical power of aesthetic language, a central concern of GDR writing throughout its history and one which writers' engagements with the language of the Stasi files throws into stark relief.[50]

In this section of the chapter I examine how these developments are particularly reflected in texts that move away from the documentary account of the victims of surveillance operations to the fictional exploration of the psyche of those who perpetrated MfS crimes. As I intimated above, one of the most viciously satirical of such 'perpetrator texts' is Thomas Brussig's *Helden wie wir* (*Heroes like us*).[51] Brussig's novel is a direct response to a reading of the GDR that sees everything that went on there as a Stasi 'Simulation', questioning such claims head on by writing a fictional history of the GDR as if this were the case. The novel tells the story of Klaus Uhltzscht, who might best be described as a GDR version of Forest Gump. Klaus, a highly ignorant member of the GDR's intelligence service, stumbles through the history of the GDR, affecting it at key moments, most noticeably on the night of 9 November 1989. A self-declared student of sexual perversion, who is obsessed with his 'Pinsel' (willy) (H, 7), Brussig's protagonist claims to have caused the first breach in the Berlin Wall by exposing himself to border guards at Bornholmer Straße. Shocked by the size of his member, the guards are stunned into silence and so are unable to hold the crowds back from passing into the West. From this brief plot synopsis, it is obvious that the novel is not to be taken at face value, but is rather, on one level at least, a sustained satire

on the GDR as 'Stasi State'. Indeed, the novel's satirical mode is immediately made clear by its narrative conceit. Klaus tells his story to the *New
York Times* reporter Mr. Kitzelstein, thus inviting the reader to relate to
the story, in the words of Kristie Foell and Jill Twark, as yet 'another
sensationalist tabloid confession' of scandalous Stasi activity, common
place in the media of the early 1990s. As such, the text can be read as an
ironic response to the predominant view of the GDR at the time, its over-
the-top conformation of the centrality of the Stasi to life in the GDR ironically questioning such readings of the past.[52]

Brussig received a good deal of criticism for his portrayal of the Stasi.
His humorous description of Klaus and his fellow officers was seen by
some as a trivialization of its activities. Reviewers such as Thomas Kraft
claimed that in the book 'The Stasi is portrayed as a low quality Monty-
Python-Show troop.'[53] This portrayal was then viewed by others as a
means of playing down the need for Stasi members to take responsibility
for their actions. Martin Ahrends, for example, felt, 'The book can be read
as a general absolution for all perpetrators and fellow travellers.'[54] Such
critics saw Brussig as nothing less than an apologist for the SED. However,
these views ignore Brussig's obviously provocative stance, which questions the overwhelming importance of the Stasi to post-*Wende* readings of
the GDR. Moreover, while these critics might, perhaps, be forgiven for not
getting Brussig's joke, it his harder to understand the fact that they ignore
the obvious critique of the GDR that the text *also* includes. The satirical
appropriation of a hybrid position adopted in the text to question the
perceived instrumentalization of the GDR, consequently, therefore, also
confirms the oppressive nature of the life under the SED.

In so doing, the text attacks what its author sees as equally worrying
mis-readings of the past by east Germans. This is shown most obviously
in the distance between the author and his somewhat unreliable narrator.
In telling his story, the banal Monty-Python-like image of the Stasi Klaus
describes fails to hide the distortion of socialism that brought about the
need for its existence and for his own collaboration with it. Klaus is
shown to be wholly a product of the environment in which he grew up.
As a child he looks at a series of maps in his atlas, which trace the course
of world history. Seeing the gradual change in colour from imperialist
blue to socialist red in the maps, he realizes, 'I was already there where
the others had to get to … I belonged to the leading, red world' (H, 95).
'I was one of us', he proudly declares (H, 106). His pride in belonging to
the 'victors of history' makes him desperate to conform to his society's
norms, norms that are symbolized in the text by what seem on the face of
it to be the decidedly anti-socialist, petit bourgeois views of his mother, a
hygiene inspector, and of his father, a Stasi officer. His mother is a prude

who will not even speak the word 'Sex', preferring to replace it with the word 'Sechs' (Six) (H, 58). Her attitude leads Klaus to perceive all manifestations of sexual activity as filthy. Unfortunately, Klaus finds it impossible to suppress his own sexual thoughts, and instead becomes fixated on the idea of sex. As a result, he is forced to see himself as 'one of the most perverse people on the planet' (H, 59). The damaging effect of his father's influence is more obvious. The man is a bully, whose authoritarian style of bringing Klaus up has more in common with the institutionalized and inhuman system Klaus imagines is to be found in the USA than with an 'enlightened' communist state. As the man informs the reader early in the novel, during his childhood, his actions were always judged by his father as if the boy was the defendant in an 'American trial by jury' (H, 34).

Klaus' desperation to conform to the GDR's wishes, as they are represented in the demands of his parents, is so great that he becomes consumed by the dream of being the ultimate conformer, a hero of the state who, in a rather confusing leap of logic, can put his sexual perversity to good use to help bring about the final victory of socialism (H, 247). This search for conformity and acceptance eventually brings him to the door of the MfS. By joining this institution he seems at last to find a satisfactory means of regaining the state's approval, providing the protagonist with a context for his feelings of perversion and alienation. The Stasi is seen as the product of the attitude of people like Klaus's parents, a reflection of the psyche of the state. Just as Klaus's mother, in attempting to suppress all discussion of her son's natural sexual urges, produces a sex-obsessed monster, the state, in its drive to suppress all natural dissent amongst the population, has produced the monster of the Stasi. Thus Klaus's sexual perversion functions as a metaphor for the perversion of socialism at the centre of the GDR.

The initial image of the Stasi presented in the text is that of a surrogate family, which is far more forgiving than Klaus's own. His father is a forbidding figure who dismisses the narrator as a failure (H, 39). While it transpires that the man is, in fact, also a Stasi officer, his domestic stance towards Klaus is not reflective of those members of the organization with whom Klaus has to deal professionally. His Stasi superior at work, for example, is a rather avuncular character who informs his young colleague on his first day, 'We're very informal here, and call everyone by their first name' (H, 48f.). Yet, as Klaus's description of the Stasi's activities goes on, one begins to suspect that it is actually far from an avuncular, Monty-Python-like operation. His sense of belonging and the matter-of-fact narration of his work starts to jar as we learn, for example, of the house searches he would take part in, where the aim of the exercise was not to find evidence but rather to let the occupant know that they had been visited, thereby leaving them with a subtle 'feeling of threat' (H, 155). Elsewhere we read of Klaus's delight at successfully kidnapping a small child. Although he himself attempts to present this in innocuous terms, claiming that he gained the greatest satisfaction out of preventing her from winning at Ludo (H, 228), this cannot conceal the cruelty of such state-sanctioned kidnaps.

Klaus is convinced that he is destined for higher things in the service of his country, dismissing his sordid activities as necessary for the greater good of socialism, and refusing to accept any individual responsibility for them:

> Someone had plans for me … I was certain that I only had to do what I was told, and beyond that I had no power whatsoever. I was waiting, and nothing that I would do during this time was intended or wanted by me. For that reason I didn't hurt anybody. *I was not the person* who committed break-ins, who kidnapped, who persecuted, who made other people insecure, who created fear. I was just waiting. (H, 169) [Brussig's emphasis]

In the light of such claims by the narrator that he was only following orders, one can perhaps understand the outrage of those critics who see Brussig as an apologist. However, such critics fail to see the clear sense of provocation in Klaus's frank account of his life in the Stasi and the subsequent claim that he has nothing to be ashamed of. Along with western reductive readings of the past, as well as the GDR's institutionalized oppressive regime itself, he also attacks those individual east Germans who now suggest that they had no responsibility for, or part to play in, the existence of the system. As Brussig's protagonist himself later asks: 'How could this society exist for decades if everyone was unhappy?' (H, 312). The text is a call to east Germans to examine honestly all aspects of their past, and their own compliance with the state, whatever form this may have taken.

The multifaceted nature of Brussig's attack comes to the fore in his representation of the events of 9 November. On the one hand, the over-the-top satirical conceit that a single member of the Stasi exposing himself could bring down the Wall questions the 'GDR equals Stasi' equation identified by Brockmann, recalling those conspiracy theorists who saw the *Wende* wholly as the result of MfS engineering.[55] On the other, it is an attack on the notion that the east German masses liberated themselves from the SED through their peaceful revolution. For Klaus such an idea is ridiculous: 'look at east Germans before and after the fall of the Wall. Before they were passive, and they're still passive' (H, 320). Thus it would appear that the 'heroes' of the title are to be read entirely ironically. It is ultimately the decadent, inhuman GDR state, encapsulated in the figure of Klaus, that destroyed itself, the perversion at the heart of the GDR eventually leading the state to implode.

Brussig's attack on the population of the GDR does not end with 'the masses'. He is particularly scathing of those intellectuals who rejected unification in favour of a socialism 'with a human face'. The main target of his scorn is the most famous GDR writer Christa Wolf. Much of Brussig's novel can be seen as a continuation of the attack on *Was bleibt*, recalling the *Literaturstreit* and its assault on the left-leaning intelligentsia in Germany. In *Helden wie wir*, we see the reverse of Wolf's story of a woman pushed to the brink of a psychological breakdown by being put under surveillance by the MfS. Brussig's narrator attacks Wolf's dramatization of events, picking up details from Wolf's book and treating them comically. For example, as Foell and Twark note, at one point in *Was Bleibt* Wolf's protagonist realizes that someone has been in her flat, due to the fact that a mirror has been broken, an event that deeply disturbs her, and which would seem to be a clear example of the type of psychological warfare the Stasi engaged in, the type of activity which Klaus himself describes.[56] However, the idea that this particular act was a calculated ploy on behalf of the MfS is subsequently humorously undermined by one of Klaus' colleague, who claims that he broke the mirror by accident, complaining of the lengths he had to go to in order to cover his tracks, concocting a story about a minor earthquake that he then had to have placed in the newspaper (H, 161).

The most concerted attack on Wolf comes in the novel's final chapter, entitled 'Der geheilte Pimmel' ('The Healed Willy'), a satirical reference to Wolf's canonical 1961 text *Der geteilte Himmel* (*The Divided Heavens*). At this point, the satirical tone of the text tends to give way to polemic. Klaus witnesses Wolf's famous speech on 4 November 1989 (reproduced in full in the novel, H, 283–5), although he confuses Wolf with Jutta Müller, the trainer of the ice skater Katarina Witt, an icon of GDR sport and still a major celebrity in post-unification Germany. Klaus is disgusted by what he sees as Wolf's defence of the GDR's socialist project, encapsulated for him in the line from her speech 'Just imagine, we have socialism and no one wants to leave' (H, 285). 'Mr Kitzelstein, it would be laughable', the narrator suggests, 'if only it wasn't so bloody tragic' (H, 287). In the conflation of Wolf with Müller, Brussig uses this speech to mock the ideals of this older generation of writers, and to distance his own generation from it. Yet, while he dismisses Wolf's position, he does not suggest that the younger generation has any better idea of how to run the world: 'Don't ask me what I was for', he claims, 'but when I heard Jutta Müller's speech, I knew what I was against' (H, 286).

Brussig's text is unremittingly defiant, with very little escaping his scorn. He rejects the older generation's defence of the GDR's socialist experiment but at the same time refuses to offer any solutions himself. Furthermore, as we have seen, while Klaus is scathing about the GDR, the west fares no better, and towards the end of the novel it is this target that finally, once again, takes centre stage. Here the notion of 'writing back' against western received views returns to the fore, suggesting that Klaus remains highly critical of the unified German state, which he sees as a wholesale colonial takeover, albeit one in which the east German population were willing participants. He notes in disgust that, as the demonstrators began to shout for 'Germany', those in the West 'acted as if everyone who said "Germany" actually meant "The Federal Republic." How unimaginative!' (H, 322). *Helden wie wir* is one of the most prominent examples of a perpetrator narrative being used as a means of defiantly 'writing back' against western colonialism. However, as well as rejecting western attitudes towards the east, Brussig also uses these same attitudes to critique his own east German society, and in particular its views of the past. Thus his 'identity of defiance' is at times self-reflexive in its rejection of the ideals of both past and present German states.

The unremittingly defiant stance adopted by Brussig's text writes large the culture of blame that Maaz suggests has dominated post-unification society. In »*Ich*« by Wolfgang Hilbig (a GDR writer whose later work was discussed in Chapter 1 of this study, also in connection with the act of 'writing back'), we similarly see the Stasi being used as a vehicle for a defiant critique of both east and west German society.[57] However, here the notion of 'writing back' goes beyond the expression of pure defiance, both through its engagement with the act of writing, and more importantly, in its gesture beyond the culture of blame, towards a more conciliatory understanding of the past. Hilbig's text would appear to be even more obviously a product of hybridity than Brussig's novel in its reflection of an ostensibly western view that constructs the GDR as a 'Stasi state'. Taking as its inspiration the scandals surrounding the outing of Anderson and Schedlinski as IMs, »*Ich*« tells the story of a manual worker, M.W., who, wishing to escape the intense tedium of factory life, takes refuge in the world of literature, obsessively spending his time reading and writing. Through both the work of his literary models and the texts he himself creates, he attempts to transfigure the banality of his daily life into art, and thus to find a less limited sense of identity than the one afforded him as a worker. His activities attract the attention of the MfS, who coerce M.W. into working for them as an IM in the underground literary scene. As an informant, he starts to be overtaken by a nightmarish, 'simulated' world in which all the inhabitants simply act out the parts given to them by the Stasi. For example, in order to force M.W. into cooperation with the MfS, his Stasi contact claims he has an illegitimate son, whom the Stasi will look after provided he complies with its wishes. M.W. protests, claiming he has no child, to which his Stasi contact responds: 'Do you really think we couldn't prove the child was yours? We could do that even if you had never had a woman in your life' (I, 105). 'Reality' is anything the Stasi defines as such.

The reason why M.W's writing attracts the attention of the MfS is explained in the novel through the apparent interconnection of the act of writing and the act of spying. Both the informant and the writer, as observers of their environment, are pushed to the margins of their world. Both are alienated from society, for, as his Stasi contact suggests: 'it is easiest to see if you look from the darkness into the light, and not the other way around' (I, 132). Furthermore, the MfS, like Hilbig's protagonist, is obsessed with writing. Consequently, in »*Ich*«, as in Scherstjanoi's *Operative Personenkontrolle »Futurist«*, the Stasi's use of language is a key concern. It is through the written text that the MfS validates the version of reality it chooses to create. Although his contact claims that 'reality' is anything he and his colleagues wish it to be, M.W.'s paternity must still be confirmed in writing. The contact demands that he enter into a written agreement with the MfS by signing a declaration of paternity (I, 66). Material reality is forced to comply with the Stasi's text, in order for the text to appear to be reflecting material reality.

M.W.'s obsession with writing had always isolated him from the other members of his class, who looked on his constant scribbling with suspicion. Indeed, they begin to suspect that he is writing about them before he ever becomes an IM (I, 87). His sense of isolation leads to a crisis of identity in which he finds it impossible to maintain any contact with the world around him or to finish any of his literary texts, until finally he descends into what he terms his 'sleeping phase', an inescapable state of perpetual daydream (I, 87). In his validation of the Stasi's 'text' he gains a new sense of belonging. He signs the paternity declaration, is given the codename Cambert and, as a result, a new feeling of 'reality' returns to his life (I, 66). Specifically, M.W. is given a new means of expression. As Martin Kane points out, whilst the narrator finds it difficult to write literary texts, he discovers a great sense of satisfaction in the Stasi reports he writes.[58] In its officialese M.W. at last finds a language within which he can operate, and that allows him to escape from the constant struggle with words he had previously experienced: 'they conjured up a structure in him … They provided his usual supply of symbols with a more complete meaning' (I, 106f.).

However, gradually M.W.'s sense of crisis returns. He grows dissatisfied with his role as an IM, finding it progressively harder to maintain any distinction between his roles as a writer and as a spy. M.W. turns into an unreal shadow as the state-given identity of Cambert begins to dominate his psyche. Similarly, the Stasi's language, which had at first allowed him to give expression to a new identity, now becomes claustrophobic and limiting. While in the office of his handler, Feuerbach, M.W./Cambert picks up a report, making a note of the following lines: '... *the establishment of the measures of subversion to be carried out according to the exact evaluation of the results achieved by the treatment of the particular Operative Process* ...' [Hilbig's emphasis] I, 23). He then proceeds to explain what fascinates him about these lines:

> what interested me about these lines was the monstrous nature of their stream of abstraction. I'll always recognize this type of language ... I'll always recognize it by the string of genitives running wild. By its string of genitives that go on until you can't remember where they start, by this boundless use of the possessive, as if it's trying to set itself up as the subject, as the real thing. (I, 23)

The action being described is suffocated in a monstrous string of genitives until it is beyond all recognition. In reading this report, M.W. begins to realize the true nature of the Stasi's language, and, by extension, the nature of the whole of its operation. It is a language that obfuscates and confines experience, rather than defining and communicating it. In advising him how to write his reports, Feuerbach urges him to remember: 'the human being is always at the centre' (I, 38). Here we might be forgiven for thinking that the Stasi officer is echoing his more famous namesake, the philosopher Ludwig Feuerbach and his call for a materialist view of the world, based on a enlightened humanist prioritization of the needs of the individual. However, as Haase has suggested, the invocation of this philosophical tradition merely throws into starker relief the oppressive banality of MfS's activities. The Stasi officer is, in fact, simply calling upon a standard piece of SED rhetoric that, within the context of the book, becomes a demand for the individual subject to be 'trapped' linguistically within the texts M.W. writes.

Although generally well received, Hilbig's exploration of the Stasi was attacked by a number of critics for jumping on a Stasi 'bandwagon'. Such critics accused him of giving an inaccurate account of life in the Prenzlauer Berg scene in an attempt to capitalize on the topicality of the subject-matter. Peter Hanenberg, for example, suggests in his unequivocally negative review that the novel is nothing more than 'journalistic history', which 'is keenly calculated to pander to a market that can't get enough of the complicity of intellectuals with the authorities in the

GDR'.[59] Hilbig is presented as having produced yet another sensationalist account of life under the Stasi, pandering to the type of 'orientalist'
discourse examined in Chapter 1 in its suggestion that the GDR was
nothing more than a 'Stasi state'. However, in actual fact we once again
find an echo of Bhahba's conceptualization of hybridity, where the copy
of the dominant discourse produced by the colonized subject begins to
destabilize this discourse. While Hilbig's text is clearly results from an
image of a Stasi-dominated GDR, in *»Ich«*, the salacious accounts found
elsewhere in the mass media finally become a means through which the
colonized other can question these very views. As such, the novel's presentation of the Stasi begins to take up the same position as Brussig's texts,
albeit, as I shall now discuss, with a somewhat different accent.

In *»Ich«*, Hilbig uses the Stasi as the location for a discussion of the
nature of identity and the relationship between language and representation, themes that run throughout his work. In his earlier pre-*Wende* texts,
Hilbig adopts the narrative personae of those who were excluded from the
official discourse of the GDR in order to examine the position of the
writer as outsider and the problem of artistic production. In so doing, the
author uses this perspective as a vehicle for a critique of the East German
state, the voices of those the state declared criminal providing him with a
means of attacking its self-declared utopian status.[60] By maintaining this
position in his post-*Wende* work, Hilbig makes a *de facto* statement of the
continued relevance of the role of the writer as social critic, seeing no
reason to change in accordance with the demands made during the
Literaturstreit. This position was subsequently confirmed in later novels
such as *Das Provisorium*. While, in these novels Hilbig continues to
engage with the nature of life in the GDR, he also goes beyond this
context, implicitly critiquing what he sees as the 'second-class' status of
east Germans in unified Germany of the early 1990s, as well as the problematic nature of the dealing with the GDR past. As Brussig does with
Klaus, Hilbig use the figure of the IM to provoke post-*Wende* German
society into rethinking its attitude towards life in the East German state.
In his Frankfurt lectures of 1995, the writer describes the new Federal
Republic, dominated by the voices of the western regions, as a 'taboo
society, in which people in the east are denounced even if they used to
belong to the Young Pioneers' (the GDR's mass youth movement for children in the first four years of school).[61] The author claims that the experience of former citizens of the GDR is being judged too quickly. *»Ich«*
can be read as a response to the summary dismissal of the experience of
easterners. Although the narrative stance Hilbig adopts initially seems to
confirm this dismissive view, he in fact forces his reader to explore ambi-
guities in the relationship between the individual and the SED dictator-

ship. As we have already seen, we are shown how M.W. is coerced into working for the Stasi and how he himself can be seen as a victim of this oppressive State organ. Thus, Hilbig calls into question any simplistic division of the GDR's citizens into perpetrators and victims of State-sanctioned oppression.

As such, Hilbig's text anticipates Brigitte Burmeister's *Unter dem Namen Norma*.[62] In this novel, published the following year, we are told the story of Marianna, a woman from East Berlin who travels to the west to visit her husband, the man having moved there for work. Marianne never feels comfortable in this new environment because its inhabitants have little understanding of her past experience, east Germany being almost a foreign country to them. At a party thrown for her by her husband's new acquaintances, her sense of discomfort becomes overwhelming. This leads her to take the drastic, if somewhat curious, step of relating a false story to another guest about her involvement with the Stasi as an IM, a story which completely dumbfounds its recipient. In a similar fashion to Hilbig, Marianne's false 'confession' is motivated by a defiant urge to challenge the perceptions of what she sees as a now western-dominated society. Of particular interest to this present study is Alison Lewis's analysis of this moment in the text, which paints this confession in overtly postcolonial terms:

> Marianne's false confession uncovers new asymmetries and forms of social distinction at the heart of the 'imagined community' of the united German nation in the virulent myth of East Germany as a deformed and perverted nation of perpetrators. In the act of telling the autobiography of Stasi perpetration – which she passes off as her own story – Marianne aims to subvert the image west Germans have of the east and to expose the operations of what could be terms a peculiarly German brand of 'orientalism'.[63]

Thus the novel, like others discussed, presents an east German deliberately taking up the position assigned him or her by the western hegemony, in order to bring this position into question. Crucially for Lewis, the perpetrator role allows her actively to escape that of passive recipient of a western version of history. However, Lewis also notes that, as a result of this stance, the woman actually goes beyond simply uncovering the type of orientalist view of the east we have already discussed because the role of the perpetrator provides an image around which a highly inclusive sense of an east German community can form, a community that can then have a broader social function than merely providing a point of identification for easterners in defiance of reductive western readings of history: 'Because the paradigm of the *Täter* [perpetrator] was less exclusive and more *inclusive* of the East German experience, it was also able to incorporate the very varied experiences of the *Mitläufer* [fellow traveller], that is the generality of the population'.[64] Consequently, the defiant act of taking on the role of the perpetrator can also become a metaphor for a more conciliatory act, through which Marianne shows not only her solidarity with, and forgiveness for, those who committed treacherous deeds on behalf of the state, but also her identification with those small acts of everyday compliance that defined the experience of a far larger proportion of the population.

Nonetheless, while adopting the position of the perpetrator might suggest a degree of forgiveness, it might also, of course, suggest that the individual can escape his or her responsibility for the past, an issue that is central to Brussig's novel. The question of responsibility, too, is highlighted in Hilbig's text, which similarly refuses to allow east Germans to ignore the actual nature of their relationship with the state. Although the GDR is presented as a hate-filled, paranoid system that attempted to control all aspects of life, the narrator suggests that, on some level at least, '*we* were the reason for this hatred' (Hilbig's emphasis) (I, 371). Like Brussig, Hilbig's text calls for the silent masses, who acquiesced to the authority of the state by withdrawing into the private sphere while publicly accepting the SED's authority, to accept the fact that they are implicated in the system's forty-year survival. However, in »Ich« there is an important difference in tone. Brussig's use of *wir* (us) in his title is part of his unremitting satirical attack. Although the word implicates the narrator in this attack, and as we have seen at times he spares neither himself nor his generation from his scorn, nevertheless, the superciliousness tone of the novel largely puts the emphasis on the *rest* of the east German community, which, unlike him, needs to be brought down to earth and reminded of the reality of the *Wende*. For Hilbig's protagonist, however, the use of 'we' is a more conciliatory gesture, a gesture underlined by the threnodic tone of the text as a whole. Rather than it being a satirical judgement on his fellow citizens, the narrator's use of *we* in Hilbig's novel is more concerned with the very act of self-implication the word implies, thereby suggesting his painful acceptance of his own measure of guilt.

»Ich« declares the continuing importance of the role of the writer as social commentator in Germany, a role challenged, as we have seen, by the debates and events of the early 1990s. In Günter Grass's *Ein weites Feld* (*Too Far Afield*), one of the most widely discussed Stasi novels of the 1990s, this position becomes overt.[65] Here Grass explores the relationship between a fictionalized version of Theodor Fontane, who in the novel is reincarnated as the east German cultural functionary Theo Wuttke, and his sinister 'day-and-night-shadow' Hoftaller, similarly a reincarnation, in his case of a nineteenth-century secret policeman *Tallhover*, the central figure from a pre-*Wende* Stasi novel by Hans Joachim Schädlich.[66] Wuttke, also known in the novel as Fonty after his forebear, is an immortal literary commentator, whose writings have given insight into political developments in German society since the mid-nineteenth century. For the same period of time, Tallhover/Hoftaller has accompanied the man, reflecting the less-lofty side of German history through his continuous employment by a variety of menacing German intelligence agencies.

Grass was one of the most vociferous west German intellectuals to defend Wolf during the *Literaturstreit*. In *Ein weites Feld* he rejects any call for writers to withdraw from public debate. On the contrary, he presents an extended literary intervention in this very debate, examining what he sees as the problematic, yet important, relationship between German writers and the state since at least the nineteenth century. In revisiting the position of those intellectuals attacked during the *Literaturstreit*, Grass actually breathed new life into this old debate, with the novel producing almost as much controversy as Wolf's text had done five years earlier.[67] What most angered critics was Grass's presentation of unified Germany. Like many of his contemporaries in the east, Grass was very sceptical of unification, and in the novel he concurs with these same intellectuals in his presentation of the GDR as having been swallowed by a western colonial power (W, 355).[68] However, at times Grass goes further than most in his criticism, suggesting, perhaps ironically, a degree of continuity in the experience of easterners from the Third Reich, through the SED's dictatorship in the GDR, to what he describes as a new form of western economic dictatorship, embodied in the THA, an institution that, in the novel's view, is heartlessly destroying the eastern population's way of life.[69] Here we see the FRG not as a moment of rupture with, but as itself a continuation of, the abject trajectory of Germany history put forward in the Enquete reports. Through his engagement with the writings of Fontane, Grass juxtaposes the work of this nineteenth-century author, writing at the time of the first German unification in 1871, with the political situation in Germany in the wake of November 1989, showing the continued relevance of Fontane's texts, and consequently highlighting the continuing relevance of literary intervention in the political sphere.[70]

In *Ein weites Feld*, Grass is clearly addressing the literary debates of the immediate post-*Wende* period that began with attacks on GDR intellectuals, but which finally also implicated his own generation in the west. This has two interesting implications for the rest of this present study, both of which will be addressed in more detail in the next chapter. First, in Grass' position we find a moment where east-west geographic boundaries become of secondary importance to political positions. Grass' left-liberal stance thus finds points of contact with, and is communicated through, the position of the GDR's socialist intellectuals. Second, the novel takes place almost entirely in the east. As such we can, perhaps, point here to a further form of 'orientalism', in which the GDR becomes an imagined space where positions that were dominant in the *West* prior to 1989 can continue to be explored and used to critique the values of post-unification society.

The Limits of Defiance and the Question of Moral Responsibility

As controversial as Grass' book was, his engagement with the role of a Stasi perpetrator, in the shape of Hoftaller, is a rhetorical strategy, a means of defending the public role of the writer, just as it is in Hilbig's exploration of the perspective of the perpetrator discussed above. Since the Stasi files have been opened, however, there have also been publications by, and about, those who actually cooperated with the Stasi. In some cases, for example Hermann Vinke's account of Christa Wolf's involvement with the MfS, these texts were produced to put the record straight, showing the limits of a particular writer's activities.[71] In other texts, such as Monika Maron's *Pawels Briefe*, we find a more problematic engagement with the past. Maron's autobiography, for example, provides what Andrew Plowman views as a highly contradictory account of her involvement with the Stasi – one that vacillates between a 'declaration of having nothing to answer for' and an 'act of self-justification'.[72]

One of the most eagerly awaited, and certainly most problematic, of these biographical and autobiographical accounts to date has been that of Sascha Anderson, the Stasi's main operative within the Prenzlauer Berg scene. Anderson was outed as an IM in a spectacular manner by Wolf Biermann during Biermann's acceptance speech on receiving the Georg-Büchner Prize in 1991. In this speech Biermann attacked the poet and literary entrepreneur as 'the ungifted chatterer Sascha Arsehole, a Stasi spy who is still coolly playing the muse's son and hoping that his dossiers never surface.'[73] As more and more victims requested access to their files, it seemed ever clearer that Biermann's accusations were well founded. Nevertheless, Anderson continued to protest his innocence, refusing to admit the extent of his involvement with the MfS. In an interview with Holger Kulick, for example, he categorically denied having ever been a fully fledged IM. He admits 'I caused a lot of shit, but never in the context in which it is now being interpreted'.[74] When asked whether he was deliberately placed as an operative within the alternative culture, he is adamant: 'I was never that. No-one ever said to me, now you go there and do this and that.' Any contact with the Stasi he did have, he insists, was on an informal basis.[75]

Many of Anderson's activities could be pieced together from a number of the victim files, but it was not until the end of the decade that a more complete picture could be established, when the shredded remains of Anderson's own perpetrator file, previously thought to have been lost, were reconstituted.[76] As already discussed, we must be extremely careful when reconstituting history from the Stasi files. Yet, while their content must be treated with caution, as I have also noted it cannot simply be ignored wholesale. In Anderson's case, even if only a fraction of its contents are true, the fraction that can be corroborated by cross-referencing with numerous 'victim' files or from other independent sources, a bleak picture of his activities is presented. The document, which runs to over 1,000 pages, details the numerous people Anderson apparently regularly betrayed to the Stasi – figures that included artists and dissidents such as Lutz Rathenow, Rüdiger Rosenthal, Cornelia Schleime, Ralf Kerbach and Jürgen Fuchs (the information on Fuchs being largely collected once Anderson had left the GDR for West Berlin in 1986).[77] Indeed, in at least one case (that of Rüdiger Rosenthal), the files suggest that Anderson's information was instrumental in an arrest, thus potentially removing the possibility of the defence common amongst Stasi IMs (and central, for example, in Maron's case) that the information they gave did not actually harm anyone.[78]

With the publication of Anderson's autobiographical text *Sascha Anderson* in 2002, commentators hoped for some answers to why Anderson worked with the MfS against the underground Prenzlauer Berg scene, of which he was such a key member.[79] This they were not to receive. Instead Anderson produced a highly confusing, fragmented account of his life that, while freely admitting his relationship with the Stasi, focuses overwhelmingly on his development as an artist and not on his life as an informant. By adopting this approach, Anderson takes the same line as those few people who defended him at the time of his outing, claiming that Anderson the poet should not be judged by the same criteria as Anderson the man.[80] Consequently, while he, like Grass, defends the validity of the role of the writer, in respect to the positions drawn during the *Literaturstreit*, he sides with the opposite camp, maintaining his artistic worth in wholly aesthetic terms. Through the type of engagement with the nature of writing and world of literature, seen in other texts discussed in this chapter, Anderson implies that he is beyond judgement, or at least that the only view of himself that matters is his own, a position that is obviously highly contentious given the very real damage that

Anderson's activities did. Indeed, as we shall see in its reception, Anderson's text perhaps suggests the limitations of defiantly 'writing back', when it is a rhetorical position that defiantly ignores the issue of moral responsibility.

The tone of the text is set in its opening paragraph. Quoting the words of Heiner Müller, the narrator claims

> A secure structure, a fixed form, that is something for the end of one's life. Or for those who confuse beginnings and ends. On stage this happens when people suddenly begin to tell their own story. That destroys the [artistic] agreement; it goes beyond the realms of the dramatic ... it is the beginning of the end of the spectacle (SA, 7)

The book is titled *Sascha Anderson*, and as such it would seem to be setting itself up as a classic autobiography, in which readers enter into a 'pact' with the writer, whereby the reader accepts that the narrator of the text is the same as person writing it, and that the text with which they are being presented is an account of this writer's life. However, in this first paragraph Müller, and by extension Anderson, seems to reject the very concept of telling one's life story, suggesting that it is an impulse that runs contrary to the imperatives of art. Consequently, he immediately thwarts the reader's expectation, breaking the autobiographical 'pact', and problematizing the status of the story we are about to read.[81]

That said, the 'plot' of this story is clearly based on Anderson's own life, and so to some extent at least must be seen as an autobiographical account. We learn of his early experiences in Dresden, his time in prison and his first flirtation with the intelligence services, of his involvement in the underground literary scene, his emigration to the West in 1986 and finally his outing as a Stasi IM. However, such episodes merely serve as a backdrop for a philosophical journey through the world of literature. In this respect, the text actually echoes Hilbig's »Ich«. Anderson, like Hilbig's protagonist, seems intent upon using literature as a means of self definition. Similarities between the two texts are on one level unremarkable, given the fact that Hilbig makes no secret that his novel is based on information gleaned from the Prenzlauer Berg IMs.[82] However, what is remarkable about *Sascha Anderson* is that the similarlities between the two texts lay not in the details of the IMs experience but in the way Anderson discusses the nature of writing, a key element throughout Hilbig's work. Yet, whereas Hilbig uses his discussion of literature as a vehicle for social critique, Anderson's focus remains the aesthetic realm. Thus, the relationship between Hilbig and the IM, which leads to the writing of »Ich«, is reversed in Anderson, with Hilbig's fictional text now providing a literary model for Anderson's 'true' account of his life. *»Ich«* uses the Stasi as a landscape for the protagonist's metaphorical journey of artistic discovery, through which he seeks a more authentic, less partial existence than he experiences in his everyday life. This search is implied in the very title of the novel, which posits an idealized version of the narrator's ego that is always at one remove, bracketed off by quotation marks from his physical self. The search for authenticity would similarly appear to be the starting point for Anderson in his autobiography. As Ijoma Mangold suggests, in *Sascha Anderson*, the author also presents his life as a search for an escape route, through the medium of literature, out of an inauthentic, partial world in which the author's psyche is being ripped apart.[83] Here again, the text's title plays a key role. The centrality of such psychological fragmentation to the author's experience is presented graphically on the book's dust jacket, where the author's name is presented in large red letters torn in two across the centre.

In Anderson's case, the key figure he meets on his literary journey is the poet Novalis, whose work he quotes throughout. Indeed, he even claims at one point, 'I am sure of the fact that Novalis wrote me' (SA, 106), his literary forebear appearing central to the construction of Anderson's very sense of self. However, once again recalling *»Ich«*, his encounter with the world of literature ultimately confirms his lack of self. In the romantic tradition of writers such as Novalis, and more obviously Fichte (whom he also cites), Anderson suggests that he can only ever discover his 'Ich' negatively. He himself exists in a state of emptiness, a void that is only ever able to find shape through his literary engagement with others, defined, in Fichtian terms, as his 'Nicht-Ich' (Not-I) (SA, 112).

Yet, the narrator often also self-consciously contradicts this reading, offering an image of himself and his literary project that is diametrically opposed to that of Hilbig's protagonist. While M.W. never finds the authenticity he seeks, he nonetheless remains committed to the quest. In *Sascha Anderson*, rather than using the medium of literature as a means of unifying the man ripped in two on the book's cover into Sascha Anderson the individual, the narrator at times argues that the search for authenticity is a fruitless task, and moreover one in which he has no interest. While he remains nothing more than a reflection of his 'Nicht-Ich', he claims that this is enough for him. There is no need for him to imbue his life with meaning through writing. Indeed, towards the end of the text, it would seem that he does not even care whether it is read or not, seeing no value in communicating with a reader. 'I'm enough for me', he declares. 'There's no point trying to explain anything' (SA, 231).

This stance becomes particularly problematic when Anderson explicity discusses his involvement with the security services. His first contact with this world comes in the shape of the KGB, to whom he is introduced by a Russian family friend (SA, 121–4). In a similar fashion to Klaus in *Helden wie wir*, the young Anderson has naïve ideas of a glamorous life as a spy, being trained to work behind enemy lines (SA, 15). However, it is again Hilbig's text that provides the most obvious point of reference. Indeed, in an overt echo »*Ich*«, Anderson describes his early life as a writer as a time when he existed in the 'twilight form of a half-sleeping person' (SA, 76), recalling the 'sleeping phase' of M.W.'s pre-Stasi life. Like Hilbig's protagonist, working for the Stasi seems to give his life meaning, meaning that is, as ever, described in highly literary terms. He calls his first Stasi contact 'Mephisto' (SA, 125). As a result, it would seem that he wishes to imbue his decision to join the MfS with all the significance of an event in a classical tragedy, the Stasi contact playing Mephisto to his Faust, promising him the whole world if only he will sign his soul away. Yet, Anderson immediately undermines this reading of his life when we learn that the officier's actual name was not Mephisto, but in fact Faust (SA, 125). Thus, the classical allusion is destroyed. The Faust/Mephisto tragedy is impossible if both men are to play the same role. This is not to be the story of one man's fateful fall through his inability, either due to hubris or fear, to escape his pact with the devil. Nor is it the story of an uneven power dynamic, of one side trying to manipulate the other. As he later insists in a meeting with his handlers, he might have been sitting on the other side of the table to them, but 'I was on their side' (SA, 252). The notion of using literary reference to imbue the banality of the everyday with new significance, through which the reader can come to an understanding of Anderson's life, collapses into a narcissistic postmodern game in which the writer's motivations become impossible to fathom.

Ultimately, then, Anderson suggests that he has no interest in communicating the 'truth'. Schooled, as he himself declares, in 'poststructuralist know-how'(SA, 262), the 'truth' for him is just another text. Consequently, he can categorically deny to Adolf Endler, for example, that he ever worked for the MfS (SA, 293) when rumours to that effect begin to emerge in the wake of the *Wende*. His version of reality is just as valid as anyone else's, and for Anderson himself it is the only version that matters. He feels no compulsion to explain his life to the reader. This is a story, he tells us in the final line of the book 'that I am telling myself' (SA, 297), the centrality of this narcissist position to the text further emphasized if we return to the dust jacket. On its reverse side we find a two images of Anderson's upper body, the one a reflection of the other, a picture that perhaps warns the reader before they ever open the book that the narrative it contains is entirely inward looking with no real intention of communicating a coherent story.

Sascha Anderson is neither an apologia, nor a confession, the two key modes of classical autobiography, and between which we see Maron, for example, vacillate. That said, there are brief moments where he does attempt to justify his role as an IM, showing, for example, how he used his position to help stop Egmont Hesse being press-ganged into working for the Stasi, or how he managed to secure a publisher for Endler's work (SA, 248). More disturbing is his claim that he was one of the least hypocritical members of the scene. Rejecting, once again, the suggestion that he was being ripped apart by his double life, as the book's dust jacket graphically implies, he claims 'I wasn't split like those who sat in their local bars, like the *Wiener Café* on Schönhauser Allee, or in *Mosaik* on Prenzlauer Allee, and waited until closing time to fuck the bar staff. Perhaps I had no morality, but I also didn't have a half morality' (SA, 231–2). Other artists in the scene might have viewed their position in moral, perhaps even noble terms, proud of their position as dissident artists, critical of the state. However, they were also normal, limited people, just like anyone else, subject to human weakness and compromise, something that Anderson had at least fully accepted.

Paradoxically, it would seem the only 'moral' statement the artist is finally able to accept is that he is amoral, and as such that he is beyond the pale of society. As a result, the judgements of others, such as Biermann, on his life are irrelevant to him (SA, 295). Anderson declares his own self worth in his rejection of what society thinks of him. This leads him to adopt a particularly obtuse version of the 'identity of defiance' in what would on the face of it appear to be yet another literary attempt to 'write back' against 'inauthentic' versions of hisoty . While he sometimes suggests that he acted on behalf of others in the underground scene, curiously he mainly paints himself in a despicable light, an image far more in tune with that to be gleaned from his Stasi file, as well as his postunification media image more generally. For example, he discusses his actual file in the following terms:

> In edition 28, volume 8 of the magazine *Horch & Guck*, files were reproduced in the year 2000, which quote from a selection of my reports for the State Security Service. In the contours revealed by the files, I recognize myself. The commentary of the author obsessed with adjectives denouncing his victims. In this commentary (not in the text of the journalist) I encounter what I never wanted to be,
> What I Was. (SA, 244)

Here Anderson appears to accept the truth of his file's content, exhibiting some degree of guilt and finding it difficult to face what he did, although, by this point in the text, the 'autobiographical pact' has been undermined to such an extent in the contradictory account of his life's motivations, that it is almost impossible to accept the author's feelings as genuine.

Although his Stasi file is only mentioned at this one moment in the text, its existence was so widely reported that it can be assumed that the reader will be aware at least of the gist of its contents. In a sense, it is the counter biography to Anderson's own account. When the accounts are read in tandem, Anderson's text is even more confusing, compounding further the sense that he is intent upon obfuscation rather than communication. As Lewis notes in her study of the Prenzlauer Berg scene, Anderson's recollection of events in his life differs both radically, and bizarrely, from his file. First, he consistently misremembers dates. For example, in the text he claims to have moved to Berlin from Dresden in 1974, while in his Stasi files the move happened a year later.[84] This might be easily explained, put down simply to a failure of memory on Anderson's part. In this connection the dates in the Stasi files, written at the time and with no fathomable reason to be inaccurate, would logically seem more reliable than Anderson's account written nearly two decades later. But such inconsistencies exist within a wider, more problematic context, in which Anderson also 'misremembers' the nature of his involvement with the Stasi, curiously painting himself at times in a far worse light than he needs to. For example, in the description of his relationship with the organization in the period immediately after his first imprisonment, Lewis notes that he describes a moment of crisis, brought about by having apparently been dropped by his Stasi contacts: 'I waited for my handlers. They did not come' (SA, 184). In the files, on the other hand, we find details of Anderson's active attempts to escape the Stasi's clutches at this time:

> According to the files Anderson held out for a total of nine months, before he succumbed to the wishes of Graupner [his Stasi contact] to keep his pledge. He did not get in touch, missed meetings, broke agreements and expressed as clearly as he could he that he was annoyed with the State Security Service.[85]

What is Anderson's motivation for painting a worse picture of himself than he needs to? As ever this is difficult to pinpoint. On one level, as Lewis argues, his counter-intuitive use of his own files is consistent with Anderson's general need to construct an air of mystery around himself.[86] On another, it can be seen as yet another use of the perpetrator perspective as an 'identity of defiance', of Anderson provocatively 'writing back' against the public's view of his life by producing a hyper-confirmation of this view, through which he might bring the truth status of files into question. More controversially, however, he may well be suggesting that it is irrelevant which account is accepted as the truth, whether it be written by him, the Stasi, or indeed Wolfgang Hilbig for that matter.

Of course, the problem is that Hilbig, who was not an IM, is writing a work of fiction. Anderson, to whatever limited extent, is not and so, as many of his critics point out, the 'truth' cannot simply be ignored because there is very much a material reality beyond the text. Any postmodern game Anderson might wish to play cannot discount the fact that his actions had highly damaging effects, effects that are never engaged with directly in his text. It is no surprise, then, that some of the most vocal critics of the book were the victims of his work for the Stasi, individuals who largely felt that their experience was completely elided in Anderson's account. Ekkehard Maass, for example, attacked the text as a wicked trivialization of the IMs past, 'as if his conspiratorial discussions with his handlers were meaningless chats over coffee and cognac'.[87] However, for others what is particularly worrying about *Sascha Anderson* is that it found such a high-profile publisher as Dumont. Lewis, for example, suggests that this text would never have been published in the early 1990s: 'Anderson's obfuscatory and romanticized account of his life working for the Stasi would have been traduced as the cynical exercise it is ... By 2002 the interest in Anderson had surely not waned, but the publishing industry's interest in the truth certainly had'.[88]

As I have attempted to show in the course of this chapter, in the years since the *Wende* there has indeed been a development in the way the Stasi has been represented in literature. The early emphasis on victim narratives, such as we find in Kunze's *Deckname »Lyrik«* soon began to be countered by texts such as *»Ich«* or *Helden wie wir*, which use the Stasi metaphorically as a means of provoking 1990s Germany into engaging with the pre-*Wende* experience of East Germans, or, in Grass' text, as a means of recuperating the beleagured position of the intellectual. These later texts clearly gesture to a sense of dissatisfaction amongst eastern, and indeed some western intellectuals, giving rise to what has been defined, often pejoratively, as an 'identity of defiance', a construction of self-understanding based on a negative reaction to what was identified in the previous chapter as the 'colonization' of the GDR past by an externally imposed version of history, against which these authors 'write back'. As we have also seen, at times this 'writing back' can go beyond pure defiance allowing writers to reflect upon their position within the new Germany, calling on both easterners and westerners to approach the historical evaluation of the GDR with honesty. As such, for most critics any attempt at 'writing back' we find in *Sascha Anderson* fails, because it elides the experience of

Anderson's victims. That Anderson's text produced such an indigent reaction clearly points to the fact that the role of the Stasi remained an important issue at the start of the new decade. Nonetheless, by this time there had clearly also been a shift away from a view of GDR history that focused largely on its oppressive institutions to one that engaged with everyday life in the east. As we shall now see, this shift made the charge ever more commonplace that writers and other cultural practitioners were intent upon trivializing the activities of the SED dictatorship.

Notes

1. This is not to say that victim narratives have disappeared completely, as, for example Claudia Rusch's *Meine freie deutsche Jugend*, Frankfurt/Main: S. Fischer, 2003, testifies, which tells of the effects of Stasi surveillance on a young child growing up in the GDR.
2. Faulenbach, 'Die Enquete-Kommissionen', p. 31.
3. For a detailed description of the structure and functions of the MfS see Karl Wilhelm Fricke, *MfS intern*, Cologne: Verlag Wissenschaft und Politik, 1991; or in English David Childs and Richard Popplewell, *The Stasi. The East German Intelligence and Security Service, 1917–89*, Basingstoke: Macmillan, 1996, Mike Dennis, *The Stasi Myth and Reality*, London: Longman, 2003.
4. Quoted in Wolfgang Emmerich, *Kleine Literaturgeschichte der DDR: Erweiterte Neuausgabe*, Leipzig: Gustav Kiepenheuer, 1996, p. 43.
5. See Dieter Schlenstedt quoted in J.H. Reid, *Writing without Taboos: The New East German Literature*, New York: Berg, 1990, p. 1.
6. This term comes from a poem by Uwe Kolbe, in which he reflects on the experience of those whose entire formative years were spent under socialism. See Uwe Kolbe 'Hineingeboren', in *Hineingeboren: Gedichte 1975–1979*, Frankfurt/Main: Suhrkamp, 1982, p. 46. For further discussion of these artists' work see Karin Leeder, *Breaking Boundaries: a New Generation of Poets in the GDR*, Oxford: Clarendon, 1996.
7. Christa Wolf, *Was bleibt*, Frankfurt/Main: Luchterhand, 1990.
8. Georgina Paul, '"Ich, Seherin, gehörte zum Palast": Christa Wolf's Literary Treatment of the Stasi in the Context of her Poetics of Self-Analysis', in *German Writers and the Politics of Culture: Dealing with the Stasi*, ed. by Paul Cooke and Andrew Plowman, Basingstoke: Palgrave, 2003, pp. 87–106 (p. 90).
9. For a survey of views expressed in this debate see, *Es geht nicht um*

Christa Wolf: Der Literaturstreit im vereinten Deutschland, ed. by Thomas Anz, Frankfurt/Main: Fischer, 1995.

10. Ulrich Greiner, 'Die deutsche Gesinnungsästhetik. Noch einmal: Christa Wolf und der deutsche Literaturstreit. Eine Zwischenbilanz', *Die Zeit*, 2 November 1990. See also Frank Schirrmacher, 'Abschied von der Literatur der Bundesrepublik', *Frankfurter Allgemeine Zeitung*, 2 October 1990.

11. For examples of the press coverage of such scandals see Paul Cooke and Nicholas Hubble, '*Die volkseigene Opposition*? The Stasi and Alternative Culture in the GDR', *German Politics*, 6(2) (1997), 117–38.

12. For an overview of this debate see Peter Böthig and Klaus Michael (eds), *MachtSpiele: Literatur und Staatssicherheit im Fokus Prenzlauer Berg*, Leipzig: Reclam, 1993.

13. The organization is now referred to the 'Birthler Agency' after Marianne Birthler, who took over from Gauck in September 2000.

14. Mary Fulbrook, *German National Identity after the Holocaust*, Cambridge: Polity, 1999, p. 224.

15. Fulbrook, p. 226.

16. Werner Mittenzwei, *Die Intellektuellen: Literatur und Politik in Ostdeutschland 1945–2000*, Berlin: Aufbau, 2003, p. 416.

17. Wolf Biermann, 'Der Lichtblick im gräßlichen Fatalismus der Geschichte: Rede zur Verleihung des Georg-Büchner-Preises', *Die Zeit*, 25 October 1991.

18. Sylvia Klötzer, '(Sub)kultur und Staatssicherheit: Rainer Schedlinski', in *im widerstand/im mißverständnis: Zur Literatur und Kunst des Prenzlauer Bergs*, ed. by Christine Consetino and Wolgang Müller, New York: Peter Lang, 1995, pp. 51–74 (p. 64). For a more critical discussion of this view see Alison Lewis, *Die Kunst des Verrats: Der Prenzlauer Berg und die Staatssicherheit*, Würzburg: Könighausen & Neumann, 2003, pp. 145–175.

19. See Klaus Michael, 'Alternativkultur und Staatssicherheit 1976–1989', in *Enquete-Kommission* III/3, pp. 1636–74 (p. 1638).

20. Mittenzwei, p. 417.

21. For further discussion of the terrible acts of psychological warfare carried out on the population by the Stasi on behalf of the GDR see Mike Dennis, 'The East German Ministry of State Security and East German Society during the Honecker Era, 1971–1989, in Cooke and Plowman, pp. 3–24 (pp. 6–7); Antony Glees, *The Stasi Files: East Germany's Secret Operations Against Britain*, London: Free Press, 2003, pp. 29–35; Anna Funder, *Stasiland: Stories from Behind the Berlin Wall*, London: Granta, 2003.

22. Mittenzwei, p. 424
23. Quoted in Mittenzwei, p. 424. This is a conceit also found in Alexander Osang's recent bestselling novel, *Die Nachrichten* (*The News*), which tells the story of a young east German newsreader whose career is destroyed when he is outed, falsely, as having worked for the Stasi. Alexander Osang, *Die Nachrichten*, Frankfurt/Main: S. Fischer, 2002.
24. Alison Lewis, 'Reading and Writing the Stasi File: On the Uses and Abuses of the File as (Auto)biography', *GLL*, 56 (2002), 377–97 (p. 378).
25. Stephen Brockmann, *Literature and German Reunification*, Cambridge: CUP, 1999, p. 83.
26. Brockmann, p. 84.
27. Brockmann, p. 85.
28. Hans-Joachim Maaz, *Die Entrüstung: Deutschland Deutschland Stasi Schuld und Sündenbock*, Berlin: Argon, 1992, p. 13.
29. Maaz, pp. 95–105.
30. Non-fictional accounts of life in the GDR were particularly prevalent in the early years of unification, with numerous writers producing autobiographical texts of their experiences. For an overview see Dennis Tate, 'The end of autobiography? The older generation of East German authors take stock', in *Legacies and Identity: East and West German Literary Responses to Unification*, ed. by Martin Kane, Oxford: Peter Lang, 2002, pp. 11–26.
31. Reiner Kunze, *Deckname »Lyrik«: Eine Dokumentation*, Frankfurt/Main: S. Fischer, 1990, hereafter (D). Other such responses include Erich Loest, *Die Stasi war mein Eckermann*, Göttingen: Steidl Verlag, 1991, and Hans Joachim Schädlich (ed.) *Aktenkundig*, Berlin: Rowohlt, 1993. For an overview of such texts, albeit one which exhibits many of the qualities of the salacious media accounts of Stasi activities I critique elsewhere in this chapter, see Edwin Kratschmer, 'GDR Writers and the *Stasi* Net', in Kane, pp. 27–49.
32. In his text, Kunze cites an interview with Böhme from *Der Spiegel*, in which Böhme claims 'Ich bin zu keiner Zeit und an keinem Ort, weder mit noch ohne Decknamen, als Mitarbeiter der *Stasi* tätig gewesen'. Kunze then goes on to cite a string of examples which clearly show that Böhme, under the names 'August Drempker' and 'Bonkarz', delivered intimate information to the *Stasi* about Kunze. See 'Anhang: "Ich tue meine Arbeit wie bisher"' (D, 113–124). For an example of press reactions to Kunze's allegation see Martin Jäger, 'Das Loch in der Wand Objekt Autor', *Deutsches Allgemeines Sonntagsblatt*, 8 February 1991.

33. The 'V' at the end of IM here is an abbreviation for 'Vorgänge', suggesting that he is an active informant. The use of 'V' has caused a number of problems in the interpretations of the files, since it is also used as an abbreviation for 'IM Vorläufe', used to describe someone who the Stasi consider might be useful to it but who it has not yet engaged. See McAdams, p. 68.

34. Quoted in Karl Corino, 'Deckname Lyrik: Die Verfolgung eines Dichters', *Stuttgarter Zeitung*, 15 December 1990.

35. Heimo Schwilk 'Ensetzter Blick in den Spiegel. Aus den Akten des Staatsfeinds', *Rheinischer Merkur*, 4 January 1991.

36. Maaz, p. 91.

37. Interview with Wolfgang Kraus for *Österreichisches Fernsehen*, 2. *Programm, Jour fixe*, 30 September 1991, in Reiner Kunze, *Wo Freiheit ist ... Gespräche 1977–1993*, Frankfurt/Main: S. Fischer, 1994, pp. 187–200 (p. 197).

38. Timothy Garton Ash, *The File: A Personal History*, London: Flamingo, 1997, p. 10.

39. Wolf Biermann, 'Die Stasi-Ballade', in *Für meine Genossen*, Berlin: Klaus Wagenbach, 1972, pp. 68–71 (p. 69).

40. Joachim Walther, *Sicherungsbereich Literatur: Schriftsteller und Staatssicherheit in der Deutschen Demokratischen Republik*, Berlin: Ulstein, 1996.

41. Karl Corino, 'Es ist unglaublich viel gelogen worden: Ein Gespräch mit dem Schriftsteller Reiner Kunze über seine Stasi-Akte', *Frankfurter Rundschau*, 16 January 1991.

42. Kant initially won his court battle, but at appeal the decision was overturned, with the proviso that any future editions of the book carry a footnote in which it would be noted that this report was never written. See interview with Jürgen P. Wallmann, *Westdeutscher Rundfunk, Köln, Am Abend vorgestellt*, 13 August 1993, in Reiner Kunze, *Wo Freiheit ist ...* , pp. 223–234 (p. 230–1.).

43. Adolf Endler, 'Gelächter im Akten-Whirlpool', in *Das Vergängliche überlisten. Selbstbefragungen deutscher Autoren*, ed. by Ingrid Czechowski, Leipzig: Reclam, 1996, p. 149.

44. Valeri Scherstjanoi, *Operative Personenkontrolle »Futurist«*, first transmitted by SDR 30 December 1996. All references in this chapter are to the manuscript of the radio play, hereafter (O).

45. Personal interview with Valeri Scherstjanoi at his home in Berlin, 13 August 1996.

46. Michael Haase, *Eine Frage der Aufklärung: Literatur und Staatssicherheit in Romanen von Fritz Rudolf Fries, Günter Grass*

und Wolfgang Hilbig, Frankfurt/Main: Peter Lang, 2001, p. 18.

47. Haase, p. 13–14.
48. Andreas Staab, *National Identity in Eastern Germany: Inner Unification or Continued Separation*, Westport: Praeger, 1998, p. 90.
49. See Bhabha, p. 89.
50. For an overview of the role of language as a site through which 'power was articulated *and* contested in the GDR' see David Bathrick, *The Powers of Speech: the politics of culture in the GDR*, Lincoln: University of Nebraska Press, 1995, p. 24.
51. Thomas Brussig, *Helden wie wir*, Berlin: Verlag Volk und Welt, 1995, hereafter (H)
52. Kristie Foell and Jill Twark, '"Bekenntnisse des Stasi-Hochstaplers Klaus Uhltzscht": Thomas Brussig's Comical and Controversial *Helden wie wir*', in Cooke and Plowman, pp. 173–94 (p. 176).
53. Thomas Kraft, 'An der Charmegrenze der Provokation – Thomas Brussigs Realsatire über 20 Jahre DDR-Geschichte: *Helden wie wir*', *Freitag*, 13 October 1995.
54. Martin Ahrends, 'General Absolution: Thomas Brussig auf der Suche nach dem großen Wir', *Freitag*, 12 April 1996.
55. One of the best-known examples of this view is that of the journalist Henryk M. Broder, who described the *Wende* as the organization's 'magnum opus', quoted in Brockmann, p. 83. This image is also satirically evoked in Günter Grass's *Ein weites Feld* where the Stasi operative Hoftaller explains how the MfS brought about unification in order to bankrupt the capitalist west, the chaos of which will eventually bring the people to realize that they need once again the strong leadership offered by the GDR (W, 16 and 473). See note 65.
56. Wolf, *Was Bleibt* , p. 20. For further discussion of this dimension see Foell and Twark, pp. 188–9.
57. Wolfgang Hilbig, *»Ich«* (Frankfurt/Main: S. Fischer, 1993), hereafter (I).
58. Martin Kane, 'Writing as Precarious Salvation: The Work of Wolfgang Hilbig', in *Contemporary German Writers, their Aesthetics and their Language*, ed. by Arthur Williams, Stuart Parkes and Julian Preece, Bern: Peter Lang, 1996, pp. 71–82 (p. 79).
59. Peter Hanenberg, ' *»Ich«* ', *Die Politische Meinung*, 288 (1993), 90–1. See also Jan Faktor, 'Hilbigs *»Ich«*: Das Rätsel des Buches blieb von der Kritik unberührt', *Wolfgang Hilbig*, ed. by Heinz Ludwig Arnold, Munich: Text & Kritik, 1994, pp. 75–9 (p. 75).
60. For further discussion of this issue in relation to Hilbig's pre-*Wende*

writing see Paul Cooke, *Speaking the Taboo: a study of the Work of Wolfgang Hilbig*, Amsterdam: Rodopi, 2000.

61. Wolfgang Hilbig, *Abriß der Kritik*, Frankfurt/Main: S. Fischer, 1995 p. 93.
62. Brigitte Burmeister, *Unter dem Namen Norma*, Stuttgart: Klett-Cotta, 1994.
63. Alison Lewis, 'The Stasi, the Confession and Performing Difference: Brigitte Burmeister's *Unter dem Namen Norma*', in Cooke and Plowman, pp. 155–72 (p. 165).
64. Lewis, p. 158, italics in original.
65. Günter Grass, *Ein weites Feld*, Gottingen: Steidl, 1995, hereafter (W).
66. Hans Joachim Schädlich, *Tallhover*, Reinbek: Rowohlt, 1986. For further discussion of this novel see Karl-Heinz Schoeps, 'Tallhover or The Eternal Spy: Hans Joachim Schädlich's Stasi-Novel *Tallhover*', in Cooke and Plowman, pp. 71–84
67. For an overview of this controversy see Oskar Negt (ed.) *Der Fall Fonty: 'Ein weites Feld' von Günter Grass im Spiegel der Kritik*, Göttingen: Steidl, 1996.
68. See for example Günter Grass, 'Kurze Rede eines vaterlosen Gesellschaft', in *Günter Grass: Essays und Reden III 1980–1997*, ed. by Daniela Hermes, Göttinghen, Steidl, 1997, pp. 230–4. For a fuller discussion of Grass's position see Martin Kane, 'In the Firing Line: Günter Grass and his critics in the 1990s', in Kane, *Legacies and Identity*, pp. 181–97.
69. The role of this institution in Unification debates is discussed in more detail in Chapter 1 of this study.
70. For further discussion see Julian Preece, 'The Stasi as Literary Conceit: Günter Grass's *Ein weites Feld*', in Cooke and Plowman, pp. 195–212.
71. See for example Hermann Vinke (ed.), *Akteneinsicht Christa Wolf: Zerrspiegel und Dialog*, Hamburg: Luchterhand, 1993, which presents files detailing Wolf's connection with the Stasi, as well as an overview of the debate this revelation sparked.
72. Monika Maron, *Pawels Briefe. Eine Familiengeschichte*, Frankfurt/Main: S. Fischer, 1999; Andrew Plowman, 'Escaping the Auto-biographical Trap? Monika Maron, the Stasi and *Pawels Briefe*', in Cooke and Plowman, pp. 227–40 (p. 231).
73. Biermann, 'Der Lichtblick im gräßlichen Fatalismus der Geschichte'.
74 Holger Kulick, 'Grautöne. Der Amoklauf Sascha Anderson', in Böthig and Michael, pp. 188–97 (p. 191).

75. Kulick, p. 192
76. For a summary of the file's contents see Holger Kulick, 'Der Dorfpolizist von Prenzlauer Berg', *Horch und Guck*, 28 (1999), 1–39.
77. Udo Scheer 'Die Maske hinter dem Gesicht', *Rheinischer Merkur*, 8 March 2002.
78. Ijoma Mangold, 'Ich ist ein Anderson: Hinter mir gibt es kein Mysterium, es stehlt alles in den Akten: Wie Sascha A. in seiner Autobiografie verschwindet', *Süddeutsche Zeitung*, 2 March 2002. See also Plowman, 'Escaping the Autobiographical Trap?', p. 230.
79. See, for example Ina Harwig, 'Krankenhaus und Weltgeschichte: Die Anwendung des Ich auf die DDR: Wo Christa Wolf und Sascha Anderson sich treffen', *Frankfurter Rundsachau*, 15 June 2002; Scheer 'Die Maske'.
80. For example, while, on a personal level Uwe Kolbe, like Biermann, saw Anderson as an 'arsehole' he still declares in his open letter to Anderson 'the difference between me and Biermann is that I don't find all your texts questionable'. Uwe Kolbe, 'Auf meine Art naiv: Literaturbegriff und Moral', in Michael and Böthig, pp. 84–92 (p. 88). Similarly Durs Grünbein, one of the youngest members of this group of poets, prioritises the aesthetic over the political, seeing Biermann as a replacement Georg Lukács, the demagogue of early GDR cultural politics, who refused to endorse any literature other than that of socialist realism. Grünbein writes 'my most recent nightmare is a library put together by Biermann'. Durs Grünbein, 'Im Namen der Füchse: Gibt es eine neue literarische Zensur?', in Michael and Böthig, pp. 325–9 (p. 326).
81. For a seminal exposition of the autobiographical past see Philippe Lejeune, *Le pacte autobiographique*, Paris: Seuil, 1975.
82. See the note on the inside back cover of the novel.
83. Mangold, 'Ich ist ein Anderson'.
84. Lewis, p. 66.
85. Lewis, p. 66.
86. Lewis, p. 54–5.
87. Ekkehard Maass, 'Und das ist geschehn: ein Betroffener über die Stasi-Mitarbeit von Sascha Anderson: Es war mehr als Freundesverrat', *Berliner Zeitung*, 25 July 2002. The one notable exception to this was Bert Papenfuß-Gorek, who has consistently stood by Anderson (see, for example, Bert Papenfuß-Gorek ' Man liebt immer die Katze im Sack: Gespräche mit Ute Scheub und Bascha Mika', in Böthig and Michael, pp. 182–8). Indeed, Papenfuß even allowed Anderson to use his bar, *Kaffee Burger*, on 1 March

2002 to launch his book. See Peter Böthig, 'Trickbetrüger der Schuld, *Der Tagesspiegel*, 2 March 2002.

88. Lewis, 'Reading and Writing the Stasi Files', p. 397.

—4—

'Productive' Hybridity:
Nostalgia and the GDR on Film

In my discussion of literary representations of the East German state, we saw how a number of authors used parody in order to critique the view of the GDR as nothing more than a 'Stasi state'. To a degree such texts might be said to exibit aspects of the so-called 'identity of defiance', often seen to be at work in post-unification east German self understanding, although, as I have suggested, the notion of 'defiance' does not fully reflect the complexity of many of the texts examined. Yet, in the parodic engagement with the theme of the Stasi in texts such as *Helden wie wir*, while the author questions the validity of certain mainstream readings of history, he nonetheless continues to use the totalitarian paradigm as his frame of reference. During the course of the 1990s, however, a shift can be identified in cultural representations of the East German state. Here we begin to see the authors of a range of cultural texts focus instead on what they view as the 'normal', everyday aspects of life in the East, aspects that are not reflected in a view of the GDR as a totalitarian 'Stasi state'. In order to examine this development in more detail, I return in this chapter to the concept of hybridity. However, instead of Bhabha's image of a potentially provocative 'hybrid' subject, which can have a destabilizing function, we start to find examples of Hall's 'productive' identity formation, examined in Chapter 1. Hall, like Bhabha, identifies the centrality of hybridity to the experience of colonized peoples. This, he suggests, is often seen as a condition that, after decolonization, must be rectified. Yet, for Hall, rather than seeing the postcolonial subject as having 'lost' their 'authentic' precolonial identity, which they must attempt to re-excavate (what he terms an 'archaeological' concept of identity formation), he argues that identity formation might better be seen as a dynamic 'productive' process. To cite Hall once more: 'Cultural identity, in this second sense ... is not something which already exists, transcending place, time, history and culture. Cultural identities come from somewhere, have histories. But, like everything which is historical, they undergo constant transformation'.[1] Hall's concept of 'productive' identity formation, which in a postcolonial context is necessarily hybrid in nature, is particularly useful in our discussion of late 1990s culture because it illustrates the extent to which east German identity cannot simply be conceived of as a 'defiant' reaction to a 'colonizing' western state. Instead, many late 1990s texts show an east German population keen to register their ownership of western culture, while at the same time carving out a space for eastern distinctiveness within this framework.

One of the most contentious aspects of this shift away from a totalitarian paradigm towards one that focuses on more mundane, everday aspects of life, has been the fact that it has ostensibly brought with it a sense of nostalgic longing for the GDR. *Ostalgie*, the term, first coined in the early 1990s, by which this phenomenon is commonly known, is found throughout contemporary culture, most obviously recently, as I shall discuss in more detail in Chapter 5, in television and consumer culture. In the present chapter, however, I focus on the place of *Ostalgie* in cinema, a forum that, at the end of the 1990s, was one of the first to bring the word to widespread public awareness. Like many manifestations of east German cultural identity in the 1990s, *Ostalgie* was more often than not seen as an unsettling influence in the new Germany, undermining both the objective historical appraisal of the GDR period and the project of inner-German unification. If we return to the views on the PDS, discussed in Chapter 2, for example, nostalgia for the GDR was seen by all the other main parties as a worrying development, helping to keep alive anti-democratic principles. For its critics *Ostalgie* is a dangerous form of selective amnesia that sees the East German state through rose-tinted spectacles, ignoring the problems of life there and idealizing it instead as a land where, for example, there was no unemployment and a strong sense of community existed. Indeed, for some critics, particularly as Lothar Fritze notes from within the western media, the impression is created that any expression of nostalgia for aspects of life in the east signals a wish amongst the population to return to the days of division and even to a rebuilding of the Berlin Wall.[2] However, as ever, it is problematic to divide views purely along geographical lines. The east German writer Inka Bach, who left the GDR before the *Wende*, for example, puts her view bluntly, suggesting that:

> Those untiring ostalgic defenders of the GDR still cry today for the lost feeling of humanity and warmth to be found there, as if living in the East was like being cosily wrapped up in straw in a stable, in contrast to the social iciness of the West…. It is true, the GDR was like a stable, but only in terms of the smell … It was never as harmless as people try to make out now.[3]

In the rest of this book, I hope to show that *Ostalgie* is, in fact, a far more multi-layered phenomenon than Bach's analysis would suggest. Specifically, in this chapter I examine its complexities in relation to the east German filmmaker, Leander Haußmann's *Sonnenallee* (*Sun Alley*), a major hit on its release in 1999 and the first mainstream east German film to engage with the issue of GDR nostalgia. My discussion of *Sonnenallee* is subsequently contrasted with examinations of Oskar Roehler's *Die Unberührbare* (*No Place to Go, 2000*) and Wolfgang Becker's *Good Bye, Lenin!* (2002). Both these films are by west German directors, and like *Sonnenallee* examine the issue of nostalgia and the GDR. However, with regard to the latter two I discuss a further important dimension: we are reminded of the fact that, when looking at GDR nostalgia, one must also remember that it is not only east Germans who at times look fondly at pre-unification days. As a study carried out by Shell in 2000 notes, while there might be 'an open *Ostalgie*' to be found in the east, it is also possible to isolate a more subtle form of '*Westalgie* for the old Federal Republic'.[4] In 1989–1990 virtually all mainstream debates concerning the future of Germany envisaged unification as the annexation of the East by the West. Whether one welcomed this development or not, no one thought that the new Germany would be anything other than an enlarged version of the postwar West German state. Perhaps West Germans would have to pay more tax than before to help build up the eastern regions but there would be no fundamental reshaping of West German society. Yet, by the end of the 1990s it was becoming clear that the events of 1989 had also had an (albeit more gradually) altering effect on the former West German population. The fall of the Berlin Wall effectively also brought about the end of the old FRG (a change finally sealed in 2002 with the demise of the *Deutschmark* – a central definer of postwar West German stability). Of particular importance to my discussion of Roehler and Becker's films is how these film-makers exhibit a nostalgic longing for aspects of the pre-unification West, paradoxically, via their representation of the East. Here we return to western conceptions of the GDR as 'Orient', where the east is again constructed as an imagined space, used to prop up and substantiate aspects of West German identity, but in a very different manner than that discussed in connection with the Enquete Commissions.

Representing the East on Film since the *Wende*

In order to contextualize the three films that I scrutinize in detail, it is first necessary to give a brief overview of developments in the representation of the east on film since the GDR's collapse. In this period, the GDR and the question of eastern integration have become key topics for film-makers in both the east and the west. Yet, as Leonie Naughton points out, until recently their approaches tended to differ radically.[5] Films by west Germans, particularly in the early 1990s, largely followed the patterns set by the filmmakers of the New German Comedy, the mode of film produc-tion that became dominant in the 1980s and that marked a reaction to the avant-garde, overtly critical *auteurist* cinema of Rainer Werner Fassbinder, Wim Wenders and other artists connected with the New German Cinema. As Sönke Wortmann, the director of a number of hit films in the 1990s (for example *Allein unter Frauen/ Alone Among Women*, 1991, *Der bewegte Mann/Maybe ... Maybe Not*, 1994) puts it 'when I was at film school in Munich, the great hero was Tarkovsky. Today it's Spielberg.'[6] No longer wishing to follow the avant-garde tradi-tion of the previous generation, these younger filmmakers emulate the fast-paced, action-driven entertainment films of Hollywood.

This change in German film aesthetics has been greeted with a degree of alarm by some critics. Eric Rentschler comments, for example, that while Fassbinder, Wenders and others produced films from the late 1960s onwards that 'interrogated images of the past in the hope of refining memories and catalysing changes', contemporary cinema lacks 'opposi-tional energies and critical voices', aiming instead for what he terms a 'cinema of consensus'.[7] The turn away from a protest tradition in film making has had particularly important implications for the representation of the east. John Davidson notes that in the early 1990s, although there was a good deal of interest in the GDR, this interest was less about the critical appraisal of the period, than about legitimizing a reading of German history that sees its culmination in the present unified state:

> The stress on the GDR as the site of coming to terms with the past, which occurs inside a film landscape generally marked by depoliticized *Beziehungskomödien* (situational comedies) and a few highly-promoted hits, indirectly legitimates West Germany's past and reunified Germany's present.[8]

Here we see film following trends found in the political and literary discourses already discussed. Although, in much west German main-stream film production the legitimization of the unified state is achieved less through an engagement with the horrors of the past (as it is, for example in the Enquete Commissions' reports) than through the presen-tation of an escapist vision of the present, promising a bright new future for the nation. For example, in the so-called 'Trabi Comedies' of the early 1990s (Peter Timm's *Go Trabi Go*, 1991 and Wolfgang Büld and Reinhard Klooss's *Das war der wilde Osten/That was the wild East*, 1992), which tell of the humorous adventures of the plucky but naïve Struutz family, or Detlev Buck's *Wir können auch anders* (*No more Mr Nice Guy*, 1993), the comic story of two brothers who travel to the former GDR to claim their family inheritance, a number of assumptions are made about the unification process that are found throughout western films of the time. On the one hand, there is an implicit belief that unification is purely an east German concern. Here we see filmmakers ignore the calls by politicians discussed in Chapter 2 to see the question of dealing with the GDR and the issue of social integration as a matter for all Germans. In Timm's *Go Trabi Go*, for example, unification is implicitly constructed as a process whereby the east must simply catch up with the west. Both the population of the east and its infrastructure are shown to be lagging behind, as we see the simple Struutz family driving through the Bitterfeld countryside in their little GDR car. At this early stage in German unification, there is, perhaps, no reason to doubt that the broken down farm buildings they pass will soon be replaced with Kohl's 'blossoming landscapes' as the divided country comes together in prosperity. On the other, the notion of the east lagging behind is at times actually celebrated. In a similar fashion to Hans Pleschinski's *Ostsucht* examined in Chapter 1, the east German population might be seen as more primitive than the west, but it is also presented as more 'authentically' German. Glossing over any potential problem of social integration, we are presented with a society in which Struutz and his family can overcome any difficulty through their indomitable German spirit, to be found throughout the east. As a result, and as Naughton notes, such films can be seen as re-workings of west German *Heimat* ('Homeland') films of the 1950s:

> *Heimat* is resurrected in western features to provide a society in ruins facing a complete political reorientation with reassuring images of harmony and integration. A genre whose *Weltanschauung* was anathema to the socio-political values and priorities of the ex-GDR has been recycled to shape impressions of what life in the east has become and what the East has to offer. A western framework is imposed on the east to define it in western terms.[9]

For Naughton such images of the east as a new German *Heimat* are primarily a comforting image for the east German spectator. However, such images of comfort can clearly also speak to audiences in the west. In films by Timm and others we are presented with a picture of the east as a pre-industrial fantasy world. As such, again like Pleschinski's text, this can be seen as a further example of the east as a western Orient. But, rather than providing the FRG with a negative, abject historical 'other', here the east becomes a repository for a more authentic notion of

Germanness, where old-fashioned German values, as well as an indefatigable German spirit, are alive and well, thereby reassuring the spectator that ultimately all will be well with the nation.

Although the New German Comedy dominated German domestic cinema, it would be unfair to say that the legacy of the New German Cinema was completely lost in 1990s, particularly with regard to the representation of the east. First of all, some of its directors, including Wenders, Margarethe von Trotta, Helma Sanders-Brahms and Volker Schlöndorff, continued to make films, although in many cases such filmmakers would appear to have lost their critical edge. Von Trotta's *Das Versprechen* (*The Promise*, 1995), for example, tells the story of a young couple separated by the building of the Berlin Wall and thus forced to grow up in two different states. Having endured great hardships, the couple are finally reunited on the night of 9 November 1989 when the Wall first opens, thereby providing a quintessential image of social 'consensus' in the unified state, to use Rentschler's term. As Sabine Hake puts it, the film 'presents the post-war division as the tragic story of two young lovers divided by ideology but meant to be united; the happy ending for the nation comes with the post-ideological identity of a unified Germany'.[10] Recalling Ingid Sharp's analysis, we see the end of division constructed as a romantic union between formerly separated lovers. Although, interestingly, in this film the gender relationship Sharp identifies is reversed, with the man coming from the East to join the woman in the West. That said, both the central protagonists actually originally come from the GDR, and while the film is about a union between a couple divided by the German-German border, its focus is almost wholly on the East. Consequently, the GDR is once again presented as the main site where unification must be negotiated.

While some of the New German Cinema's filmmakers were still working in the 1990s, their abrasive engagement with German society was perhaps more obviously at play in the work of the younger west German filmmaker Christoph Schlingensief. Schlingensief's films fly directly in the face of Rentschler's 'cinema of consensus'. In his comedy slasher movies *Das deutsche Kettensägermassaker* (*The German Chainsaw Massacre*, 1990), and *Terror 2000* (1992) Schlingensief dismisses any attempt to see the events of 1989–90 as the inevitable triumph of the 'correct' German state. In *Das deutsche Kettensägermassaker*, for example, unification is presented in overtly colonialist terms, as a dangerous takeover by a barbaric west, embodied in the deranged owner of a sausage factory, who literally devours the citizens of the former GDR as they pour over the border. The evil *Wessi* cuts up his poor eastern cousins with his chainsaw and turns them into the raw ingredients for his products, thereby enacting a gory parable of Marxist economics. On the face of it, Schlingensief seems to leaves us in no doubt about the tradition he is working within, styling himself the new Fassbinder, with *Kettensägermassaker*, and *Terror 2000* forming two parts of what he calls his 'Germany Trilogy', a direct invocation of Fassbinder's 'FRG Trilogy'.[11] However, as John Davidson has noted, as far as Schlingensief himself is concerned, his self-proclaimed connection to the New German Cinema is a wholly provocative stance, through which he wishes to challenge the legacy of this earlier generation.[12] Indeed, aesthetically, his work has very little in common with Fassbinder, and in fact is far more reminiscent of Lloyd Kaufmann's 'Troma' films, those grotesque, at times pornographic, low-budget American films that brutally satirize mainstream Hollywood cinema.[13]

While it might be an oversimplication to paint the whole of west German film production in the 1990s as a 'cinema of consensus', it was within the context of east German film making that a critical *auteurist* cinematic tradition was most clearly to be seen, particularly in the work of a number of east German directors who were among the last to be trained by the GDR's state film company, DEFA. With the demise of the GDR and the winding up of DEFA in 1992, these filmmakers were forced to adjust to a completely new artistic environment in which the political censorship of the East German authorities was replaced with a culture dominated by commercial imperatives that manifest themselves in a predilection for mainstream genre film. As Daniela Berghahn notes, it is perhaps not surprising that many of these GDR artists found it difficult to embrace western forms in an attempt to make this adjustment:

> ex-Defa filmmakers were ill-equipped to cater to this new agenda. Genre cinema had never been one of DEFA's fortes ... and, as the scriptwriter Wolfgang Kohlhaase had already noted in 1977, to beat a capitalist film industry at what it did best would be impossible.[14]

Many of these filmmakers did not make the transition successfully to the new artistic environment. However, in the work of those that did one finds a clear engagement with *auteurist* aesthetic values, as well as a far harsher critique of German society at the time, than is found in much 1990s mainstream western film production. The most successful of these filmmakers, who nonetheless remained on the margins of the popular cine-matic landscape, are Andreas Dresen (*Nachtgestalten/ Night Shapes*, 1999; *Halbe Treppe/ Grill Point*, 2002), and Andreas Kleinert (*Verlorene Landschaft/Lost Landscape*, 1992; *Wege in die Nacht/ Paths into the Night*, 1999). Both filmmakers point to strong feelings of social exclusion

and alienation in postunification German society, particularly among easterners. Dresen's *Nachtgestalten*, for example, charts the interlinked jour-
neys of a number of social misfits one night as they move around Berlin.
Although coming from a GDR tradition, a number of critics have made
links between this film, as well as Dresen's work more generally, and the
western tradition of the New German Cinema. *Nachtgestalten*, for
example, has been termed a welcome 'return of social concerns to the
German screen, a theme that has been abandoned since the demise of the
New German Cinema'.[15] That said, it is also possible to place the work of
these filmmakers within an eastern European and Soviet tradition, to
which they would have had readier access before unification. Kleinert's
Wege in die Nacht, for example, the story of a former GDR citizen turned
leader of a vigilante group, who metes out rough justice on the thugs he
encounters on the night trains of postunification Berlin, shows obvious
points of correspondence with the work of Andrej Tarkovsky, about whom
Kleinert wrote his undergraduate dissertation, and who is cited, as we have
seen, by Wortmann as an important influence at the time of the New
German Cinema. His representation of Berlin's industrial landscape as a
beautiful yet disturbing postapocalyptic vision of urban decay seems, for
example, to be deliberately reminiscent of Tarkovsky's futuristic urban
world in his 1979 film, *The Stalker.*

In the 1990s, then, German domestic cinema was dominated by
western filmmakers who, through the use of comedy and the *Heimat*
tradition, construct an idealized and escapist view of a unified German
community, largely confirming Rentschler's view of German cinema
since unification being dominated by images of 'consensus'. On the
periphery, however, one found filmmakers, particularly east Germans
trained in the GDR, who continued (and, indeed, still continue) an
auteurist tradition, producing far more abrasive images of the state of
German unity. In all these films, we tend to find unification presented as
a wholly eastern issue, one with which the former GDR is, more or less,
successfully dealing, but that need not make the citizens of the old FRG
rethink their relationship to the unified state. However, as I shall explore
in the rest of this chapter, by the end of the decade, with the arrival of
films such as *Sonnenallee, Die Unberührbare* and *Good Bye, Lenin!* we
see a change, even a reversal in the pattern of film making outlined above,
a reversal that has important implications for each film's representation of
the past, and specifically for their engagement with the issue of nostalgia
for the pre-unification German states, both East and West.

Leander Haußmann's *Sonnenalle*

The reversal suggested above is, perhaps, most obvious in Leander Haußmann's *Sonnenalle*, where we see an east German filmmaker adopting many of the traits of the western New German Comedy. The film is an adolescent 'rights of passage' narrative, telling the story of a group of teenagers in their final year of secondary education living on Sonnenallee, a street that was divided by the border between East and West Berlin. Set in the 1970s, we see the humorous ways they negotiate the authorities in the GDR, their search for illegal Western contraband, in particular Western rock music, and above all their clumsy attempts to form relationships with the opposite sex. The film was a major hit in terms of German domestic box-office, with over 1.8 million spectators in its first year, only being beaten by *Star Wars Episode One: The Phantom Menace* and *The Mummy*, and making it the biggest grossing German film of 1999.[16]

Although a commercial sucess, this romantic comedy set in the shadow of the Berlin Wall was viewed by many reviewers as proof positive of the 'dangers' of *Ostalgie*. Hans Christoph Buch, for example, writing in the Tagesspiegel claims that the film 'turned the GDR into a musical, with Erich Honecker as the "Fiddler on the Roof"' in which the 'real tensions' of life in the East had been covered up 'with cheap *Ostalgie'*.[17] The Berlin listings magazine *Tip* went so far as to compare the film's presentation of the GDR with propagandistic comedies made under National Socialism.[18] The film even provoked a lawsuit from an organization for victims of political violence, Help e.V., which claimed that *Sonnenallee* was an insult to those who had suffered at the hands of the former East German regime.[19] The view that *Sonnenallee* is simply an exercise in ostalgic wallowing would, moreover, seem to be confirmed in an interview with the writers of the film's screenplay, Haußmann himself and Thomas Brussig, whose *Helden wie wir* was discussed in the previous chapter and which has (if less successfully) also been turned into a film.[20] Brussig declares: 'I always said that it was supposed to be a film which would make westerners jealous that they weren't allowed to live in the East.'[21] The opening of the film appears to underline this intention. Micha, the narrator and hero of *Sonnenallee*, claims in a voiceover, 'Things aren't too bad. We haven't got any homelessness and at least no one starves to death here.'[22] Although Micha uses the present tense, thus speaking from the temporal perspective of the film itself, the sentiment concurs completely with the type of post-unification articulations of *Ostalgie* attacked by Inka Bach, pointing to the ostensibly caring, community-oriented nature of GDR society, which, it is often lamented, has been lost since the state's demise.

Initially, then, the film seems to confirm its detractors' criticism that it is simply an exercise in reactionary *Ostalgie*. However, it soon becomes apparent that the film's main concern it to examine the underlying tensions competing within the phenomenon of *Ostalgie* itself. First, and perhaps most obviously, Haußmann explores the reasons why east Germans feel the need to recall their past. As I suggested in previous chapters, in the early 1990s the focus of popular examinations of the GDR was almost exclusively on its insidious structures of control, and in particular on the role of the Stasi. The result of representing the GDR as nothing more than a 'Stasi state', in which it was impossible to have a 'normal' life, led to a growing sense of alienation amongst many ordinary east Germans, who felt that their everyday experience in the East was being devalued and ignored.[23] On one level, *Sonnenalle*, like Brussig's earlier novel, is a response to this sense of alienation. However, rather than directly responding to the GDR as 'Stasi state', the film attempts to move beyond this image. As the publicity information for the film suggests: 'It's high time that people talk about what else the GDR was other than the Wall, the Stasi and the Central Committee.'[24] *Sonnenallee* represents an attempt to give a voice to the experience of ordinary GDR citizens. In so doing, the film seeks to de-exoticize the lives of east Germans. Thus, although its approach differs, the film, like many of the Stasi narratives discussed, is ultimately also concerned with deconstructing a view of the former East German state as a tamed 'Orient'.

The prevalence of what I have identified as western 'orientalist' tendencies in 1990s German society is satirized throughout Haußmann's film, most obviously in its construction of the GDR as a zoo. On a number of occasions, we are shown West Germans on observation platforms treating the Easterners they look down upon like animals trapped behind bars for their amusement. At the beginning of the film, for example, we see a group of Western tourists calling over the wall to Micha: 'Youhoo, *Ossi*, give us a little wave!' The use of the term *Ossi* is revealing here, since it (along with its partner term *Wessi*) is a word that has only come into common usage since the *Wende*, thereby placing the apparent representation of preunification relations between Easterners and Westerners within the context of postunification stereotyping, flagging up the present-day lack of sensitivity that the filmmaker feels many *Wessis* exhibit towards the experience of east Germans.

The film goes on to suggest that much of this western exoticization is predicated on ignorance, which is constantly mocked by the inhabitants of the GDR. Here the film turns on its head the image of the naive easterner, evident in the western 'Trabi comedies' of the early 1990s. In one sequence, for example, Micha and his friend Mario run behind a bus of

Western tourists, arms outstretched, cheeks sucked in, shouting 'Feed us, feed us!' The perspective of the film then switches from outside the bus to the inside and from colour to black and white, suggesting that the boys' satirical gesture is being filmed by someone in the bus. Consequently, the joke is now presented almost as if it were a piece of newsreel footage, that is, as part of the West's official conception of life in the GDR. The ignorance of Westerners reaches its pinnacle in the character of Uncle Hans, a regular visitor to the family, who takes great pride in his ability to smuggle contraband into the East. But what is this contraband – Western music, newspapers? No, tights and underpants, products that are completely legal in the East.

Apart from the film's overtly satirical presentation of western misconceptions about life in the GDR, *Sonnenallee* also attempts to de-exoticize eastern experience more subtly through its very choice of subject. Rather than the nature of life in the East being the central focus of attention, the GDR becomes the context for the presentation of the universal experience of adolescent growing pains. As a result, Haußmann normalizes the experience of easterners while preserving the specific differences in the historical context of the GDR. The main plot revolves around Micha's attempts to woo his dream girl, Miriam. We first meet Miriam in a moment of humorous sentimentality as she walks towards camera (constructed as Micha's point of view) in soft focus and slow motion to the sound of an Elvis-like crooner. She is presented as a paragon of beauty. The world around her freezes, cars come crashing to a halt, until, with a flick of her long golden hair, she turns and disappears into a building. The music comes to an abrupt end and the world starts up again. This gently mocking evocation of teenage love is one that is readily understandable by both easterners and westerners alike, a point underlined by Haußmann himself: 'When a boy sees a girl for the first time- that's something that everyone can understand'.[25] The focus of the film becomes, therefore, the nostalgic recollection of the experience of first love, rendering Micha's warm memories of the GDR more acceptable: 'This was the nicest time of my life, because', he claims, 'I was young and in love.'

What is particularly interesting, however, in Haußmann's presentation of this 'universal' story is his propensity to use specifically western forms and conventions, through which he again seeks to normalize the eastern experience for a western audience. Here we find Haußmann move unequivocaly beyond any notion of an 'identity of defiance' towards what Hall sees as a more 'productive', hybrid identity, in which the filmmaker suggests a version of east German identity that can also signal its ownership of western culture, a degree of 'ownership' that David Chioni Moore suggests can be found across the post-Soviet bloc. If we look, for example, at his representation of women, this differs markedly from the East German DEFA tradition of film making. Andrea Rinke notes:

> Ever since 1945, mainstream cinema in the Federal Republic has been dominated by Hollywood and its female stereotypes: the housewife, the glamorous sex-symbol and demonized temptress. By contrast, an initial overview of DEFA films reveals an altogether different variety of female protagonists ... Films in the GDR tended to portray their heroines at their workplace, as ordinary average people, avoiding glamorous extremes. The majority of women on screen are working mothers with one or two children, more often single than married.[26]

Throughout *Sonnenallee* all such traditional images of GDR women are avoided. Helen Cafferty points out, for example, that Micha's mother is only ever seen in a domestic role, abandoning her one attempt to escape to the West in favour of returning to her family and her roles as a housewife and mother.[27] Marriage is viewed as an ideal state and, as we have already seen in the presentation of Miriam, the film can hardly be attempting to avoid 'glamorous extremes' (to quote Rinke once more) in its female protagonists.

The use of western forms is also found in the film's wealth of cultural allusions. Micha has a rival in love, a West Berliner who turns up at a school disco where Micha has already made a failed attempt to dance with Miriam. The school dance scene is, of course, a standard trope of Hollywood teen films. However, specifically here, there is an overt intertextual echo of Franc Roddam's 1979 film *Quadrophenia*. The West Berliner is a reworking of the 'Ace Face' (played by Sting), who dominates the dance-hall sequence in this earlier film, and who similarly flouts the authorities when challenged. The allusion continues when it transpires that Micha's rival is not a rich Western playboy but, again like 'Ace Face' in *Quadrophenia*, a bellboy, the expensive cars we see him driving having been 'borrowed' from rich hotel guests.

As well as film citations, Western music also plays an important role. Wuschel, for example, is obsessed with the Rolling Stones, his central aim in life being to find a copy of *Exile on Main Street*, the Holy Grail of all Western contraband. As in the representation of women, the use of pop music translates the experience of east German youth into understandable terms for a west German audience by highlighting the common features of life in the east and west. In pointing out the importance of groups like the Rolling Stones to this generation in the east, the film evokes the sounds and styles of the 1970s as it was experienced on both sides of the Wall. Or, more accurately, it indulges in the type of nostalgic re-appropriation of this period which was in vogue at the time in both the east and west of Germany. Nostalgia for 1970s fashion and music was, of course, a key feature of much 1990s European and US youth culture, reflected in a surge of 1970s nostalgia films – see for example the film remakes of the 1970s television shows, Betty Thomas's *The Brady Bunch Movie* (1995) or Damien O'Donnell's *East Is East* (1999). That said, it is important to note that Haußmann is not suggesting that growing up in the East was the same as growing up in the West. Rather, by normalizing the experience of ordinary GDR citizens the film in fact attempts to preserve the specific differences in everyday life in the East. Consequently, the film implies that happy memories of living in the GDR should not necessarily be seen as a dangerous form of revisionism.

On one level, then, *Sonnenallee* attempts to overcome a process of historical elision that many east Germans feel is taking place in contemporary German society, by normalizing and de-exoticizing the experience of everyday life in the GDR. The film views the East German state through a western cultural lens, thereby constructing a 'productive' image of east Germanness which can embrace both cultural traditions. However, competing with this impulse is the film's critique of *Ostalgie*, which questions what it sees as the fetishization of the GDR by some easterners. Here the film becomes reminiscent of Brussig's earlier novel, in which he criticizes, albeit far more harshly, eastern attitudes to their past. Nevertheless, as I shall discuss below, this critique in the film can in fact also be viewed within the context of a 'productive' notion of identity formation.

Central to the film's more critical invocation of *Ostalgie* is the use of irony as a means of distancing the audience from the world the film presents, through which it forces an east German audience to reflect upon their use of the past. Initially, *Sonnenallee* appears to present a highly accurate image of East Berlin in the 1970s. In the opening shot, the camera pans slowly across the walls of Micha's bedroom, showing all the paraphernalia of 1970s youth culture. It moves across posters of The Beatles and Bat Man to a record by Omega, the Eastern bloc's answer to the Rolling Stones, until finally pausing on Micha's prized possession, an East German reel-to-reel tape recorder. His room becomes the spectator's entrance portal to this lost world of the past, and has all the qualities of a living museum. As one finds throughout much contemporary *Ostalgie*, and as I shall discuss in more detail later in this study, the film fetishizes certain GDR artefacts. In fact, at times the focus on a particular item seems almost to become a form *of ostalgic* product placement, advertising certain prized exhibits in the filmic museum and allowing the east German audience a celebratory moment of *jouissance* as they recognize a now forgotten object. A good example of this is the film's presentation of the 'Multifunktionstisch' ('Multifunctional table') in Micha's family's living room. The mother asks the father to open up the 'Mufuti', to which the man responds with confusion. She then repeats 'Open the multifunctional table can't you?', thus drawing the audience's attention of this now strange GDR artefact. This celebratory moment of product placement is then, however, undercut as the father struggles with what he calls this 'Eastern crap!' Nevertheless, a few moments later the advertisement for the table is bravely resumed. The local policeman pays the family a visit. Now set up, the table dominates the room. All goes quiet as the policeman sits down. Then, with some solemnity he examines the table and asks, 'is that a Mufu … ti?'[28]

Through such moments of over-the-top, comic *ostalgic* product placement east German spectators begin to sense that they are not being presented with a straightforwardly mimetic representation of life in the East, but rather a hyper-real simulation, through which their sense of nostalgia is indulged, but at the same time, gently challenged. As Haußmann suggests, 'If you look closely, you see that the film is completely unrealistic. The décor, the street-everything looks like it's been built.'[29] In a sense, the film's attention to detail is too perfect, too well constructed to be real. Its presentation of the GDR is overcoded, and therefore ironically draws the spectator's attention to its artificiality.

This overcoding actually begins with the film's manipulation of genre. As Cafferty notes in her analysis of the film's use of humour, 'the business of mainstream romantic comedy is to produce a heterosexual couple', and in *Sonnenallee* such couples abound. Not only do Micha and Miriam find love, Mario marries his existentialist, anti-establishment girlfriend, Micha's mother and father's marriage is revitalized. Indeed, in practically every scene where we see Micha's friends there is also a constantly kissing couple, a continual reminder of the film's romantic credentials.[30] This overloading of the film's generic features, which highlights *Sonnenallee*'s light-hearted romantic element, mirrors the film's overtly overindulgent nostalgia towards the paraphernalia of the GDR. This, in turn, suggests that east German spectators are not to take the film at face value, but are rather being invited to explore critically their relationship with their preunification experience.

Through an overcoded representation of the GDR, the past is effectively bracketed off from the present. As a result, the film's use of nostalgia ultimately refuses to be simply *ostalgic* escapism, and becomes, rather, a self-conscious revisitation of the past through the lens of the present. To return to Hall's dichotomy, we see, once more, the overt rejection of a backward-looking, 'archeological' instrumentalization of the past, implictitly suggested by many critics of *Ostalgie*, in favour of a more 'productive', dynamic appropriation of the GDR within cultural memory. A central moment of such productive re-visitation of the past comes in the film's evocation of Heiner Carow's 1973 DEFA youth film *Die Legende von Paul und Paula* (*The Legend of Paul and Paula*). In this film's climax Paul takes an axe to his lover Paula's door in order to break it down and to be with her. Although made three decades later, *Sonnenallee* is set in the same period as *Paul und Paula*. In the climactic moment in the Micha/Miriam romance plot line, Micha runs to his would-be lover's house to the growling music of the Puhdys' hit from the earlier film, 'Geh' zu ihr und laß deinen Drachen steigen' ('Go to her and fly your kite'). On the stairs of her building he then bumps into Paul from the DEFA film (played by Winfried Glatzeder), who is even wearing the same frilly shirt he has on in *Paul und Paula*. Yet, at the very moment when the evocation of the GDR past seems to be complete, it is also undermined. Glatzeder might be wearing the same clothes, but he is nearly thirty years older. Thus our attention is deliberately drawn to the fact that the film is not actually taking place in the 1970s. The reference to *Paul und Paula* is used to show that the past is being recontextualized. This is further emphasized when Paul asks Micha if he needs an axe to get to Miriam. The violent denouement of the earlier film is immediately satirized as Micha tries the door, which opens readily. 'No thanks, it's fine!', he replies.

Through such distancing devices, *Sonnenallee* explores the changing function of the past in the present. In so doing, the film suggests that it is not only westerners who are guilty of eliding East German history. As we see in *Helden wie wir*, easterners themselves are not above using the past creatively and selectively. This becomes most obvious when Micha, in a final attempt to win Miriam, writes a fictional diary, through which he hopes to show that he is worthy of her love because he has suffered at the hands of the authorities. We see him go back to his early childhood: 'Dear Diary, at last I can write what I really think, because I now know all the letters. Today we learnt the β. At last I can write a word that I often think about *Scheiße* (shit)!' As he develops his diary style, his entries become more and more daring. In the manner of Helmut Dietl's 1992 film *Schtonk*, which tells the story of the forging of Hitler's diaries, Micha uses his environment to help construct imagined past events. Specifically in this case, a power cut and gunfire at the Wall are used to fabricate an escape attempt. The diary writing sequence has a double effect in the film. First, although individual events in the diary are made up, the overall image of life in the GDR is actually far more hard hitting than in the rest of the film. Ironically, the writing of a fictionalized version of his life actually becomes a mechanism through which the film escapes its direct thematization of *Ostalgie* to explore the negative aspects of life in the East in a more realistic, less romantic, way than they are treated in much of the rest of the film. Here we see, for example, Micha discuss overtly the oppressive, dehumanizing effects of the GDR's state institutions. The force of this discussion is then underlined by the fact that the diary-writing sequence ends with the shooting of Wuschel. We are shown the boy rushing home during the power cut, having finally obtained a copy of *Exile on Main Street*. He is ordered to stop by a policeman, but fearing that the record will be confiscated he runs away. The next sound we hear is a gunshot, and suddenly the nostalgic façade of the film is ruptured as we see the boy lying motionless on the street. Although the harshness of this sequence is subsequently softened when it transpires that Wuschel has been saved, the bullet having been blocked by his prized record, a rose-tinted impression of the GDR can never be fully restored. Although Wuschel is not dead, his youthful dreams, embodied in the Rolling Stones album, have been shattered by the state. Furthermore, the spectator is powerfully reminded of the fact that this is a country where people were shot for trying to escape, and where owning a piece of music could be considered a criminal offence.

Second, the diary sequence shows how the past has always been, and is always, used as a means of bestowing meaning on the present. The writing of the diary is a self-referential moment that highlights the relationship of the film itself to the east German viewing public and their use of the past. Here we see the film point to the broader issue of the relationship between nostalgia and the construction of cultural identity. While the film questions the role of *Ostalgie* in contemporary society, it by no means dismisses it. As a result, the criticism of easterners in *Sonnenallee* is far less vicious than that of *Helden wie wir*. This change is made explicit in Brussig's literary reworking of the film:

> Whoever wants to preserve accurately what actually happened shouldn't rely on memory. The function of memory is not simply to fix the past ... Memory can do much more than this. Memory miraculously allows people to make peace with the past, by allowing the soft veil of nostalgia to fall over every painful experience.[31]

For Brussig, who has now obviously softened in his tone, nostalgia is a normal and necessary function of social development, and consequently, east Germans should not necessarily be reprimanded for exercising it in their appraisal of the past. That said, Haußmann also give clear warning that easterners should not simply wallow indulgently in their

past. Instead their GDR experience should be seen as a dynamic, productive element in their contemporary cultural identity.

Oskar Roehler's *Die Unberührbare*

In Haußmann's film we find a nostalgia for the East German past based
on a visceral, deliberately apolitical, representation of everyday life in the
GDR. *Ostalgie* in *Sonnenallee* is less about the recuperation of the GDR's
socialist project, such we find in some of the policy statements of the PDS
discussed in Chapter 2, and which have been widely criticized, than a call
for a more inclusive reading of German history. Moreover, it is also used
as a self-reflexive vehicle for exploring the complex relationship of easterners themselves to this history. However, as I suggested in the introduction to this chapter, since the late 1990s there has also been a wave of
nostalgia by west German authors and filmmakers for West German
society of the 1970s and 1980s, a phenomenon that has not been
discussed to anything like the extent of *Ostalgie*. In novels such as
Matthias Politycki's *Weiberroman* (1997) Frank Goosen's *Liegen lernen*
(2000), or Sven Regener's *Herr Lehmann* (2001), subsequently turned
into a film by Haußmann, we see a similar evocation of past music and
fashions to that of *Sonnenallee,* but here in reference to the FRG.

There are, however, some important differences between such *Ostalgie*
and what the Shell report calls *Westalgie*, not least of which is the question of generational shift. As Stuart Taberner notes, the *Westalgie* texts
mentioned above are written by the so-called 'generation of 78', who
came of age in the late 1970s and 1980s. For Taberner, the nostalgia to be
found here reveals an attempt by this generation to mark its difference
from the politically engaged 'generation of 68' – which found its voice
during the student movement of the late 1960s, as these young people
began to question their parents about their role in the rise of National
Socialism – and the hedonistic generation of '89', often seen as a lost
'Generation X' for which political idealism has been completely replaced
by pop culture:

> Wedged between 'the good old 68ers' ('den guten alten 68ern') and 'Neon-
> kids of the generation of 89' ('den Neonkids der 89er-Generation'), to cite
> Matthias Politycki, it was time for this generation to come of age and to begin
> to shape the country in a fashion more to their liking.[32]

However, as Andrew Plowman suggests, nostalgia for the old FRG
present in contemporary west German culture is not only found among

the '78ers'. On the one hand, certain members of the 68 generation have begun to look again at their past. In literary works such as *Ulrike Kolb's Frühstück mit Max* (*Breakfast with Max*, 1999) and Uwe Timm's *ROT* (*RED*, 2001), or in Volker Schlöndorff's film *Die Stille nach dem Schuß*, (*The Legends of Rita*, 2000) one finds, 'the legacy of "1968"... re-assessed following the advent of younger generations'.[33] As I shall examine here, in such nostalgia one finds points of correspondence with certain ideologically based types of *Ostalgie*, that is, the type of nostalgia criticized in connection with the PDS, but which can also be found in the views of some former GDR intellectuals such as Christa Wolf. On the other hand, and perhaps more curiously, one finds a nostalgia for the 68ers in certain manifestations of 89er pop culture, seen, most obviously, in this generation's recycling of the symbols and insignia of the 'Red Army Faction', or Baader-Meinhof terrorist group, which rose from the student movement's ashes. These West German urban guerrillas are recalled in a number of popular cultural phenomenon, from the joke 'solidarity' parties organized in Berlin for the 'WAF' ('Wasser Armee Friedrichshein', whose posters replace the rifles of the RAF insignia with water pistols), to the 'Prada Meinhof' clothes range.[34] Such nostalgic kitsch revisionism by this generation is highly ambivalent. It might be read as the ultimate rejection of this past, an ironic statement that the radi-calism of this generation was a pointless gesture because the memory of this terrorist group now lives on as a manifestation of the very consumer culture it sought to undermine. Or, it might be seen as statement by the 89ers of their feelings of loss, an attempt to recuperate certain aspects of the 68ers political radicalism, which they feel is missing from their own lives, in the only cultural language to which they have access. Of course, it is probably a mixture of both.

Although perhaps a rather minor cultural phenomenon, it is interesting to note that the *westalgic* 'WAF' parties mentioned above take place in the *east* Berlin borough of Friedrichshain. As such they have much in common with the '89er' director Osker Roehler's *Die Unberührbare*, a film that traces the last days of a fictional West German writer, Hanna Flanders, from the events of 9 November to her suicide in the early days of 1990. A central issue in the film is its representation of the East, and specifically the place of the former GDR in discussions of contemporary west German culture, a discussion that leads to a far more fraught engagement with recent German history than is to be found in Haußmann's film. *Die Unberührbare* received wide critical acclaim. It won the coveted German Film Prize in 2000 (*Sonnenallee* was the runner up), and was also selected as the country's entry for the best foreign-language film Oscar. One of the main reasons cited for the film's critical success was its return to the tradition of the New German Cinema and its rejection of 1990s filmic pop culture. 'The best thing to happen to German film since Fassbinder,' was typical of comments by the critics.[35] Thus, we see the reverse side of the aesthetic shift between filmmakers of the east and west discussed in relation to *Sonnenallee*. While Haußmann embraces, however subtly, western genre norms, Roehler rejects genre filmmaking, and returns to the *auteurist* tradition of the New German Cinema, the praise given to his film echoing that already cited in connection with Andreas Dresen's work. However, Roehler has a similarly ambivalent relationship to this generation of filmmakers, and particularly towards the political radicalism of the 68ers from which they came, to that already identified in '89er' pop culture more generally. In *Die Unberührbare*, Roehler questions the contribution of this earlier generation to German society. At the same time he seems to long for the sense of purpose that political engagement gave its members.

Roehler himself leaves us in no doubt as to the importance of this older generation of artists, and in particular of Fassbinder, to his development as a filmmaker, claiming in an article he wrote for the *taz* that when he was introduced to Fassbinder's work as a child he immediately became fascinated by his films.[36] What attracted him, he claims, was the filmmaker's portrayal of marginal figures, whose treatment cast a light on the nature of the whole of society. Specifically, there are two obvious points of comparison between Fassbinder's work and Roehler's film. The first is Fassbinder's *In einem Jahr mit 13 Monden* (*In a Year with 13 Moons*, 1978), a film that traces the final days of Elvira Weishaupt, a trans-sexual whose life consists of a catalogue of rejections, from her mother as a child, to the man she loves and for whom she changed sex. Unable to find acceptance in society, Elvira finally decides to take her own life. The importance of this film to Roehler is made explicit in his introduction to the screenplay of *Die Unberührbare*. Here he mentions *13 Monden* as one of the films 'that had such an impact on my impressionable eyes that after seeing it twice I thought I could recall every shot',[37] and as we shall see, there are clear points of correspondence between Fassbinder's and Roehler's protagonists. However, in Roehler's film there is an added dimension of generational conflict, a crucial dissimilarity which links the film perhaps more obviously to the second part of Fassbinder's 'FRG Trilogy', *Die Sehnsucht der Veronika Voss* (*Veronika Voss*, 1982). Recalling Billy Wilder's *Sunset Boulevard* (1950), *Die Sehnsucht der Veronika Voss* tells the story of the last days in the life of a has-been star from the Nazi era, driven to ruin by a corrupt doctor who keeps her addicted to morphine in order to rob her of her wealth. Shot in high-contrast black and white, the film straddles the traditions of both the Ufa movies of the 1930s and 1940s and American film noir in order to explore continuities between the barbaric behaviour of the National Socialist period and the institutionalized corruption of the apparently Americanized Federal Republic of 1950s. The film's anti-heroine is isolated by a world that superficially rejects Nazism, embracing the culture of its American conquerors, while in reality having done very little to overcome the fundamental societal traits that enabled Hitler to take over.[38]

Die Unberührbare similarly traces the trajectory of a woman who has outlived her day. As Fassbinder does in both *Veronika Voss* and *13 Monden*, Roehler portrays a figure living on the edge of society, who becomes a symbol of a wider sense of crisis in Germany as a whole. The inspiration for the film's narrative came from the life of Roehler's mother, the West German leftwing writer Gisela Elsner who gained success on both sides of the inner-German border in 1964 with her first novel *Die Riesenzwerge* (*The Giant Dwarves*), a book that grotesquely depicts what she views as the obscene consumer culture endemic to Western patriarchal bourgeois society.[39] Seen as an early torchbearer of the 68 generation, Elsner rode the wave of the student movement, until in the 1970s and 1980s her style became more and more esoteric, and Western interest in her work waned. In the GDR, however, she continued to find acclaim, being valued as a socialist 'fifth columnist' within the capitalist West.[40] After 1989, Elsner was deeply troubled by the demise of East Germany, which she had always seen as the better of the two postwar German states (although she never chose to live there). Once again, the east functions as a western orient. However, here the GDR is constructed neither as part of Germany's abject past nor as part of its more 'authentic' tradition. Rather, it becomes the repository for a critical, leftwing value system that she can use to attack her own society. As a result we find a further point of correspondence between leftwing critical intellectuals in the east and west, already discussed in connection with Grass's *Ein weites Feld*. On a more pragmatic level, the end of the GDR plunged her into not only an ideological, but also a financial crisis, since it meant that she lost the only remaining market for her books. By the early 1990s she was becoming evermore psychologically disturbed and overtaken by ill health. Increasingly, she chose to escape into a haze of drugs and alcohol, until in 1992 she took her own life.

Die Unberührbare presents a highly condensed, fictionalized account of Elsner's (here called Hanna Flanders) final days, from the fall of the Wall to her suicide. The film's opening sequence is deliberately disorienting, thwarting the spectator's expectations, and evoking from the outset the same feeling of confusion that is at work in the film's central protagonist. The credits appear on a black background to the sound of people celebrating the opening of the Wall. We hear the familiar voices of joyous incredulity we remember from the media coverage of that night, voices that immediately conjure up images of celebrating revellers drinking *Sekt* and dancing on top of the Wall. However, what we are then presented with visually is completely out of step with the soundtrack. The first shot of the film is an extreme close up of the top of a medicine bottle containing arsenic, a shot that gives the illusion that we are staring into the barrel of a gun. The noise of the revellers fades and is replaced by a telephone conversion between a man and a woman. The film then cuts to the first shot of Hanna, hair dishevelled, drawing desperately on a cigarette and drinking wine. 'I'm putting the phone down. I'm going to kill myself', she informs her interlocutor (U, 28). This is a threat that she does not put into action until the end of the film. Nevertheless, it sets the tone for the whole of the narrative. The joy that seemed ubiquitous that night is replaced by a moment of utter despair.

Echoes of Fassbinder abound. First, like *Veronika Voss, Die Unberührbare* recalls the style of Film Noir in its use of high-contrast black and white and symbolically laden camera angles. More importantly, Hanna Flanders, like Voss, is an anachronism, a hangover from an earlier age. However, in this later film there has been a generational shift. It is not 1930s fascism but rather Fassbinder's contemporaries who are now under the spotlight. The leftwing interrogators of the late 1960s are now themselves being interrogated. As the camera pans around Hanna's flat we see her walls covered with pictures of her heroes from the Russian Revolution. But these silent images from the beginning of Marxism's rise to power are impotent in the face of the television coverage that flickers away in the corner of her living room bringing news of Marxism's decline. Hanna is an individual in crisis, unable even to contemplate adapting her life and beliefs to this new society. As a result, she nostalgically clings to her old image from the 1960s, a wholly backward-looking notion of identity formation, far removed from the 'productive' use of nostalgia found in *Sonnenallee*. The final shot of Hanna on the night of 9 November is of a distraught, nervous woman staring painfully into the bathroom mirror and searching for the tablets to which she is addicted. The film then cuts to the next morning where the bathroom mirror now holds the reflection of an elegantly dressed woman, wearing thick 1960–style white make-up with wide black eyes and a huge Cleopatra-like wig. This is Hanna's public face. In interviews Hannalore Elsner, who plays the film's central protagonist, consistently describes her character's make up as 'war paint', seeing the woman as a powerful, independently minded individual.[41] Yet, it is abundantly clear that the confident, defiant persona, constructed through her make up, is extremely fragile. It is in fact a defensive gesture based wholly on a nostalgic longing for the past. Hanna can never be anything more than a grotesque pastiche of her 1960s self.

This fragile defensiveness is then further reinforced by her smoking. She is never seen without a lit cigarette, which she holds boldly in front of her face, defiantly announcing her presence in a room. However, it gradually becomes clear that this defiance is a sham. First, as I shall discuss below, at crucial moments, her defiant façade cracks and we see her as she truly is, a nervous addict drawing the smoke desperately into her lungs. Second, when at the end of the film she collapses in the street (an image that clearly recalls *13 Monden*, which is punctuated throughout by the central protagonist falling to the ground) we realize that cigarettes have actually brought her to the point of death. Her aggressive defence mechanism is eating away at her from within. Consequently, both through her use of make up and cigarettes it is clear to the spectator that, unable to move on, Hanna Flanders is ultimately unable to live.

Without doubt, the last thirty years have taken their toll on this particular 68er. This is highlighted in the film's re-examination of key motifs of this earlier period. As in Fassbinder's work, conflict between this generation and their parents is central. This is, for example, directly dramatized in his contribution to the ensemble film *Deutschland im Herbst* (*Germany in Autumn*, 1978), which features an interview between Fassbinder and his mother, during which the filmmaker questions the woman about her views on fascism. Here we see a confident, if disturbing, Fassbinder browbeat his mother, dominating their exchange and finding holes in her political position. In Hanna's relationship with her parents, however, the power dynamics are entirely reversed. She visits her mother and father late in the film. By now she has been rejected by her publisher and so, facing financial ruin, she goes to her parents to ask for money. Hanna sits in their expensive living room, which is cluttered with ornaments, and which strongly gestures towards the type of bourgeois excess that she and the rest of her generation ostensibly rejected. Flanked by her parents, she nervously draws on her cigarette, while her father tries to pretend that there is no tension in the room as he pours them all a drink. But the mother knows that Hanna only comes to visit when she needs money and is immediately provocative, asking her daughter whether the penny has at last dropped, whether the end of the GDR has at last convinced her that her 'radical' leftwing views cannot work. Unlike the confident interrogative son in *Deutschland im Herbst*, Hanna cannot fight back. Any attempt she makes to take up a position against her mother fails, fundamentally undermined by the fact that she is still reliant on her parents' money, in turn suggesting that she has never really grown up. Furthermore, in the

film's revisitation of this generational encounter, we are also given a far
more sympathetic image of Hanna's father than we might have found in
the work of the 68ers themselves. The authoritarian patriarch seen, for
example, in Gizela Elsner's own *Die Riesenzwerge* is replaced by a frail
old man, who, although rather obsequious, evokes the spectator's sympa-
thy by his selfless wish for his daughter to be happy and his frustration at
her self-destructive hatred of the world.

Throughout the film Hanna comes off poorly. Nowhere would this
seem to be more obvious than in her response to the *Wende* and her view
of life in the East. As we have already seen, Hanna is distraught by events
in the GDR. In an interview with a journalist, her feelings erupt as she
viciously attacks the East German population for embracing the
consumer society she despises:

> It makes me sick to see how these unification types are taking over. I find it
> disgusting how they root around in their underpants, how they snatch at
> things. I've suddenly become aware of the depressing truth that they are fight-
> ing for *Mon Chére* chocolates and for the right to stuff Western tampons up
> their cunts. They're not fighting ... not in the sense Lenin means it ... for the
> truth. (U, 42)

However, after this outburst, when she is pressed on what this 'truth'
might be, she finds it impossible to answer. Hanna's socialism would
appear to be all form and no content. Indeed her attack on consumer
society seems to be nothing less than brazen hypocrisy, given the fact that
we have already seen her spend a fortune on a Christian Dior coat. She
would seem to be the worst type of champagne socialist, a view held by
many she meets in the East. When, for example, she travels to her old
publisher in East Berlin, she immediately realizes she is not welcome. On
arrival she is attacked by a member of the staff, who is still celebrating
the opening of the Wall: 'You're that Flanders. I know you. You're that
spoilt cunt from the west, who knew nothing about our political reality
except for a few champagne receptions in Moscow' (U, 71). Having
struggled to reject the trite Marxist rhetoric of their former masters, the
people in the East have no time for Westerners who have lived a life of
luxury telling them they should not have their turn.

Hanna Flanders has always constructed the East as a utopian other,
through which she defined her dissident position within the FRG, giving
her an ideological point of comparison, which she employed to critique
western capitalism but which did not correspond to the experience of
those who lived there. Now this imagined 'Orient' has become real, it
refuses to act in accordance with her wishes, ultimately leading to the loss

of Hanna's own sense of self. This loss eventually leads to her suicide and which, in turn, writes large a crisis that, as we saw in the previous chapter in our discussion of the *Literaturstreit* and to which I shall return in connection with *Good Bye, Lenin!*, faced much of the west German cultural landscape in the aftermath of the *Wende* as the values of earlier generations gave way, ultimately, to those of the 89ers.

The second generational shift, from the 68ers to the 89ers, is also explored in the film through the prism of familial conflict. However, in his examination of this generational encounter Roehler's position would seem to be rather more ambivalent than it is in Hanna's meeting with her parents. While in Berlin Hanna visits her son, a would-be writer and representative of the 89er generation. The pair meet in the young man's flat. He is excited by recent events, the fall of the Wall inspiring him to start a new life, symbolized by his declaration to his mother that he has given up smoking. Both sit at his desk where the conversation soon moves from being polite to being aggressive. The camera pans from one speaker to another, the long take giving the spectator no respite from this fraught family scene as Hanna, in full 'war paint', draws with casual defiance on her cigarette, ignoring her son's obvious cravings. Hanna's smoking is used here as a means of stamping her authority on the discussion (a far cry from her use of cigarettes at her parents' house, where her smoking is a highly defensive gesture). On one level, as in the scene with her parents, one senses that Hanna has not grown up. She childishly goads her son, patronizingly asking him if he is still 'trying' to write. Yet, although the spectator is disturbed by her lack of respect for her son, it is nevertheless impossible to sympathize wholly with the son's position, his decision to give up smoking due to the events in Berlin seeming to be crassly naive. Also, if we compare this sequence to Hanna's encounter with her parents, she exhibits a far greater strength of character with her son than she does in her conversation with her mother. Consequently, one feels that while Roehler seems to be questioning the values of his mother's generation, he is not suggesting that his own has any more satisfactory answers.

In this sequence one sees that Hanna is still a force to be reckoned with and as the film goes on one begins to sense that, while Roehler questions Hanna's worldview, he does not completely reject it. Indeed, he may, to a degree, even be attempting to recuperate it. Fundamental to the film's tentative recuperation of Hanna is the difference between the temporal perspective of the film and that of the spectator. If we return to Hanna's visit to the East, as we have already seen, her views have been fundamentally challenged by the collapse of the GDR. Nevertheless, as she wanders through East Berlin, her utopian dreams appear, at least partially, to be fulfilled. There is clearly a far stronger sense of community here than is to be found back in the West. When an Eastern woman sees that Hanna is troubled, she welcomes her into her home, where she and some friends, like the rest of the population, are celebrating. They treat her immediately as if she were one of the family. Unfortunately, this utopian moment is soon shattered when Hanna airs her political views. The assembled group cannot understand why the fall of the Wall should have unsettled her so much and when Hanna suggests that she has greatly suffered under capitalism her hostess is clearly aggravated. Within the context of the film, such a statement would seem to be, at the very least, insensitive to the family that has taken her in, who are celebrating their newly found freedom. Such views are completely out of step with the mood of the times. Nevertheless, for the spectator, looking back on these events a decade or so later, there is a strong sense of irony, because we know that many of Hanna's statements would soon be heard in the mouths of east Germans themselves as they began to realize that life under capitalism was not necessarily as rosy as it had appeared on the television programmes beamed in from the West that they used to watch. Consequently, rather than being completely dismissed by the film, Hanna can almost also be viewed as a tragic Cassandra-like figure. What she says still has validity but the world is not ready to hear it.

In his representation of a West German intellectual's critical response to the end of the GDR and the demise of socialism, Roehler looks to the tradition of Fassbinder, constructing a 68er version of his Veronika Voss, through which he attempts to revisit and renegotiate the generational tensions explored in the work of the New German Cinema, as well as the relationship of parts of this generation to unification. Through its critique of Hanna's nostalgic refusal to live in the present, the film initially appears to reject the 68ers, seeing their views as anachronistic within unified German society. It would seem that Hanna Flanders has a wholly backward-looking, in Hall's terms 'archaeological', relationship with the past – one that cannot engage productively with the present. Gradually, however, the film's treatment of Hanna, reveals itself to be more ambiguous. During her trip to the east, Hanna's anachronistic views are shown to have continued relevance, and as such become a vehicle through which the film presents a critique of post unification society. In the tragedy of her final suicide, it is made clear that there is no room for such views in the new Germany. In so doing, Roehler seems to point to a lack in his own culture as well as that of his contemporaries. Ultimately, he seems to lament the demise of the protest generation, suggesting the continuing need for an art of dissent that has been lost in the pop culture of this '89er' 'Generation X', a generation to which he uncomfortably belongs.

Wolfgang Becker's *Good Bye, Lenin!*

Roehler's film uses the issue of unification and the nature of life under socialism to explore tensions in the sensibilities of his generation of west Germans, pointing to an ambiguous nostalgia he feels for the worldview of the 68ers. As a result, the film largely ignores the type of *Westalgie* one finds in the work of the generation that divides them, the 78ers, discussed by Taberner and Plowman above. One rather curious example of a nostalgia film by just such a 78er is Wolfgang Becker's tragicomedy *Good Bye, Lenin!*[42] This is curious because it is a film that would seem to have very little to do with west German nostalgia and everything to do with *Ostalgie*. Indeed, it was often discussed by reviewers in the same breath as Haußmann's *Sonnenallee*.[43] However, for the remainder of this chapter I will explore how the film develops themes from *both* Haußmann and Roehler's films. Like *Sonnenallee*, *Good Bye Lenin!* reconstructs, with a good deal of humour, aspects of everyday GDR culture. But, in a similar fashion to *Die Unberührbare*, it also employs the east as a discursive space where Becker can explore aspects of Roehler's nostalgia for the political engagement of his mother's generation. In *Good Bye, Lenin!*, however, this it taken further, since Roehler's ideological *Westalgie* is implied through the recuperation of aspects of the East German state's socialist project, such as can be found in the work of some former GDR intellectuals. Thus while Becker's film, like *Sonnenallee*, presents the spectator with aspects of daily life in the GDR, it is a politically-inspired version of *Ostalgie* that is central to the picture of the East, rather than the more visceral manifestation of the phenomenon we see at work in *Sonnenallee*. That said, Becker has a far less tortured relationship with Germany's past than that suggested by Roehler in his ambivalence towards the legacy of the 68ers. This is shown particularly clearly in the different ways the two films represent the death of their central mother figures, the tragedy of Hanna's suicide being replaced in Becker's film with a family funeral, an image that is used symbolically to mark the passing of both former states, bringing with it an implict call to embrace the new Germany which Becker's generation has been at the centre of shaping. We see here, I suggest, a west German filmmaker taking up Hall's 'productive' notion of identity formation, showing that unification has brought changes which the whole of German society must accept. In so doing, he ultimately highlights the 'hybrid' status of the very unified state itself, a state which is made up of two different, but interlocked, cultural traditions, both of which must be understood and respected if 'inner unity' is to be achieved.

    Good Bye, Lenin! was extraordinarily successful for a German film. It massively outstripped the popularity of *Sonnenallee*, with an audience of

6.5 million in its first year, and took €35 million at the German box office, to become the biggest hit of 2003, ahead of blockbusters such as *Gangs of New York* and *Harry Potter and the Chamber of Secrets*.[44] Like *Die Unberührbare* it was nominated as Germany's entry for the Oscars. However, its international success was far greater than that of Roehler's film. Indeed, the only comparable German film since unification, in terms of its global impact, is Tom Tykwer's *Lola Rennt* (*Run Lola Run*, 1998), or Caroline Link's *Nirgendwo in Afrika* (*Nowhere in Africa*, 2001). However, *Good Bye, Lenin!* has easily surpassed the popularity of both these films. [45]

The film tells the story of Christiane Kerner, a fiercely 'devout' citizen of the GDR, and her two children, Alex and Ariane, whom she is forced to bring up on her own after her husband escapes to the West. Shocked by seeing her son arrested at a demonstration just before the *Wende*, Christiane suffers a heart attack, and as a result falls into a coma. She remains unconscious for eight months, during which time we witness the end of the GDR and the rush of its population to embrace the West. When she eventually awakes the doctor tell her children that their mother's heart remains very weak. She is to be confined to bed and above all must not be upset in any way. Since the news of the end of socialism would be devastating to her, Alex decides that he will have to keep this from her by recreating the GDR in her bedroom. He brings back the drab old Eastern furniture that Ariane has already disregarded in favour of new Western fittings. He plays her videos of old editions of *Aktuelle Kamera*, the GDR's news programme, and when required even films, with the help of a work colleague, new fictional stories in order to stop his mother becoming suspicious of the changing world around her. To complete the illusion, he feeds her GDR groceries such as *Spreewald* gherkins and *Moccafix Gold*, products that he hunts down with increasing desperation because they are now almost impossible to find due to the population's rapid turn towards Western consumer culture.

While many critics drew comparisons between *Good Bye, Lenin!* and *Sonnenallee*, there are a number of obvious differences between the two films, the first being that *Good Bye, Lenin!* was written, directed and has its lead role (Alex, played by the rising star Daniel Brühl) filled by west Germans. This is often seen as one of the most remarkable aspects of film. In numerous reviews and interviews, critics wonder at the fact that Becker and Bernd Lichtenberg, two *Wessis*, could have produced a story that presented such an accurate image of the GDR.[46] Second, reviewers noted *Good Bye, Lenin!*'s success across the whole of Germany, as well as abroad. The success of *Sonnenallee* was largely down to its popularity with eastern audiences, and internationally the film had very little impact.[47] These differences aside, however, points of correspondence between the two films abound, particularly, for most critics, in the films' attitude towards the GDR. Becker and Lichtenberg insist in numerous interviews that the main aim of *Good Bye, Lenin!* is not to examine critically the nature of life in the GDR and its collapse, but to tell a family's private history. Consequently, like *Sonnenallee* it would appear that the GDR is intended simply to provide a backdrop for a universally applicable story. 'You don't have to know a thing about German history to understand it', Becker suggests, 'a son who loves his mother – it's a story you find everywhere'.[48] Indeed, the family theme is central to much of the rest of Becker's work, which not set in the East. *Good Bye, Lenin!* has, for example, a good deal in common with his earlier highly-acclaimed film *Das Leben ist eine Baustelle* (*Life is All You Get*, 1996) which similarly revolves around a family in crisis.

Like Haußmann's film, Becker's is a rights-of-passage narrative, in which Alex, the film's narrator, emerges from the shadow of his problematic childhood and his relationship with his mother to start a new life with his girlfriend Lara. To a degree, Becker's film exploits a story that anyone can recognize to express, yet again, the 'normality' of citizens of the GDR. Claudia Schwartz, for example, suggests that *Good Bye, Lenin!* is unashamedly sentimental, in order to show that 'the memories of former GDR citizens can be emotional. And that they have nothing to do with an ideology, and everything to do with a lived life'.[49] As we saw in *Sonnenallee,* it would seem that the normality of everyday family life is to be revealed to us from behind the official façade of the GDR's public face. This is suggested quite literally during the GDR's fortieth birthday celebrations. The camera pans up one of the huge red flags that hang from one of the block of flats lining the route of the GDR's military parade. It slowly zooms in on one of the windows covered by the flag, at which point the film cuts to Alex's bedroom, cast in a deep red shadow by the same flag, which is covering his window. Moreover, in similar fashion to Haußmann's film, the normality of eastern experience is highlighted in the film's ironic presentation of the west's exoticization of the population. After the GDR has begun to implode, Alex's sister falls for a westerner, Rainer, whom she meets a work. This westerner's attitude to the east early in their relationship is soon made clear when we see Ariane dress up as a belly dancer for the man, her performance of Rainer's erotic fantasy being a particularly overt evocation of western orientalism.

However, in *Good Bye, Lenin!* there is a subtle, but important, shift in the focus of the film's nostalgic invocation of everyday life in the GDR.

Unlike Haußmann's film, the majority of cultural markers included in Becker's film, from the songs people sing to the language Alex uses in his voiceovers which punctuate the narrative thoughout, are products of the official ideology of the GDR. As Haußmann has pointed out in connection with the sort of *Ostalgie* one finds in *Good Bye, Lenin!*, 'things are coming back that we hated during GDR times, or didn't know about and didn't consume. In my film *Sonnenallee*, the kids don't listen to a single Eastern song.'[50] Thus, it would seem that Schwartz's view of *Good Bye, Lenin!* being an accurate portrayal of the everyday life of ordinary East Germans, for Haußmann at least, is wide of the mark, since it ignores the importance of Western points of reference within the GDR, particularly for its youth culture.

Indeed, one of the main aims of the film is an engagement with the effects of the very ideology Schwartz claims *Good Bye, Lenin!* ignores, rather than the experience of 'ordinary' GDR citizens, such as we find in *Sonnenallee*. As a result, the picture of life in the GDR presented is very different. In Haußmann's film we see an image of the East German state that explores aspects of life ignored, for example, in the Enquete Commissions' reports. In Becker's film, while there are ironic moments where western orientalism is challenged, a view of the GDR as a totalitarian state, and as such part of Germany's abject 'other' history, is also at times confirmed. Alex's father is forced to leave because of the intolerable pressures put on him at work, in the words of Alex, 'just because he wasn't in the party' (GBL, 110). We see Alex's mother being interrogated by the Stasi, an event that causes her to have a nervous breakdown, and that in turn has a profoundly damaging effect on the rest of the family, particularly on her young son. Finally, as we see the GDR coming to an end, we witness the violence of the state's repressive institutions against the people in the early mass demonstrations as the regime tried, increasingly in vain, to maintain its grip on power.

On one level, then, *Good Bye, Lenin!* endorses the official readings of GDR discussed in Chapter 2, a view that is further underlined by the fact that the film, unlike any of the others discussed in this chapter, was taken up by the Federal Government's Agency for Political Education (*Bundeszentrale für politische Bildung*) as a text to teach students about GDR history.[51] The fact that the film seems to fit officially-sanctioned readings of the GDR was also noted by reviewers. The British journalist Peter Bradshaw, writing in the *Guardian* argues that the sentiment of the film 'has less to do with politics, and more with nationhood and the great family of Germany. The *Ossi*s are the naughty black sheep who strayed and are now forgiven. This was the triumph of the reunification at the time.' Thus Bradshaw sees in the film a representation of life in the GDR

which, like many mainstream filmic representation of unification, celebrates the triumph of the 'good' German state over the 'bad'.[52]

However, there is clearly more to this film than simply celebrating the
victory of unification. The film might well be unambiguous in its
condemnation of the negative aspects of the GDR state. Nevertheless, it
is similarly unambiguous in its recuperation of the utopian impulse
behind the GDR's socialist project, an impulse that seems to counter any
unproblematic celebration of the West the film might contain. As Alex's
project of reconstructing the GDR for his mother becomes more complicated, and ever more of the family's neighbours are brought in on the
deceit, he begins to realize that 'the GDR that I built for my mother was
becoming more and more the GDR that I would have liked to have' (GBL,
104). The importance of this utopian version of the state's ideology is
symbolized throughout in the motif of space travel, and in particular the
figure of Sigmund Jähn, a GDR cosmonaut, the first German in space and
Alex's childhood hero. After the *Wende*, Alex actually meets his hero in
the flesh (or at least a man he takes for Jähn), who is now working as a
taxi driver in Berlin. As his mother grows weaker, Alex decides to
complete his imagined GDR by making Jähn its new president, through
which act he sets the seal on the philosophy of his illusory version of the
socialist state. In his inaugural speech, filmed by Alex and his friend for
one of their faked *Aktuelle Kamera* reports, Jähn declares, 'Socialism is
not about building walls. Socialism is about approaching the other person
and living with the other person. It's not about dreaming of a different
world. It's about making it happen' (GBL, 127). In the words of Jähn we
have Alex's conception of what the GDR should have been about: socialism with a human face, which could urge the population onto new heights
of achievement.

Alex builds his utopian state for his mother, who is consequently at the
centre of this new GDR. Here we find further confirmation of a shift in
focus away from the recollection of the 'normal', everyday life of East
Germans found in *Sonnenallee*, to an engagement with socialist ideology.
Rather than being a representative of the majority of 'ordinary' East
Germans, who had little emotional investment in the GDR's socialist
project, Alex's mother would seem to have far more in common with the
state's intellectuals. Christiane, like Christa Wolf, for example, is a reform
socialist, who, although critical of the SED, has not lost faith in its original ideological project. Her position is neatly summed up in the promi-
nence of Gorbachov's *Perestroika* book on her bookshelf, a figure whose
writings, although solidly socialist, were anathema to the GDR's ruling
gerontocracy. At the same time, Alex's mother, like Wolf, is fêted by the
Party. She is invited to major state functions, and even receives the GDR's

Gold 'order of merit'. Consequently, the mother occupies a similar position in the film to intellectuals such as Wolf, a position for which, as we have already seen, such figures were attacked during the *Literaturstreit*. By idealizing the mother's utopian impulses the film attempts to recuperate these intellectuals' position. Indeed, even Jähn's words, written by Alex, would seem to be evocative of Wolf's 4 November speech ('Just imagine, we have socialism and no one wants to leave'), ridiculed by Brussig in *Helden wie wir*. Gunnar Decker, in his review of the film for *Neues Deutschland*, makes explicit reference to this process of recuperation: 'The way the West German literary papers attacked Christa Wolf in 1990 and her attempt at self justification in *Was bleibt* was vulgar arrogance ... The cultural elite of the GDR was dismissed as being too beholden to the state. GDR history was ghettoized, and only aspects of it allowed.' In this film, however, aspects of the GDR's political project are celebrated that could not be before, in particular, he suggests, those aspects that infused 'the spirit of those who stayed' and helped bring about the change.[53] Unsurprisingly *Neues Deutschland*, the former official organ of the SED, does not focus on the film's representation of the GDR as a totalitarian society. Instead, Gunnar argues that Becker's film celebrates the GDR's utopian ideology. In something of a logical stretch perhaps, GDR socialism becomes the tool through which a population that was oppressed by this very ideology could liberate itself.

Linking Alex's mother's position to that of intellectuals in the East has an important knock-on effect for the film's representation of West German society, returning us to Roehler's film, and the question of *Westalgie* for the 68ers. Just as the *Literaturstreit* initially centred on the East, but soon became about the role of leftwing intellectuals in the West as well, *Good Bye, Lenin!* is not simply a nostalgic recuperation of the GDR's utopian socialist project. It also looks at the nature of unified German society, and, like *Die Unberührbare*, the continued importance of a leftwing value system, which would appear to be in the process of being dismantled in the new Germany. Implicated in this is the film's subtle critique of globalization, suggested in its representation of American consumer culture in present-day Germany, the influence of which, as we have seen in our discussion of a number of West German texts, from *Veronika Voss* to *Ostsucht*, has long been feared by writers and filmmakers. The negative effects of contemporary perceptions of Americanization are most obviously suggested by Ariane's decision to leave university and to start working for *Burger King*, the US Hamburger chain standing in for the influence of global capitalism on the postunification society. Specifically, Becker suggests that the values held dear in pre-*Wende* society, such as education, are being eroded in a world where the neo-liberal value system of the market is the main definer of what is important.

In Roehler's film, the GDR acts as a repository for ideological views that can counter the rush to consumerism, in so doing, he sets up a link between intellectuals on both sides of the German divide, his western protagonist's view having much in common with those expressed in texts by east German writers such as Christa Wolf or Wolfgang Hilbig, discussed in Chapter 1. Similarly, throughout *Good Bye, Lenin!*, Becker uses GDR socialism to question the centrality of consumer culture to this new society. After the *Wende*, we see the population of the GDR rush to embrace western goods, disregarding anything from the east. Here the film highlights the irony of much contemporary *Ostalgie*, pointing out the fact that those east Germans who are now turning back to eastern products were initially more than happy to disregard them in favour of western ones, many of which are shown simply to be different from, but not better than, east German goods. We see, for example, Ariane's new, highly fashionable, western Venetian blinds come crashing down from the window after a gentle tug. Moreover, the fact that easterners have now turned back to their GDR products in search, perhaps, of a more 'authentic' sense of easterner identity is also shown to be a somewhat pointless gesture. For example, although Alex is unable to find the *Spreewald* gherkins his mother asks for, he does eventually manage to track down an empty jar, which he fills up with gherkins from Holland and serves to her. His mother does not notice the difference. Consequently, the film suggests that the contemporary fetishization of consumer products from GDR is all form and no content, and the effort Alex expends trying to find authentic products, while a noble gesture of love for his mother, is really a waste of energy. However, the continued relevance of utopian leftwing views, as a corrective to Germany's present-day value system, is most obviously communicated during one of Alex's editions of *Aktuelle Kamera*. Unable to keep the evidence of Western influence from his mother, he rewrites history to present the *Wende* as one in which Westerners want to join the East. The reasons the news report gives for the West taking this step – mass unemployment and concomitant social instability – are, of course, key concerns for the whole of contemporary German society, as the country attempts the painful process of social restructuring to face the imperatives of neo-liberal globalization.

While at times *Good Bye, Lenin!* paints a very negative picture of life in the GDR, in which the population lived under the thumb of the Stasi, it also goes beyond such a view of the past by engaging with aspects of everyday life in the east. As such, it would appear to have much in common with *Sonnenallee*. However, it also differs from Haußmann's film, which is largely concerned with presenting a visceral understanding of what it means to be an east German, and becomes, instead reminiscent of *Die Unberührbare*, recuperating the GDR's ostensibly utopian socialist ideals and allowing links to be draw between them and the project of leftwing intellectuals across the nation. Like Roehler, Becker uses his representation of the east to lament the loss of much of the pre-*Wende* political agenda. That said, the film finally seems to accept this loss, as well as the changes that Germany is currently undergoing, thereby marking a further development in *Good Bye, Lenin!* not found in Roehler's film.

In Becker's film we see a moment in German film making that views unification not soley as an eastern issue, but as a process in which *all* members of the German community must accept both their differences and, most imporantly, that they all have to change. Through leaving university, Ariane meets her western boyfriend, and by the end of the film we learn that they are to have a child together. Although there are some fraught moments in their relationship, particularly when Rainer does not understand his new family's eastern ways, at times exhibiting an exotic fascination for them, by the end of the film he comes to respect that they have a different, but equally valid cultural tradition. Furthermore, he clearly loves Ariane, and will make a good parent. Indeed, he is already a caring father to her first child, which she had during the GDR period, but with whom her east German ex-partner has very little contact. As a result, although the film takes place almost wholly in the east, unlike much post-unification film making, it does not see the project of unification as a wholly east German issue. Instead, the film suggests that 'inner unity' is to be achieved through a process of mutual respect and a willingness on all sides to adapt. This is then underlined in its closing moments, during Alex's mother's funeral, a moment that also distances the film from that of Roehler in its radically different way of marking the death of its central female figure. In *Die Unberührbare*, the final focus is on the shocking tragedy of the woman's suicide. In *Good Bye, Lenin!*, on the other hand, a more consilatory tone is struck. At the funeral, the entire family, from both east and west, comes together to mourn Christiane's passing. Alex fires his mother's ashes into the sky using a rocket he built at school, a gesture that makes clear that the woman's worldview, like the utopian vision of Alex's cosmonaut led-GDR, belongs in the heavens. The rest of the family remains on Earth. With their mother's time past, they must move on, accepting the challenges this new society will bring all Germans. In this funeral sequence we see the final message of the Becker's film. The film is this '78er's' eulogy for Germany's divided past. It is an act of mourning, and like all acts of mourning it involves fondly remembering this past time, allowing the mourner to indulge their nostalgia. But it also involves drawing a line under the past, forcing him or her to realize that it can also never be regained. In Hall's terms, we might see this as a further image of 'productive' hybridity, evident in Haußmann's presentation of life in the GDR, but which has now been extended to the whole of German society. The memory of the mother, and the value system for which she stood, should not be dismissed, but neither can they be kept alive artificially. They must, instead, be incorporated 'productively' into this reunified German family's collective self-understanding, as it attempts, along with the rest of the nation, to negotiate its future.

Notes

1. Hall, p. 112.
2. Lothar Fritze, *Die Gegenwart des Vergangenen: Über das Weiterleben der DDR nach ihrem Ende*, Weimar: Böhlau, 1997, p. 111.
3. Inka Bach, *Wir kennen die Fremde nicht*, Berlin: Ullstein, 2000, pp. 119–20.
4. Arthur Fischer et al., *Jugend 2000 13. Shell Jugendstudie*, Opladen, Leske & Budrich, 2000, p. 284.
5. See Leonie Naughton, 'Wiedervereinigung als Siegergeschichte: Beobachtungen einer Australierin', in apropos: *Film 2000*, Berlin: DEFA Stiftung, 2000, pp 242–53.
6. Sönke Wortmann, interview with Stephen Kinzer, quoted in Ute Lischke-McNabe and Kathryn S. Hanson, 'Introduction: Recent German Film', *Seminar*, 4(33) (1997), 283–9 (p. 84).
7. Eric Rentschler, 'From New German Cinema to the Post-Wall Cinema of Consensus', in *Cinema and Nation*, ed. by Mette Hjort and Scott Mackenzie, London: Routledge, 2000, pp. 260–77 (p. 263–4)
8. John E. Davidson 'Overcoming Germany's Past(s) in Film since the Wende', *Seminar*, 4(33) (1997), 307–21 (p. 308).
9. Leonie Naughton, *That Was the Wild East: Film Culture, Unification, and the 'New' Germany*, Ann Arbor: University of Michigan, 2002, p. 138.
10. Sabine Hake, *German National Cinema*, London: Routledge, 2002, p. 189. See also Stuart Taberner, '*Das Versprechen (The Promise)*', in *European Cinema: an Introduction*, ed. by Jill Forbes and Sarah Street, Basingstoke: Palgrave, 2000, pp. 157–68.
11. The first part of his *Deutschland Trilogie* is *100 Jahre Adolf Hitler*

(1989). For further discussion of Schlingensief's work see Julia Lochte and Wilfried Schulz, *Schlingensief! Notruf für Deutschland: über die Mission, das Theater und die Welt des Christoph Schlingensief*, Hamburg: Rotbuch, 1996.

12. John E. Davidson, *Deterritorializing the New German Cinema*, Minneapolis: University of Minnesota Press, 1999, p. 158.

13. For further discussion of Troma films see Lloyd Kaufman, James Gunn, Roger Corman, *All I Need to Know About Filmmaking I Learned from the Toxic Avenger: The Shocking True Story of Troma Studios*, New York: Boulevard, 1998.

14. Daniela Berghahn, *Hollywood behind the Wall: The Cinema of East Germany*, Manchester: Manchester University Press, 2005, p. 223.

15. Georg Seeßlan, quoted in Berghahn, p. 245.

16. Reinhard Wengierer, 'Vertracktes Leben', *Die Welt*, 21 December 1999.

17. Hans Christoph Buch, 'Schönen Gruß von Charlie Chaplin', *Tagesspiegel*, 9 November 1999.

18. Cited in Thorsten Stecher, 'Sexy DDR', *Die Weltwoche*, 18 November 1999.

19. See Jens Bisky, 'Beleidigend', *Berliner Zeitung*, 29 January 2000.

20. *Helden wie wir* (1999), directed by Sebastian Peterson.The film opened to largely hostile reviews. See, for example, Peter von Becker, 'Hier riecht es nach Lysol', *Der Tagesspiegel*, 9 November 1999. Brussig also reworked the screenplay he co-authored with Haußmann into the novel, *Am kürzeren Ende der Sonnenallee*, Berlin: Volk & Welt, 1999. This generally follows the plot of the film, although it adds the story of a love letter that Micha loses in the no man's land of the Berlin Wall and which he spends much of his time trying to retrieve. The cinematic references found in the film, discussed in this chapter, are largely omitted in the book. Also, the end of the novel, which involves a cameo appearance by Mikhail Gorbachov who aids in the birth of Mario and his existentialist girlfriend's child, differs from the film (p. 156).

21. Sandra Maischberger, 'Sonnenallee– Eine Mauerkomödie: Interview mit Leander Haußmann und Thomas Brussig', in *Sonnenallee: Das Buch zum Farbfilm*, ed. by Leander Haußmann, Berlin: Quadriga, 1999, pp. 8–24 (p. 22). Indeed, even the film's release date, 7 October 1999, appears to confirm this reading, timed as it was to coincide with what would have been the fiftieth anniversary of the founding of the GDR. See Berghahn, p. 245.

22. All quotations are the author's translation from the video-released version (2000).

23. For a good discussion of this aspect of *Ostalgie* and its relation to what Fritze sees as crass western criticism of the phenomenon, see Fritze, pp. 93–114.

24. Quoted in Helen Cafferty, '*Sonnenallee*: Taking Comedy Seriously in Unified Germany', in *Textual Responses to German Unification: Processing Historical and Social Change in Literature and Film*, ed. by Carol Anne Costabile-Heming, Rachel J. Halverson and Kristie A. Foell, Berlin: Walter de Gruyter Verlag, 2001, pp. 253–71 (p. 254).

25. Maischberger, p. 21.

26. Andrea Rinke, 'From Models to Misfits: Women in DEFA Films of the 1970s and 1980s', in *DEFA: East German Cinema, 1946–1992*, ed. by Seán Allan and John Sandford, New York: Berghahn, 1999, pp. 183–203 (p. 183).

27. Cafferty, p. 258.

28. The fetishization of this particular product is further suggested by the film's official website, where one finds a computer game based around the action of unfolding and folding this table. See www.sonnenallee.de, accessed 23 March 2000.

29. Maischberger, p. 12.

30. Cafferty, p. 258.

31. Brussig, *Am kürzeren Ende der Sonnenallee*, p. 156–7.

32. Stuart Taberner, 'Introduction: German Literature in the Age of Globalization', in *German Literature in the Age of Globalization*, ed. by Stuart Taberner, Birmingham: University of Birmingham Press, 2004, p. 5.

33. Andrew Plowman, '"Was will ich denn als Westdeutscher erzählen?": The "old" West and Globalization in Recent German Prose', in *German Literature and the Age of Globalization*. See also Ingo Cornils, 'Long Memories: The German Student Movement in Recent Fiction', *GLL*, 56 (2003), 89–101.

34. For further discussion, see Coco Drilo, 'Das RAF-Mode-Phantom', www.salonrouge.de/raf-hype2.htm, accessed 13 May 2002.

35. *Aspekte*, first broadcast ZDF 24 March 2000.

36. Oskar Röhler, 'Die übergroße Sehnsucht', *Die Tageszeitung*, 2 August 2001.

37. Oskar Roehler, 'Ein freies Strömen der Gedanken', in *Die Unberührbare: Das Original Drehbuch*, Cologne: Kiepenheuer & Witsch, 2002, pp. 13–22 (p. 21), hereafter (U). All quotations from the film are taken from this edition of the screenplay.

38. For further discussion of Veronika Voss see Thomas Elsaesser, *Fassbinder's Germany: History Identity Subject*, Amsterdam: Amsterdam University Press, 1996, pp. 108–15.

39. Gizela Elsner, *Die Riesenzwerge*, Hamburg: Rotbuch, 1964.
40. See Wend Kässens and Michael Tötenberg, 'Gizela Elsner', *KLG*, 2 (1992), pp. 1–12.
41. See for example, Ronny Zeller, 'Hannelore Elsner: Die Wahnsinns-Frau', *Eurogay*, http://www.eurogay.de/artikel/0300/promi_elsner. html, 15 March 2000.
42. The importance of his generational position is suggested in an interview given by Becker, where he insists that his position is informed by belonging 'to the "Post-68er-Generation", the so-called Intermezzo Generation'. Quoted in Rainer Gansera, 'Das Leben ist ja kein Genre: Wolfgang Becker über alte Kameraregeln, junge Ganzkörperschauspieler und seinen Film "Good Bye, Lenin!"', *Süddeutsche Zeitung*, 13 March, 2003.
43. See, for example, Jan Schulz-Ojala, 'Eins, zwei, drei', *Tagesspiegel*, 20 February 2003.
44. Editor, '*Good Bye, Lenin!* Big winner at German "Oscars"', *Guardian*, 9 June 2003. Audience figures taken from the German *Filmförderungsanstalt*, www.ffa.de, accessed 19 January 2004.
45. See Fritz Göttler, 'Der Renner: Auferstanden aus Ruinen- Kinokult um 'Good Bye, Lenin!', *Süddeutscher Zeitung*, 27 February 2003.
46. See for example, Michael Toteberg, 'Eine Familiengeschichte: Gespräch mit dem Drehbuchautor Bernd Lichtenberg', in *Good Bye, Lenin! Ein Film von Wolfgang Becker*, ed. by Michael Toteberg, Berlin: Schwarzkopf & Schwarzkopf, 2003, pp. 148–51 (p. 148), hereafter (GBL); Birk Meinhardt, 'Dich muss man rütteln und schütteln! Katrin Saß in 'Good Bye Lenin!', und das unverhoffte Glück in einem Leben, das schon fast zu Ende war', *Süddeutscher Zeitung*, 12 April, 2003.
47. For André Mielke, the trans-regional success of *Good Bye, Lenin!* was most clearly symbolized in a showing of the film organized for the entire *Bundestag*, with the journalist presenting this event as evidence of east and west politics coming together, in turn pointing to a broader reconciliation between the populations of the former FRG and GDR. See André Mielke, 'Der Bundestag ist auch nur ein Mensch', *Die Welt*, 4 April 2003
48. Quoted in Meinhardt, 'Dich muss man rütteln'. See also Gisa Funck, 'Im Auge des Sturms: Wird ein Autor entdeckt: Bernd Lichtenbergs *Good Bye, Lenin!*, *FAZ*, 15 February 2003.
49. Claudia Schwartz, 'Das wahre Leben im falschen: GBL- Wolfgang Beckers komischer Wendefilm', *Neue Züricher Zeitung*, 17 March 2003.
50. Ralf Geizenhanslüke, 'Hefe oder Kristall, das ist hier die Frage!

Leander Haußmann und Sven Regener unterhalten sich über *Herrn Lehmann*, die Vorzüge des Flaschenbiers und die 80er-Jahre', *Der Tagespiegel*, 1 October 2003.
51. Cristina Moles Kaupp, *Good Bye, Lenin! Film-Heft*, Berlin: Bundeszentrale für politische Bildung, 2003.
52. Peter Bradshaw, '*Good Bye Lenin! Ostalgie* ain't what it used to be', *Guardian*, 25 July 2003.
53. Gunnar Decker, 'Vielfalt statt Einfalt: Zum Ost-West-Kinoerfolg von *Good Bye, Lenin!*', *Neues Deutschland*, 3 August 2003.

–5–

Re-exoticizing the Normal:
the *Ostalgie* Industry
and German Television

In the summer of 2003, following on from the success of *Good Bye, Lenin!*, There was an extraordinary renaissance of interest in the GDR throughout Germany, central to which was discussion of *Ostalgie*. Now the term was beginning to be used by the media in a far less pejorative manner than it had been previously. Indeed, it had developed into nothing short of a craze. The most obvious example of this new *Ostalgie* craze was the plethora of television shows about the GDR. Programmes on the former East German state were not a new phenomenon. Throughout the 1990s, the television schedules regularly featured documentaries and news items about the machinations of the SED regime. However, the difference now was that for the first time the GDR became the focus of light-hearted entertainment shows. ZDF, Germany's second public-service channel, set the tone with its *Ostalgie Show*, broadcast on one evening in August. This was followed a few days later by *Ein Kessel DDR* (*A Pot of GDR*), produced by MDR, the public-service channel for the eastern regions of Thuringia, Saxony and Saxony-Anhalt. The very next evening, the privately funded channel SAT 1 broadcast *Meyer und Schulz: Die ultimative Ost-Show* (*Meyer und Schulz: The Ultimate East Show*). Finally, at the beginning of September, RTL, another national privately-funded channel, brought out its offering, the four-part *DDR Show*.[1] And the decision by these channels to produce their programmes clearly paid off in terms of viewing figures. ZDF's *Ostalgie Show*, for example, had an audience of 4.78 million viewers, 21.8 per cent of the viewing public as a whole, with 34 per cent of eastern viewers tuning in.[2] By the time RTL aired its programme the popularity of the genre had grown still further. The *DDR Show* achieved an audience on its first night of 6.32 million, 23.3 per cent of viewers in Germany (38 per cent of those in the east), and was only just pipped at the post for first place in the ratings by the German version of the 'reality' talent show *Pop Idol*, RTL's

Deutschland sucht den Superstar (*Germany looks for its Superstar*, 6.47 million viewers).[3]

Although there are some subtle and important differences between these programmes, they all have strong generic similarities. These are neatly caricatured by Antonia Kränzlin writing in *Der Tagesspiegel*:

> The principle of a GDR show is easily explained. You take a studio with a live audience, decorate it as colourfully as possible with lots of eastern items, put two presenters on the stage (preferably an *Ossi* and a *Wessi*) and then have as many eastern celebrities chat about the 'good old times in which perhaps not everything, but lots of things were better' … From time to time have the obligatory *Trabi* roll across the screen. Accompany the whole thing with hits from the East German charts. Let the *Wessis* guess the meaning of GDR abbreviations. Regularly fade in 'original pictures from the GDR'. Then add in a pinch of Spreewald Gherkins, FKK holidays and FDJ summer camps- that's the East German Show finished![4]

The tone of this piece, which ridicules the very concept of a nostalgic GDR show, was to be found throughout the newspaper debate these programmes engendered. Particularly vocal in their criticism were some former east German civil-rights activists, who in many cases had also been involved in the state-led processes of dealing with the past discussed in Chapter 2. The focus of the programmes on items such as the *Trabant* motor car, standard issue during the GDR period and now a cult collector's item, or the widespread practice of FKK (naturism) caused Rainer Eppelmann, for example, to condemn them as a 'dreadful trivialization of the GDR'.[5] The former east German dissident and now CDU politician, Günter Nooke went so far as to pose the question: 'What sort of a hullabaloo would there be if, instead of Kati Witt presenting a GDR show, we had Johannes Heesters presenting 'The Ultimate Third Reich Show'.[6] Here we see echoes of the sort of attacks I have already discussed in connection with Haußmann's *Sonnenallee*. The GDR is talked of in the same breath as Nazi Germany, the former Olympic ice-skater Katarina Witt, the presenter of RTL's *DDR Show*, and a figure who caused some controversy by her involvement in this project, being compared to a star of the National Socialist period.

That Eppelmann and Nooke were critical of the shows is not surprising, since the shows' approach to looking at the GDR is far removed from that of the Enquete Commissions' reports. More curious, however, was the fact that some of the shows' detractors were the very people who had previously defended certain manifestations of GDR nostalgia. The starkest example of this shift came with Leander Haußmann's comments in

Der Spiegel, in which he seems to take up the position of the very critics who attacked his film *Sonnenallee*:

> The reality of life in the GDR is obviously being completely forgotten – and now everyone's coming out of the holes they crawled into out of fear, frustration and shame: those old braggarts and 'fellow travellers' (*Mitläufer*). Instead of keeping their mouths shut happy that they got away with it, today they are mischievously indulging in *Ostalgie*.[7]

Haußmann's co-scriptwriter Thomas Brussig was also vociferous in his condemnation of the programmes. His bone of contention was that they were largely made in the west, or by western producers. The reason for this, he argues, is that the west is attempting to atone for its earlier treatment of eastern history, and of its poor management of eastern restructuring. Such programmes are, for Brussig, 'the expression of a bad western conscience and of a German unification that has been messed up'.[8] Whether one accepts this criticism or not, it is unarguably the case that these shows did largely take their impetus from the west (a criticism, as we have already seen, which was often, at times rather more unfairly, levied at some of the other processes of historical appraisal discussed in this book). This is even true for MDR, which is often viewed as one of the only real east German channels. The producer of Ein Kessel *DDR*, Hans-Hermann Tiedje, former editor of the tabloid newspaper Bild, was described by one interviewer as an 'Oberwessi' (Superwessi). Indeed, in the same interview Tiedje goes to some lengths to insist upon his right to make the programme, thereby implicitly revealing, perhaps, that he too found his western credentials somewhat problematic.[9]

To compound the irony of the shift in position by Brussig, Haußmann and others, their opinions were generally countered by the western programme makers themselves, along with a small number of primarily western journalists, with the types of arguments that Brussig and Haußmann themselves had used to defend *Sonnenallee*. The director of ZDF's *Ostalgie Show*, Martin Keiffenheim, for example, claimed that

> the media presents a very bad image of east Germany. With the GDR we only connect oppression, an illegal regime, Stasi files, an economy of shortages, pollution. It's high time that we approached it differently: through the culture of everyday life.[10]

Harald Martenstein, writing in the *Tagesspiegel*, evokes no less a philosophical heavyweight than Adorno in his defence of the *Ostalgie Shows*, taking issue with Nooke's comparison of the GDR to Nazi Germany. He turns Adorno's critique of National Socialism in *Minima Moralia* on its head, rhetorically asking if it is surely not possible to have a 'true life in a false one ... People try under all circumstances to be happy. In their false lives they look for the true'. The shows are, for Martensetein, potentially the long-awaited start of a genuine process of historical appraisal for the GDR. He even makes a rather bold comparison between the *Ostalgie Shows* and the effect that the student movement and the extra-parliamentary opposition (APO) in the 1960s had on the process of dealing with the Nazi period: 'The West needed 20 years, from 1949 to the APO. In the east it has taken 13 years, from the collapse to *Ostalgie.*'[11]

As we can see, the debate these programmes provoked was drawn along familiar lines. On the one hand, we have those who argue that the GDR was an oppressive dictatorship and that these programmes do not show this clearly enough. On the other, we have those who claim that we should not ignore the everyday, 'normal' experience of GDR citizens. However, crucially, some of the actors in it appeared to have switched sides. In this chapter, I argue that while Haußmann and Brussig might not be pleased about the appearance of these shows, on one level they can be seen as the end of point of a process set in train by the type of critical discourse we see in their film.

In television's *Ostalgie Shows* we find evidence that the GDR past has now become a part of the mainstream, in which the everyday experience of easterners has been incorporated into unified German television culture. However, their criticism also points to the limits of this process. The reason why some of the actors in this debate seem to have changed sides can to a degree be explained in terms of the question of ownership of the past, an issue that, as we have seen throughout this study, is central to claims of western colonization. In the critical response to these shows, there was a good deal of hostility to what was seen as another western appropriation of the GDR, even though this appropriation was ostensibly in response to an eastern call for a more differentiated view of the past. Indeed, although the shows were watched by many in the east, Brussig and Haußmann were not alone in their criticism of them. In an opinion poll carried out by Emnid, 59 per cent of those surveyed claimed they disapproved of the image of the GDR these shows presented.[12] The notion that high viewing figures might not suggest general approval is also indicate in an interview with one of the RTL show's eastern viewers, who claimed that 'lots of people enjoy these shows because it gives them something to get annoyed about'.[13] It would appear that many people only watched the broadcasts in order to get annoyed about the image of the GDR that was presented in them, It would seem that what was being perceived as a western appropriation of *Ostalgie* allowing easterners to confirm their opinion that they are still being misunderstood by their 'colonial' masters.

For the discussion in this chapter, the comments by the RTL viewer are particularly revealing, as they point to an aspect of these programmes that was largely ignored by the media debate, but which is crucial to an understanding of their purpose. While people might have been annoyed by them, they obviously still found them entertaining. If they had not, why would they have tuned in?[14] And this is ultimately their point. Although the programme makers insist that their intention is first and foremost educational, their underlying aim is neither to present an authentic, nor a revisionist representation of life in the GDR but to attract viewers – that is, to make the GDR entertaining, and ultimately sellable. In this connection, Martenstein's reference to Adorno is particularly illuminating, since we have here a working example of what he and Max Horkheimer term the *Culture Industry,* in which an ostensible engagement with GDR history is in fact a means of commodifying it.[15] What is interesting about this process of commodification, is the way *Ostalgie* has been re-appropriated within it. Rather than seeing nostalgia for the GDR as a barrier to the long awaited 'inner unification' of the German people, as it had been previously, most obviously in western discourses, in these western-produced *Ostalgie* shows, it was now seen as a means of achieving this unity.

Although the reason why the programmes were made specifically at this time was largely due to the success of *Good Bye, Lenin!*, they have none of the critical distance of Becker's film towards present-day consumerism. Instead, the use of *Ostalgie* within the context of these television programmes implies the existence of a unified 'community of consumers', in which east German experience appears to have been brought into the cultural mainstream and normalized. As we have seen in other cultural discourses, particularly in my discussion of 'productive' hybridity, television is not alone is suggesting that east Germans are both a part of, and understand, western consumer culture. However, the reason some commentators in the east responded so negatively to the shows is, I suggest, due to the fact that a hierarchy is maintained in which eastern experience remains peripheral to the west, to the extent that GDR normality is in actuality firmly re-exoticized. Consequently, we see in the shows yet another 'orientist' use of the GDR, here as a space in which unification under the FRG can be further legitimized. However, instead of achieving such legitimacy by viewing the GDR as a totalitarian 'Stasi state', East Germany is now constructed as an alien consumer world, from which the population has, nonetheless, been similarly liberated.

Consumer Culture and *Ostalgie*

The idea that consumer culture might be important to debates on German national unity is not a post-*Wende* invention. From at least the 1970s the SED understood that the battle for the hearts and minds of the population was more likely to be won in the supermarkets and department stores of the GDR than by force-feeding its citizens Marxist-Leninist ideology. Unlike many Eastern-bloc countries, East Germans were very aware of social, economic and cultural developments on the other side of the Iron Curtain. With the exception of the Dresden area, commonly termed the 'valley of the clueless' (*Tal der Ahnungslosen*), Western television programmes and advertising were available throughout the GDR and had a huge impact on Eastern attitudes. As West Germans began to enjoy the profits of the post-war 'Economic Miracle', and with them an ever-increasing range of consumer goods, Easterners listened and looked on through their radios and television sets, fully cognisant that their government was failing to keep up. Initially, the Party attempted to stem the influence of the Western media, encouraging members of the FDJ to report households whose television aerials were set to receive West German stations. However, by the 1970s the practice was so common that the SED largely stopped trying to prevent the population from watching them. Instead, they attempted (albeit once more in vain), to counter Western influences by improving the quality of their own media output and by providing Eastern alternatives to highly prized Western products.[16]

In the immediate aftermath of the *Wende*, as we saw in Becker's film, the failure of the SED to produce goods that could compete with the West became blatantly apparent. The GDR population could not wait to 'Test the West', as they were encouraged to do by the advertisers of *West* cigarettes. Eastern brands were ignored as the GDR population was able to experience first hand what some of them had only seen on television. However, the euphoria for Western products was short lived. Andreas Staab notes that even as early as 1991 nearly three-quarters of households surveyed in the eastern regions stated they preferred eastern products to western ones.[17] Once again this tendency could be seen particularly clearly in tobacco advertising. The advertisers of *Juwel* cigarettes told us, for example: 'I smoke Juwel because I've tested the West: *Juwel* – one of our own'.[18] From the early 1990s there was a growth in demand for eastern products. Along with cigarettes, famous examples are the increased market share of *Rotkäppchen Sekt* and *Club Cola*. Paul Betts suggests that consumer culture in fact became the battle ground for east Germans attempting to mark their sense of difference. Although it would not become the widely discussed phenomenon we saw in the previous chapter until the end of the decade, from the early 1990s, he comments, one begins to find a 'revived romance between east Germans and their own material culture', a product, he suggests of 'political pessimism, coupled with economic recession, rising unemployment and growing social anxiety', all of which 'inspired a new nostalgia for the stability and solidarity for the old days'.[19] The growth in the popularity of such products is, for Betts, an example of east Germans looking back to a romanticized version of the past, making connections between GDR consumer goods and a perceived set of values at the heart of their way of life before they were faced with the problems of dealing with the western market economy.

The centrality of an idealized image of pre-unification GDR values becomes clear if we return to the world of marketing. Advertising agencies were amongst the first institutions in the 1990s to understand that everything that 'belonged together' might not be 'growing together' quite as quickly as envisaged, and that perceptions of difference between the populations of the GDR and the FRG, whether real or imagined, could not simply be ignored. Patricia Hogwood cites the example of *Persil* washing powder, which came unstuck with one of its publicity campaigns in the eastern regions:

> The advert showed a middle-aged woman executive returning to work. Her husband and children couldn't cope without her until she discovered new Persil capsules. Eastern women, who until unification were accustomed to working all their adult lives, were offended at the implication that it was somehow wrong to 'leave' your family to go back to work. Faced with structural and gender-biased unemployment problems, they were insulted at the suggestion that such a woman could find a good post as soon as she chose to work.[20]

The prioritization of western cultural norms was alienating the eastern market. In order to find a better means of accessing this market *Persil* turned to the Fritzsch und Mackat agency, who have made a name for themselves producing campaigns specifically for the east. Instead of playing to the prejudices of patriarchy, a typical strategy in western washing-powder advertising, they highlighted the functionality of *Persil*. This allowed east Germans to identify with an 'honest-to-goodness' lifestyle, which in turn could be contrasted with a perceived superficiality of life in the west.

The need to highlight 'down-to-earth' values is, as Hogwood notes, at the heart of much east German advertising. The marketing material for

Lichtenauer mineral water, for example, suggests that the product is 'beautifully normal'.[21] In a similar vein and returning once again to tobacco advertising, one finds Cabinet cigarettes billed as 'authentic and unperfumed', thereby constructing the product in opposition to western 'perfumed', 'inauthentic' blends of tobacco.[22] The reason why these values should be seen as 'east German' perhaps reveals a residual legacy of the population's socialization within the GDR, showing that the state's cynicism towards capitalist consumer culture had more impact than one might have though in the early 1990s. Or, perhaps more accurately, it points to the legacy of having to make do with limited resources, the GDR period now being looked back on as a more frugal, simpler time, when communities readily came together to share what they had, thus seeming to live by a more 'humane' set of values than is possible in the hustle and bustle of capitalism. This might not be a time that they want to relive, nonetheless, it remains one upon which they can look back with a degree of fondness in a similar fashion to the way the British who lived through the Second World War might remember warmly the 'spirit of the *Blitz*'.[23]

While most commentators view this longing for a more wholesome, less superficial way of life in the 1990s in terms of *Ostalgie*, Fritzsch und Mackat suggest the word is ill-fitting. *Ostalgie* for them is a negative term, suggesting a resentful wish to return to the past. By the mid 1990s they claim that such backward-looking *Ostalgie* is being replaced by what they call '*Ostimismus*' (from the words for 'east' and 'optimism'): 'people are looking for an optimistic identity through which they can be proud of what they have achieved'.[24] Here Fritzsch and Mackat highlight what Hogwood identifies as a growing sense of '*Ossi* Pride', in which negative stereotypes of easterners by westerners are reinterpreted positively, in order to give value to, and ultimately normalize, their experience. While some westerners might, for example, stereotypically construct easterners as 'lazy', or 'workshy' this is inverted in eastern advertising discourses to present them as 'easy going'.[25] The impulse to de-exoticize the experience of east Germans is, of course, a familiar one, seen most obviously in east German film. In advertising discourse we find this normalization strategy confirmed. East Germans are, or at least like to be told in advertisements that they are, just as good as west Germans, that their products are just as valid, if not more so because they are 'down to earth', everyday, and not subject to the superficial and trivial whims of western fashion.

The Fritzsch and Mackat agency places great store in the importance of accepting east German distinctiveness and in particular the continuing impact of past socialization on the present. This is not surprising given the fact that their business is built upon this very notion of difference. However, others suggest that the eastern and western advertising markets have largely converged. 'Although there are still subtle differences between advertising campaigns in east and west Germany, they are getting smaller', claims Steffi Hugendubel in the weekly business magazine *Werben & Verkaufen*.[26] It would seem that, if a process of colonization has taken place, it is reaching completion, or that the east German population is showing ever more clearly its ownership of western culture, highlighting that it is fully competent in the ways of late-capitalist society.

Yet, while east and west advertising markets might be converging, this does not seem to be leading to a downturn in interest in eastern products. On the contrary, in the same article Hugendubel notes that in 2001 – two years before the release of *Good Bye, Lenin!* or the production of the *Ostalgie* shows – interest in east German goods was starting to increase. On the Internet, particularly, there was a huge growth in the number of sites specializing in such products.[27] Media interest in the GDR in 2003 caused this growth to rocket, which, ironically, led to the collapse of one of the biggest Internet suppliers of GDR items. *Ossi-Versand* (www.ossiversand.de), the company, famous for their tag line 'Kost the Ost' ('Taste the East', a deliberate echo of 'Test the West') saw its turnover increase by 60 per cent in 2003. As a result, it expanded too quickly and was finally unable to keep up with demand.[28]

Along with a general increase in the consumption of specifically eastern products, there have also been developments in both their clientele and the range of products available, developments that suggest that the role of east German consumer culture is going beyond that of simply marking east German difference. First, much of this recent growth in interest comes from the west. By the time of its collapse, 85 per cent of '*Ossi*-Versand's' customer base was in the old Federal states. Thus, it would seem that the popularity of east German culture in the west has caught up with the east, because the regional demographic of its customer base now broadly reflects that of the population as a whole. Further, a recent study by the Institute for Applied Marketing and Communication in Erfurt (*Institut für angewandte Marketing- und Kommunikationsforschung*) found that a growing number of east German products have become just as important to western as they are to eastern consumers, with brands such as *Radeberger* beer and *Rotkäppchen* being recognized by over 90 per cent of those surveyed.[29] Evidently, this may be due in no small part to the fact that many of these brands have been bought out by western companies who are keen to escape the description of their products as purely eastern.[30] Moreover, it suggests that eastern culture has become part of the mainstream, at last achieving the 'normality' advertisers have long exploited, and many east Germans ostensibly wish for.

Second, and seeming to contradict this normalization process, there has been a development in what is being marketed as east German. It is in this connection that we see the word *Ostalgie* once again used widely by the mass media. However, now it is commonly evoked to describe a more positive form of nostalgia than it had been previously. Along with the examples already mentioned there has long been an interest in certain other eastern objects, most obviously perhaps the *Trabi*, but also, for example, the GDR's *Ampelmännchen*, or pedestrian-crossing figures. These differ markedly from those found in the west in the fact that they wear a hat and so look as if they belong to the 1950s rather than the present. Although initially replaced by their western counterparts, they soon started to reappear in the east by popular demand. Recently, interest in these and other items has increased, but also changed. Specifically, such items have become important tools of the tourist industry. The *Ampelmännchen* are now iconic figures to be found on a range of items from t-shirts to table lamps, taking up a good deal of space in the capital's souvenir shops.[31] Interest in Trabis used to be largely confined to their proud owners from GDR times who would meet up at rallies, like many other cult car enthusiasts. But now the Trabi is also being instrumentalized as a Berlin tourist attraction, with people being encouraged to go, for example, on 'Trabi Safaris', hiring the car to travel around the city centre for the day.[32]

The notion of a 'Trabi Safari' clearly suggests a shift in the marketing of eastern products. In this new proliferation of interest in GDR consumer goods we see the complete rejection of GDR objects as being 'normal' or 'down-to-earth'. Instead, such objects are turned into cult items, a process that then allows the tourist *Ostalgie* industry to foreground, indeed to fetishize, their 'abnormality', or exoticism. Other examples of this trend towards exoticization within the tourist industry as well as within the leisure industry more generally, include the popular novelty item, the *DDR-Box*, produced in time for Christmas 2003. This was a tin box that provided the consumer with what its producers call a complete GDR 'starter-pack'. The box included a range of *ostalgic* items, from a fold-up model of a Trabi and a certificate to prove one's loyalty to the GDR, to a bag of *Mokka Fix Gold* coffee, made famous, along with Spreewald gherkins, by Becker's film. Indeed, the influence of this film is made abundantly clear on the box's lid. While the advertisements for *Good Bye, Lenin!* claimed that the film reproduced the 'GDR in 79 m^2', the *DDR-Box* was far more practical, allowing you to have 'the east in 0.05 m^2'. However, the most telling example of the trend by the leisure industry to exoticize the GDR is the planned GDR theme park to be built by the Massine Production Company in Berlin. The declared aim of this park is to recreate a day out in the GDR, starting with the 'compulsory' exchange of Western money at its entrance gate, recalling the first step of any Western tourist's day trip to East Berlin before 1989. Like the makers of the *Ostalgie* shows, Massine insists that their motives for building the park are educational. It is not intended, the company argues, to trivialize the GDR, but rather to present to its visitors everyday life behind the Wall.[33] Yet, from the available publicity surrounding the park, it would instead seem to be simply a rather extreme version of the *DDR-Box* or the *Trabi* safaris, that is, another leisure item aimed at entertainment and profit making, not education.[34] To suggest that the visitors Messine Productions hope to attract to the park are looking to learn about the reality of life in the GDR would seem to be as misguided as to suggest that visitors to Disneyland in California are seeking to learn about the everyday 'real' life of Mickey Mouse or Goofy. Rather than looking to recreate empathetically the mundane experience of east Germans, such products seek to distil and commodify the *strangeness* of a world that no longer exists, 'to elicit surrealized East German life', as Betts puts it.[35] For the tourist industry normality is the last attribute a product wants. The *Ostalgie* Industry has become big business. It has become mainstream within German culture, precisely because it is different. This difference can then be commodified, marketed, put on a t-shirt, or as we shall see, made into a light-entertainment television show.

Television and the Eastern Regions

Before turning to the shows specifically, however, I wish first to examine more generally television culture in the eastern regions, as well as the representation of the former GDR on television since 1989. As I noted in the previous section, Western television had always been an important source of information for the population of the GDR, who largely shunned its own television channels, the state controlled DFF1 and DFF2, in favour of Western stations. In the immediate aftermath of the *Wende*, these channels did enjoy a brief moment of popularity. For a short interval, once-derided news programmes such as *Aktuelle Kamera*, whose journalists were now freed from the yoke of political censorship, began to produce more objective reports and, as Peter J. Humphreys notes 'a novelty, to attract large audiences'.[36]

As it became clear that unification was on the cards, many members of the East German media lobbied to have the DFF network turned into a third national public-service broadcasting channel.[37] However, this idea came to nothing and the eastern television frequencies were given to western stations. The failure to acknowledge pre-unification GDR television culture is seen by some commentators as one of the most unambiguous examples of unification as a western takeover. John Sandford, for example, suggests, 'many Germans in the East saw the whole operation as one of the most blatant examples of arrogant Western colonization'.[38] Indeed, it became commonplace to describe the former GDR as a 'media colony'.[39] Western stations, eager to get their hands on the prize of 'relatively scarce broadcasting frequencies and the future east German advertising market' rapidly moved in, bringing with them their own personnel, and thereby forcing the majority of the former workforce into unemployment.[40] That said, as ever one must balance such emotive claims of colonization with comparison to the pre-*Wende* situation. It would be hard to suggest that the range of television in the east is worse than it was during GDR times, when media was tightly controlled, and freedom of speech largely impossible. As Humphreys also notes in his summary of the present situation, 'the positive far outweighs the negative'.[41]

Instead of becoming a third national channel, public-service broadcasting in the east was restructured into a number of regional stations that, like their western counterparts, became part of the ARD network. The northern region of Mecklenburg-West Pomerania was absorbed into the west German regional company NDR. Saxony, Saxony-Anhalt and Thuringia were covered by the newly formed MDR. East Berlin was included within the remit of the West Berlin broadcaster SFB, and in Brandenburg ORB was set up. Consequently, the only stations with a completely eastern constituency were MDR and ORB. In 2003 this was then reduced to one when ORB merged with SFB to become RBB. Interestingly, many executives of the former SFB have seen this recent merger as an 'easternization' of Berlin's broadcasting culture, thus seeming to show a shift away from the clear westernization of the early 1990s and perhaps pointing to a development in German television culture in which the eastern regions are beginning to assert themselves. This might also be reflected in the inclusion of east German culture as part of the mainstream, even if, as we shall see, this is taking place according to a fixed, and at times somewhat problematic, agenda.[42]

Shortly after the introduction of western public-service broadcasting, the east also gained access to the main western private stations. Although there were some delays in stations such as RTL and SAT 1 gaining terrestrial frequencies in the east, they nonetheless quickly enjoyed massive popularity through cable and satellite broadcasting, easterners seeming far more willing than many in the west to take advantage of new media providers.[43] Holger Briel notes:

> After unification, the first visible changes in the East occurred on the rooftops. The old aerials – all of them trained in a westerly direction – vanished. Even before many houses received a new coat of paint or the *Trabis* and *Wartburgs* had been exchanged for a western-made car, a satellite dish would appear. East Germans, it seems, had fewer problems with accepting the new media than their western compatriots.[44]

While on an institutional level the unification of German television might be seen as an aggressive western takeover, here we are reminded that the notion of western 'colonization' is at times more complex than it might at first glance appear. If we examine television *use*, we find that easterners themselves were more than willing to accept a western takeover. Indeed, we perhaps see here further evidence that, rather than being the backward 'colonized' cousins of the west, in quickly embracing the new media the east could be leading the way in a broader process of social change, further echoing Engler's view of easterners as Gemany's 'avant garde', discussed in Chapter 1. With regard to television culture, one might also point to the fact that those in the east are at the forefront of a general tendency in Germany to spend more time viewing. In a survey from 1993 it was found that easterners watched on average 209 minutes of television per day, whereas westerners watched only 168 minutes.[45] By 2000 both groups were watching more television, but the west was slowly catching up, easterners and westerners watching on average 223 and 198 minutes respectively.[46] Furthermore, the east seems to be at the vanguard of a shift in taste away from news and information-based programming towards light entertainment. This propensity amongst easterners could, however, simply be an effect of the continuing higher unemployment in the east than in the west, leading to viewers watching more daytime television, the schedules of which are dominated by soap operas, drama series and other such entertainment programming.[47]

Although easterners are watching more television than westerners, the majority are nonetheless still dissatisfied with what is available to them, particularly in regard to its coverage of eastern issues. In a recent study, Manuela Glaab notes that '57 per cent of east Germans generally [felt] ignored in the media'.[48] To a degree this criticism would seem to be unfair. If one looks at Werner Früh and Hans-Jörg Stiehler's 2001 study, they suggest that for every story specifically about the eastern regions one finds 2.9 stories about the west. Since easterners constitute approximately one fifth of the German population, this coverage would, in fact, appear rather generous. Nevertheless, what Früh and Stiehler also find constantly problematic across a number of surveys is the nature and tone of much of this coverage. In a study from 1999 they summarize the representation of the east on national television since the mid 1980s, drawing on work by Thomas Bruns and Frank Marinkowski. Here, they comment that if one looks at coverage of the east in the early 1990s, one finds a similar trend in the representation of the east to that found in the state-led processes of historical appraisal examined in detail in Chapter 2. In the immediate post-*Wende* period, they found that the GDR was being

> presented as a phase which had to be dealt with (mainly legally) ... charac-
> terized by the terms Stasi, violence at the Wall and doping. The news and
> magazine programmes examined ... offer[ed] the viewer no starting point for
> a more positive relationship to his or her past.[49]

Television coverage tends to underline the hegemonic value system we saw at work in the Enquete Commissions' reports. This is, of course, unsurprising. As John Fiske and John Hartley point out in their seminal study of the medium, in general television tends to reflect and reinforce, rather than question, society's dominant organizing principles. This it achieves by consciously constructing its messages as reflecting society's centre:

> Television is one of the most highly centralized institutions in modern
> society. This is not only a result of commercial monopoly or government
> control, it is also a response to the culture's felt need for a common centre, to
> which the television message always refers.[50]

With the introduction of digital satellite media and a far wider range of channels, television and television audiences have become far more frag-mented than they were in the early 1970s, when Fiske and Hartley were writing. Nevertheless, the need to represent what it perceives as society's centre remains an imperative of much mainstream television. As such, television continues to be one of the most important media 'through which society finds self-confirmation and understanding'.[51]

If we accept this is a major function of television, it is interesting to look at the representation of east Germany more recently. As discussed in the previous chapter with regard to film, or in aspects of the marketing of material culture examined above, there has been something of a shift away from focusing on the legacies of the GDR's dictatorial regime to an exploration of the everyday experience of easterners. To this we might add certain literary texts that are beginning to appear, suggesting that the same can be said of this cultural sphere.[52] However, Früh, Stiehler *et al.* comment that, by the end of the 1990s at least, such a shift was not generally evident on television, thereby suggesting that, although there appeared by this time to be a wish amongst the population to look at East Germany in terms of its everyday culture (as reflected in marketing campaigns), with regard to the region's cultural representation in the mass media, this shift largely remained within what might be seen as more self-reflective discourses, such as literature and (some) cinema. In the 1999 survey, we see that on television east Germany continued to be presented as a problem, with what Früh, Stiehler *et al.* call everyday eastern 'society' (*Gesellschaft*) topics, that is coverage of social occasions (such as marriages and public events) being almost entirely absent in comparison to the coverage of such events in the western regions – they suggest a ratio of 1 to 71 in favour of the west. The fact that this aspect of life was being largely ignored by the national media for these commentators betrays a dominant western perspective in news coverage. More recently this would seem to have dissipated. In 2001, Früh und Steihler found that there were more 'non-problem-based' stories being presented. Indeed, on ARD, for example, they suggested that the number of eastern cultural items actually outnumbered those about the west.[53] Nevertheless, they also argue that while the east may be receiving more coverage, a western perspective continues to dominate, claiming that in many cases eastern stories are presented as if they were 'foreign news'.[54] As a result, eastern views still appear in much television coverage as if they were peripheral to the west. The one exception they mention to this general trend is MDR (ORB did not form part of their survey, although the same could be said of this station at the time). This channel's focus is solely the eastern regions. Unsurprisingly, therefore, it spends more of its time covering east German-specific issues.[55] Interestingly, this station has probably received more national opprobrium than any other, often seen as being nothing more than a 'Long-term advertisement' for *Ostalgie*, as the journalist Jens Schneider put it in the *Süddeutsche Zeitung*, the term *Ostalgie* here being used completely negatively.[56] Others criticize what they see as its homely, sentimental view of the world, which seems to betray a thoroughly conservative value system and does nothing to face the problems of inner unity.[57]

The *Ostalgie* Shows

With the arrival of the *Ostalgie Shows* in the summer of 2003, it would appear that this western perspective had finally been overcome. At last, the everyday experience of east Germans had entered mainstream culture, thereby suggesting, as certain members of SFB management claimed, that an 'easternization' of German television was taking place. In my discussion of these shows I suggest that there is indeed evidence of an attempt to bring the GDR past into the mainstream. However, I also suggest that this is ultimately achieved by the re-establishment of a western-dominated value system. Central to this is a focus on consumer culture, and more specifically the construction of the eastern population as consumers. In so doing, the shows embed the former citizens of the GDR firmly within western society. At the same time, they suggest the continuing existence of a hierarchy within this 'united' society in which western experience remains central, a curious state of affairs given their subject matter. I argue that the east is, in fact, ultimately re-exoticized from within the mainstream, and pushed once again to the margins. The tension between an impulse to bring the GDR into the mainstream, while concurrently maintaining its exotic cache, is one which, as I shall also examine, at times put an extraordinary strain on the programmes' light-entertainment structure.

Of the four shows, the two that were the most similar were ZDF's *Ostalgie Show* and SAT 1's *Meyer und Schulz: Die ultimative Ost-Show*. This connection is curious given the different remits of these channels. ZDF is usually the home of more highbrow television culture. SAT 1, on the other hand, is a commercial, populist channel. Nevertheless, the material both shows covered was almost identical. ZDF's content can best be summarized by reference to the programme's trailer. Here we see its two east German presenters, Andrea Kiewel and Marco Schreyl, standing in front of the camera while they compete to 'out-remember' each other on their knowledge of the GDR, rapidly calling out a string of items in turn, one after the other:

AK: *Club-Cola*	MS: *Steppke-Jeans*
AK: *Dederon-Beutel*	MS: *Goldbroiler*
AK: *Trabi*	MS: *FKK*
AK: *Action-Haarspray*	MS: *Inka*

The GDR is evoked by reference to everyday life, and more specifically to its consumer and leisure culture. A similar stance is taken in the *Ultimative Ost Show*. In its first part, we are shown a range of GDR scenarios, in each of which, as with ZDF, the focus is on the role played by consumer items. We see, for example, a GDR living room, where we are introduced to furniture concepts such as the 'Mufuti', already familiar to spectators of *Sonnenallee*, as well as to a strange GDR cocktail. Or we are presented with an east German bathroom, where we are told of the dangerous lengths young people went to dye their hair, or the problems of using GDR toilet paper.

In both shows, features about cars, leisure activities and bathroom products are then interspersed with celebrity interviews. In line with Antonia Kränzlin's comments, quoted above, personalities from the east talk about their experience of life in the GDR, while west German guests parade their ignorance. The ZDF programme focuses particularly on the use of studio guests, featuring some twenty-nine in its 90-minute programme. These include actors (for example, Saskia Valencia and Udo Schenk) singers (such as Wolfgang Ziegler and Ute Freudenberg) and sports personalities (for example, Kornelia Ender and Wolfgang Behrendt). SAT 1 has fewer studio guests but makes up for this by including a number of inset montage sequences, during which high-profile *Ossis* such as the dancer Detlef 'D!' Soost, television presenter Kai Pflaume or singer Nina Hagen appear in front of original footage from the GDR as 'talking heads', in a style familiar to viewers of British nostalgia shows such as the BBC's *I love the 1970s,* or Channel 4's *Top 10 series.* These figures then reminisce, at the obvious prompting of an off-screen interviewer, on topics such ranging from their favourite GDR music, to the problem of trying to find fashionable items of clothing.

As we have already seen, the reasons given for adopting this approach to the remembrance of the GDR by the director of the ZDF show are highly reminiscent of those stated by Haußmann in defence of his film. The shows, like *Sonnenallee,* are ostensibly aimed at 'normalizing' the experience of living in the GDR, a justification which is reiterated at the beginning of the first SAT 1 show. Ulrich Meyer, one of the show's co-presenters, a journalist from the west, summarizes life in the GDR, informing the viewer that the main point to remember is that 'between all the mass meetings and waiting in queues for food' people in the GDR had a life that was not 'half as grey' as many think. Although 'some people had at lot of problems, some people were happy'. He even suggests that the experience of living in the East was ultimately 'the same as in the West', while also being 'just a little bit different'. The aim of the programme is educational. Over the next two hours, both Meyer and the viewing audience will 'learn a great deal about the GDR'. Through this educational process of normalization, he claims, the programme will play its part in helping Germany to at last find inner unity, a point made

explicit in the final sentence of his welcome statement, which is framed
as a rhetorical question to his co-host Axel Schulz: 'we are one people,
are we not?', the revolutionary call for unification chanted by the people
of the GDR in November 1989, 'wir sind ein Volk', here re-invoked as a
declaration of SAT 1's commitment to a unified German television
culture.

In SAT 1's case, this commitment was also highlighted in the show's
scheduling. It was broadcast on a Saturday night, the 'high altar of entertainment television', as Thomas Gottschalk, Germany's highest profile
television presenter, puts it.[58] By placing the show at this time, the
channel's schedulers show their commitment to bringing the GDR into
the mainstream of public memory. This commitment towards presenting
GDR experience as normal is, however, perhaps most clearly communicated through the format adopted by all the programme-makers. All of the
programmes follow the rules of German light entertainment talk shows to
the letter, providing the viewer with a mixture of musical items and
celebrity interviews, in front of a live studio audience. In such
programmes, the relationship between the presenter and the audience is
key. The studio audience stands as a proxy for the viewers at home.[59]
Generally, the studio audience is shown at regular intervals, singing and
clapping along to the musical items, and laughing at the presenters' jokes.
The audience's performance of obvious enjoyment provides a ready-made
point of identification for the viewer, guiding him or her to accept the
show's message, promulgated by the presenters, and thereby creating, as
Andreas Garaventa in his study of the genre puts it, the 'illusion of a
large, harmonized television family'.[60] In both these programmes, as well
as in the MDR and RTL shows discussed below, the audience is used in
a classic German light-entertainment manner. However, as we shall see
with regard to ZDF's offering, this at times also becomes somewhat problematic, and indeed one of its key flaws.

In both the ZDF and SAT 1 shows, we seem to see what Fiske and
Hartley term the 'claw back' function of television. Mainstream television, they argue, tries to occupy the central ground of a society. In order
to achieve this, it constantly 'strives to claw back into a central focus the
subject of its messages'. Anything that might be seen as an aberrant, or
eccentric cultural position, once it has been adopted by entertainment
television, is turned into something that society's mainstream can understand and with which it can identify.[61]On the face of it, this is precisely
what both the ZDF and SAT 1 shows are intent upon, in turn marking an
important sea change in mainstream attitudes, away from the perceived
exclusion of east German experience we find bemoaned in earlier chapters in this book, as well as in television in the 1990s.

While these programmes ostensibly try to include in the mainstream and thus normalize the experience living in GDR, it soon becomes apparent that their real focus is to normalize the experience of GDR citizens as *consumers*, and by extension to embed their position within the consumer culture of present-day German society. The whole of the GDR is viewed through this optic. Whatever the shows discuss, be it going on holiday or the role of political institutions, the t-shirt to be bought or the CD to be plugged is never far away. Consequently, rather than giving a more differentiated picture of life in the GDR than the one afforded by the totalitarian 'Stasi state' model, the GDR is once again constructed as 'other' to the Federal Republic, but this time as a world full of humorous or bizarre consumer products. The shows' guests then look back upon this world with nostalgic condescension, able to indulge their consumer cravings, while distancing themselves from it and in turn further legitimizing the present German state. This is shown most obviously by the fact that many of the items the shows foregrounded are already completely mundane and therefore would hardly appear to need 'clawing back' into the centre of culture. By clawing back the already mundane and mainstream, in a similar fashion to the marketing of *Ostalgie* in the tourist industry, the programme-makers fetishize certain GDR objects, pushing them, instead, back to the fringes from which they ostensibly have just been rescued.

One of the many examples of this in the SAT 1 programme is the presenters' examination of bathroom items. Schulz brings out his old wash-bag from the GDR and the east German guests revel in its contents, including a stick of deodorant, and apparently most curious of all, a bar of soap in a plastic holder. But, there is very little that is strange about such items. The soap holder appears perfectly normal, only made worthy of examination by the 'oohs' and 'aahs' of the studio guests who laugh at this apparently strange artifact. As Christoph Schutheis puts it in his review of the ZDF show, 'Who says that a chocolate bar called "Schlagersüßtafel" is funnier than one called "Ritter Sport"'.[62] Thus, while the rational for these show is to normalize the GDR past, the underlying reason would seem to run in the opposite direction, namely to endow this past with an exotic chic.

In both shows we find the commodification of GDR culture, a culture that is paradoxically being both brought into the mainstream while also being confined to the margins in order to maintain its exotic appeal. As such, one finds a reconfiguration of the orientalist attitudes one sees in discussion of the GDR in the early 1990s. Although not stated explicitly, this resurgence of orientalism is hinted at by a small number of commentators in the media debate the shows sparked, particularly by those on the left from the former GDR. Peter Hoff, for example, writing in *Neues*

Deutschland, claims the the very idea that SAT 1 has produced an 'Ost Show' is misplaced. For him, it would better described as 'a west-Show about the exotic east'.[63] A similar point was made by Loskar Bisky, the leader of the PDS, on a discussion programme about the *Ostalgie* craze, where he suggests that far from being about a nostalgia for the GDR, the television programmes are in fact '*Westalgie* in the colours of the east'.[64] As we have seen in previous chapters, in other cultural discourses there is a tendency amongst some west Germans to use the GDR as a space through which they can critically engage with developments in present-day German society. In many such *Westalgie* texts, we see artists attempting to recuperate a critical left-liberal agenda, which they feel is now being lost. For Bisky, however, the problem is that these programmes are not attempting to use nostalgia to engage critically with either the past or the present. Instead, they simply reinforce a social order in which western consumer culture is constructed as central and east German experience peripheral.

Evidence for this tendency is indeed readily available, particularly in the SAT 1 show. The programme's stated aim is to teach viewers about the GDR. From the language used it is clear that the viewers in question are primarily those from the west. Representing this group is the show's west German presenter, Meyer, who rejects any notion of western dominance before it is uttered. He insists that the show is wholly about the GDR and its people. 'We' will learn, he tells the viewers, about 'their [the eastern-ers'] home', 'their stories'. The programme's co-host, Schulz, is to be the east German representative, the voice from the GDR who will ensure that authenticity is maintained. In terms of the show's implied learning process, then, Schulz is to be the teacher, Meyer the pupil.

Yet, everything about the actual roles these presenters play in the show points to the inverse of this relationship. If we return, for example, to the opening sequence of the first show, it is Meyer, dressed smartly in a suit and tie, who outlines the rationale of the programme to the audience, even explaining what life was like in the east. Meanwhile Schulz ignores Meyer's introduction, wandering around behind him, dressed more casu-ally in an opened-necked shirt and baseball cap, kissing members of the show's chorus line, whose dance routine has just announced the entrance of the two men. He makes just two brief contributions to this opening welcome sequence. First, he interrupts Meyer's speech in order to tell a joke, only to be gently asked to be quiet while Meyer finishes talking. Then, at the end of the sequence he responds with a confused 'yes', to Meyer's rhetorical question about whether all Germans are 'one people'.

Meyer and Schulz adopt classic comedy double act roles, with the former playing the straight man to the latter. Consequently, the show turns the logical teaching relationship on its head, if we are to believe Meyer's aim of wishing to learn about the GDR. From their demeanour, the figure of authority and knowledge is clearly Meyer, a position reinforced by the fact that Schulz consistently addresses him as 'Herr Meyer', while Meyer addresses the east German by his first name, 'Axel'. Curiously, much of the information we learn about the GDR comes from Meyer. It is Schulz's role to tell funny anecdotes about his life in the GDR, while relating, through the medium of humour, to the other east German guests. When it comes to imparting more general judgements about the GDR such as we see in the opening welcome sequence, or when more detailed, technical information about GDR products is required, this is left largely to Meyer. It is he, for example, who explains to the viewer the consistency of the fabric in the *Präsent 20* suits the presenters wear, or the engine capacity of the GDR sports car they feature. Thus, the notion that the show might be concerned with realigning the place of eastern experience within mainstream society is undermined through the construction of a power dynamic in which the westerner, Meyer, is the holder of authority and of factual knowledge about the GDR. The easterner, Schulz, is then confined to the role of the comic buffoon, suggesting the humorous, primitive nature of life in the east.

In the ZDF show, a potentially patronizing relationship between the east and west is avoided by having two eastern presenters. However, here too the marginality of eastern experience is finally writ large, this time through the programme's obvious failure to communicate with its studio audience. As Kränzlin notes, the programme was filmed in Mainz in front of an audience with very little experience of the GDR, a fact that is revealed in its obvious 'stiffness'.[65] Such stiffness breaks the German light-entertainment programme's pact, as outlined by Garaventa above. As a result, the audience highlights not the normality of the material to which it exposed, but rather its confusion by it. Without a *Wessi* presenter to *translate* eastern experience for it, as Meyer does for SAT 1, this west German audience cannot understand it. Consequently, the programme finally casts into doubt the mainstream status of the topic it discusses.

MDR's *Ein Kessel DDR*, like the ZDF *Ostalgie Show*, was presented by two east Germans. However, in this case the use of solely eastern presenters is constructed as one of the show's main strengths. All the editions were filmed in Leipzig, transmitted terrestrially only within the eastern regions, and thus could avoid any didactic need vis-à-vis a western audience. MDR, as an overtly eastern channel seems to buck the trend of national television in its prioritization of eastern issues. And as one might expect, the channel saw itself as perfectly placed to produce this genre of show. Unlike the others, this was to be a programme for east

Germans by east Germans (although, as already mentioned, its producer was in fact a high-profile west German). The show's stated aim remained educational. Nevertheless, this was not going to be the type of *ostalgic* 'education' we saw on ZDF and SAT 1. In its first opening sequence Franziska Schenk, who like Witt is a former GDR Olympic ice-skater, asks what was by now becoming the usual opening question for these programmes: 'naturally we asked ourselves if we ought to be allowed to make a funny programme about the GDR', to which her co-presenter Gunther Emmerlich, a television personality from GDR days, responds in the affirmative, quoting some key figures from the state's socialist tradition: 'During GDR times we laughed, and now we can laugh more freely. Karl Marx even said, it is through laughter that people can say farewell to their past. I'm often asked "what remains"? Memories will remain.' Here Emmerlich cites Karl Marx, with perhaps a sideways glance at Christa Wolf in his invocation of the *Was bleibt* debate, figures who would be very familiar to an audience socialized in the GDR. Unlike other GDR shows, MDR will examine the GDR past on its own terms. This is in fact suggested in the very title of the programme. *Ein Kessel DDR* draws deliberately on the title of *Ein Kessel Buntes* (*A Pot of Colour*), the most popular light-entertainment programme on GDR television, which ran from the early 1970s until 1992, being taken over briefly after the state's collapse by ARD.[66] Indeed, *Ein Kessel Buntes* is remembered in a variety of ways in *Ein Kessel DDR*. The opening credit sequence, for instance, includes a number of clips from this older programme, and Emmerlich himself was a regular guest on the show during the GDR period.

Unlike the repeated use of the 'their' pronoun we find in the SAT 1 show, here we find the constant use of 'we' and 'our'. MDR will present 'our stories', 'our history'. There is no amusing examination of the *Trabi*. Instead, in the first instalment we are given a detailed presentation of the life of Eva Maria Hagen, a film star in the GDR in the 1950s and the mother of the singer Nina Hagen. In an inset film we hear from her former partner, Wolf Biermann. We learn how the whole of society viewed her as a sex symbol in the 1950s, no different from Marilyn Monroe or Brigitte Bardot in the Western world. The 'normality' of her position within Eastern popular culture is, however, balanced by a discussion of how her status was manipulated by the government. We are told, for example, that she was used for propaganda purposes by the SED, who sent her to the newly built Berlin Wall in August 1961 in order to show GDR's stars supporting the state's policy to close the border. Finally, we hear of the difficulties she faced through her connection to Biermann in the wake of his expulsion in 1976. Thus, we are given a far more complicated image of life than that presented in the other shows discussed so far.

The 'normality' of Hagen's position as a teen idol in the GDR is carefully contrasted with the problems she faced negotiating the SED's policies.

To a degree, the MDR show would seem to fulfil its educational remit. It does indeed appear to be concerned to give as honest an appraisal as possible of the GDR period, normalizing the experience of east Germans, while also avoiding a rose-tinted view of life. Yet, although the show does not focus solely on consumer items to the extent others do, one of the main methods used to achieve this balance is still to filter the past through the prism of present-day consumer values. One of the regular ways the show undermines a revisionist image of history is in its comic 'hidden camera' feature. In this item, contemporary members of society are faced with situations that would have been normal to easterners during the GDR period, but that are now completely alien, due primarily to changes in German service and consumer culture. Remaining for the moment with the first show, we watch the reaction of customers wishing to eat at the restaurant in the Leipzig Town Hall when they are faced with the kind of rude waiter who was commonplace during the GDR period. We see the man casually leave customers waiting for long periods of time while he reads his newspaper. Even when he does decide to take his customers' orders, more often than not he tells them that the dish they have selected is not available. As a number of the guests mention in the film, this is the sort of treatment they hoped had disappeared with the end of the GDR, highlighting the fact that, with regard to their status as consumers, a core value of the new society, the situation is vastly better than it was before the *Wende*.

Although the programme suggests that, unlike the other *Ostalgie* shows, it will present an image of the GDR on its own terms (whatever these terms might be), nonetheless, at times it too tends towards exoticization. The educational aim of the programme is regularly undermined by an overwhelming need to provide populist entertainment. This tendency leads to much of the material covered being sensationalized, a tendency that at times jars with the programme's apparently loftier aims. Such jarring is particularly apparent in some of the show's studio interviews, during which the presenters often put the guests into confusing positions, where they find it difficult to conform to the presenters' obvious wishes, in turn undermining the smooth linking of items.

If we return to the interview with Hagen, at the end of this segment the former sex symbol is asked by the presenters if she ever enjoyed FKK, or naturism, which, as already mentioned, is a staple of these programmes generally, and the next item to be discussed. To their surprise, Hagen responds with 'no, FKK wasn't really my thing', clearly unhappy about being associated with this phenomenon. As a result, she disturbs the transition to the next feature. Nevertheless, Emmerlich and Schenk carry on regardless, introducing a short film of original GDR footage and interviews with celebrity 'talking heads' who recount their experiences. We see, for example, the singer Gerhard Schöne make the case for FKK as an expression of the natural beauty of the human body. He claims that it is a liberating experience and rejects any notion that it was sleazy or voyeuristic. FKK within the GDR context, it is suggested, was as a moment of liberalism that escaped erotic connotations, once again highlighting the show's aim of normalizing apparently exotic GDR experiences. The nonvoyeuristic aspect of FKK is then further emphasized by an interview with the photographer Günther Rössler who took 'art-house' pictures of nudes in the GDR, and who maintains the emphasis on the natural beauty of the human form.

However, this reading of FKK is simultaneously undermined throughout the item. First, from Hagen's disparaging response during its introduction, it is clear that she does not think that it was devoid of voyeuristic sleaze. Yet far more curiously, the entire feature is punctuated by shots of a topless model, who sits at the side of the stage in a deckchair sipping a cocktail. Eventually, we are told that the woman's name is Nicky, a favorite to win Germany's 'Most Beautiful Summer Girl' contest. The presentation of Nicky is completely out of step with the item's overt message. She herself could have very little memory of FKK in the GDR, being obviously in her early twenties. Her presence, therefore, can have nothing to do with the programme's avowed aim of remembering 'our' past honestly. Furthermore, when Rössler is asked to comment as a photographer on Nicky's picture in one of the tabloids, he completely distances himself from it, explaining that he has no interest at all in such photography, offering to give the presenters an explanation as to why, but warning them that this would take some time, to which Emmerlich responds by suggesting he had better not. The guests fail to stick to the script that would endow the show's presentation of FKK as a moment of titillating exoticism with a veneer of respectability, thereby revealing the show's non-educational agenda. Indeed, it is not only the guests who are confused by this item. The bizarre nature of Nicky's appearance also dumbfounds the studio audience, which has no idea how to respond to the woman, forcing Emmerlich, with a degree of embarrassment, to ask for applause after he has made his introduction. As with the ZDF programme, at times throughout the show the pact of compliance between the studio audience and the presenters is stretched to breaking point, undermining the mainstream 'centrality', in Fiske and Hartley's terms, of the show's message.

In all the episodes of *Ein Kessel DDR*, the MDR presenters attempt to hightlight the authenticity of their offering, in the face of what they present as other, inauthentic western-dominated GDR shows. The need to show that this is not just another GDR show reaches its zenith in the fourth instalment, which is dedicated largely to the discussion of state oppression, and in particular the role of the Stasi. This is an issue that is almost completely ignored on the other channels. As usual, in the show's opening the presenters try to maintain a balance between addressing the oppressive nature of life in the East, and avoiding reductive readings of the past which focus wholly on this area. We hear of the massive size of the organization, of the 6 million files it produced and of the fact that it had influence in every corner of society. However, Emmerlich also makes the point that if the MfS had up to 150,000 employees at the end of the GDR, and if the population of the state was roughly 16 million, this still means that well over 15 million members of society were not members. Thus, Emmerlich attempts to recuperate the biographies of a population often seen in mainstream discourse as having been tainted on mass by the influence of this organization.

Yet, as with the FKK item, the show's examination of this aspect of history is undermined by its entertainment imperative. The presenters seem at times to wallow overindulgently in some of the organization's more salacious activities. The first item of this edition focuses, for example, on the Stasi's use of prostitutes to blackmail foreign visitors. This is introduced by the sort of film montage to which we have by now become accustomed, much of the footage being taken from a Stasi training film. The original material is inter-cut with a high-contrast black-and-white image of a woman wearing only stockings and dancing erotically in slow motion with her back to the camera. The impact of this overtly voyeuristic image is reinforced by a deep male voice-over commentary, which tells us that such women were both 'sex objects and objects of state desire'. The film is followed by an interview with a 'Martina X', a former Stasi prostitute whose name and voice have been changed to protect her present identity. The woman clearly finds it difficult to talk about her experiences. Nevertheless, she is gently pressed into giving evermore explicit details about her activities. After first describing how she would be taken to conferences in Leipzig, she breaks off. With further prompting she is then coaxed into explaining that she would be introduced to men and go up to their rooms. Again she stops. Finally she is asked by Schenk, 'And what happened then?', to which the woman responds with the rather obvious answer 'I had to get undressed and fulfil [the man's] sexual desires'. While prostitution in the GDR is obviously a topic worthy of investigation, in the MDR show what is framed as an honest engagement with the past here comes dangerously close to salacious exploitation. The interviewers voyeuristically focus on the act of illicit sex rather than on the broader issue of the political exploitation of the sex industry by the GDR authorities.

The educational aim in the programme is often used, therefore, as a vehicle to indulge in what is at times salacious, but always generally popularist, entertainment television. This tendency towards popularism is also suggested in this same edition of the show in the inclusion of an interview with Princess Maja von Hohenzollern. Born in Dresden, Von Hohenzollern suffered at the hands of the GDR authorities when at the age of eight her parents were put in prison for a failed attempt to escape to the West. Von Hohenzollern gives an eloquent account of the hypocrisy of a state that officially allowed the emigration of its population, while in reality persecuting those who tried. Then, towards the end of the interview, we again see the prioritization of entertainment over education as the focus shifts from an examination of life in the GDR to her recently acquired status as a princess in the Hohenzollern family.[67] Still more curious is the appearance at the side of the stage of a range of wedding dresses. The reason for their presence is never mentioned. One can only presume that they belonged to an item that was finally cut from the programme. However, from the trace of the item that remains, the viewer is perhaps given a glimpse of the actual reason why von Hohenzollern agreed to come on the programme. As was well known at the time, she had recently launched a line of designer wedding attire, a line that she was, presumably, keen to advertise. Once again, we find consumer culture as a driving force behind the programme's content, leaving the viewer with the curious juxtaposition of an historical account of the GDR's painful past with life as a princess who sells wedding dresses.

While the MDR programme does not focus as heavily as SAT 1 or ZDF on *Trabants* and other *ostalgic* consumer items, as we have seen it does, nonetheless, still construct life in the GDR largely in terms of consumer values. Although it attempts to distance itself from other *Ostalgie* programmes, claiming it will not 'confuse' the good and bad aspects of life in the way some of the others do, as Emmerlich puts it in the fourth instalment, it is at times very similar to them, also attempting to commodify and exoticize the GDR past, while concurrently claiming to normalize it. In this case we see the GDR used as a means of indulging in salacious sexual stories and royal gossip, areas that have a huge popular appeal. The content of the MDR programme is in fact very close to that of the *Superillu* magazine, which is a highly popular example of the *Ostalgie* industry, selling approximately 600,000 copies weekly, and having a market share of 18.2 per cent in the new Länder.[68] As Manuela Glaab notes, by using the subtitle, 'One for us' (*Eine für uns*), the magazine plays to the perception amongst east Germans that their everyday life and concerns are under-represented in the media.[69] If one looks at the type of stories covered by the magazine, there are clear points of correspondence between its content and the MDR show. For example, a major focus of interest for its readership remains Stasi scandals – recent stories at the time of writing the present study included the unearthing of new evidence about a suspected Stasi hit man and the 'outing' of a number of members of the Leipzig Olympic bid for 2012 as IMs.[70] Furthermore, again as reflected in the MDR programme, one finds a fascination for royal gossip, shown in the number of articles on topics ranging from the life of Princess Diana to the activities of the Spanish royal family.[71]

Of course, royal gossip is a staple of much of the popular media in Germany, as it is across Europe, being regularly featured in the tabloid press. Consequently, despite attempting to maintain a brand identity of eastern specificity, *Superillu*, like the *Ostalgie* shows, is happy to resort to the tried and tested selling points of the popular mass media. In fact, a good deal of its content is no different from other mainstream, non-eastern-specific women's magazines, such as *Gala* and *Bunte* in Germany or *Woman's Weekly* and *Now* in Britain. Thus, we find that an eastern readership is, perhaps unsurprisingly, attracted to features and issues universally appealing within this genre, and which, in turn, suggests that it need not require special representation. However, for *Superillu* to maintain its market share it must also, to a degree, undermine the 'normality' of its readership. In order to sustain its 'unique selling point', the key to the survival of any successful brand, it must insist that it is representing a marginal, 'exotic' social position not catered for elsewhere in the mainstream media. At the same time, it claims, somewhat paradoxically, to speak for 'normal' east Germans.

The discussion of *Superillu* leads us neatly to an examination of the final, and most watched GDR nostalgia show, RTL's *DDR Show*, which was supported by a special tie-in edition of the magazine, again suggesting points of contact between what is perceived as the eastern and western mass media.[72] RTL, like the magazine and the other shows, sought to walk the tightrope between the need to normalize the former GDR population on the one hand, and to exoticize its consumer culture on the other. As with the ZDF and SAT 1 programmes, we are presented with simulated GDR bathrooms and living rooms. We are introduced to curious GDR drinks as well as the world of GDR music. In the RTL show, music plays a particularly important role, an emphasis that is probably largely due to the fact that the channel produced a tie-in CD of GDR pop music, which it advertised repeatedly during commercial breaks.

The main presenter of the RTL show is the west German Oliver Geißen, a choice that further shows a commitment by a national channel to bring the GDR into the mainstream. Geißen is well known in Germany as the presenter of, amongst other things, *Die 80er Show* on RTL, the format of which is identical with the *DDR Show*. This suggests that the channel sees no difference in nostalgia for the 1980s, or for the GDR. However, we also see many of the weaknesses to be found elsewhere, particularly with regard to the MDR show, which undermine the channel's attempts to normalize this aspect of German history. This is revealed once again in the obvious failure of certain guests to act according to the wishes of the presenters, but which disturbs the tone of the show far more than we saw with MDR. In the first instalment, for example, Geißen interviews Katrin Saß, who plays Christiane in *Good Bye, Lenin!*, asking her to compare her role in the film and her experience of the *Wende*: 'How was your *Wende*?'. Saß pauses for a moment, then thoughtfully suggests, 'My *Wende* ... mmm, that was 1989', sarcastically suggesting that she experienced the events just like everyone else in the east, and that Geißen, as a *Wessi* would have to be reminded of when it took place.

As the interview progresses another of the show's guests, the boxer Henry Maske joins the discussion, saying that the events of that year felt completely 'unbelievable' to him, a view that is met with approval by the other east Germans present. At this point, Geißen attempts to empathize with them, claiming that in the west the events felt equally 'unreal', to which Saß quickly retorts, 'but you lot didn't want it to happen!', a statement which Geißen then attempts to laugh off, but which clearly makes him feel uncomfortable. Like SAT 1, RTL claim that the DDR Show is their contribution to the process of inner unity. 'This is all Germany. This is all us', runs the refrain of the show's title music, a refrain that is used throughout the programme to introduce its guests. However, in successive interviews, the programme cannot hide the obvious feelings of disunity exhibited by guests who seem openly irritated at being interviewed on the subject of the GDR by a westerner. This irritation would, it must be said, seem somewhat disingenuous. First, of course, the guests presumably knew who would be interviewing them and were keen to have the exposure such a show would give them. Second, Geißen does try his best to be sensitive to his guests. His style is deliberately naïve, and although, like Meyer in the SAT 1 show, this western presenter is the central focal point, he is very adept at giving his guests room to speak. He consciously tries not to dominate, playing far more successfully than Meyer the role of the interested layperson eager to learn about life in the east.

Clearly, RTL learnt from some of the criticism of the earlier shows. From its very first programme it includes one item a week which presents the dictatorial nature of the GDR. In the first edition, for example, we watch a film about Erika Reimann, who was imprisoned for 14 years as a schoolgirl for drawing a moustache on a picture of Stalin (her appearance on the show tying in with the recent publication of her account of the incident).[73] Yet, while the show's creators insist that this type of item was always to be included, the journalist Marcus Theurer points out that this particular film sequence was made very late in the programme's production, and as such can perhaps be seen as a response to the attacks on the ZDF programme.[74] Yet, while RTL was in a position to avoid some of the pitfalls of the other programmes, ironically the *DDR Show* probably received more criticism than any of the others. This was mainly due to RTL's presentation of some official GDR institutions. As already mentioned, along with Geißen, the show's co-host was Katarina Witt, one of the biggest Olympic stars the state produced, and as we see in *Helden wie wir*, a woman who for many was a major sex symbol. Indeed, recently she has received more publicity for appearing as a *Playboy* centrefold than for her sporting achievements, an event that certainly impressed Geißen, who makes much mileage out it in the show.[75] In her opening interview she appears on stage with her hair in pigtails and dressed in a tight-fitting Young Pioneer's uniform, although she is at pains to tell the audience that it is not an original uniform as her adult figure would not have been able to fit into it. She explains how one joined the organization and what one did. It is presented as an idyllic moment in her life. We see her sing its songs and her response to its call 'Be Prepared!' ('Sei Bereit!'), 'Always Prepared!' ('Immer Bereit!'). The presentation of the Young Pioneers is overwhelmingly nostalgic, with Witt revelling in the chance of wearing the uniform again, as well as recalling other aspects of the state's ideological paraphernalia, concluding simply that the whole experience 'was lovely'. The apolitical nature of this item is then further reinforced, as Martenstein also points out, by the lightly-charged eroticism of Witt's appearance in her uniform, which seems to foreground not the experience of being in the Young Pioneers, but Witt's status as sex symbol.[76]

The show's focus on institutional aspects of life in the GDR, and specifically the state's use of uniforms and flags would seem to betray particularly clearly the western perspective of the programme. As Betts notes, with regard to the presence of GDR material culture in the west, 'West Germans tend to collect not old consumer goods but, rather, more political memorabilia (SED pins and flags) as the preferred emblems of their imagined GDR.'[77] This is also reflected in the difference between the types of *Ostalgie* exhibited in *Sonnenallee*, and *Good Bye, Lenin!* respectively, the latter focusing much more closely on the question of the state's ideology than the former. Although, once again, it is clear that the television manifestation of this ideological *Ostalgie* is far less reflective than that of the Becker's film. Instead, in the RTL show, we find the commodification of an old, exotic political culture, far removed from the world of present-day German consumerism, but which can continue to be indulged through that very consumerism. As such, this *Ostalgie* would seem to be reminiscent of the type of consumerist *Westalgie* we see, for example in the 'Prada Meinhof' phenomenon. That said, any of the potential ambiguity discussed previously in connection with this type of *Westalgie* is wholly avoided in the *DDR Show*. Rather, the consumerist optic becomes a means of neutering this aspect of the GDR past, turning the potentially problematic question of participation in GDR institutions into an action that can now be understood in terms of material culture.

The normalization/exoticization of GDR political culture in the *DDR Show* was specifically picked out for vilification in the press debate the *Ostalgie* craze sparked, and got RTL into a good deal of hot water. As well as wearing a Pioneer uniform, in the show's publicity material Witt wore a FDJ shirt.[78] This caused an outrage amongst some east Germans who felt that no 'normal' person would willingly wear such a shirt unless they absolutely had to, a position illustrated, for example, in the FDJ meeting we see in the film *Sonnenallee*, where the film's romantic heroine, Miriam, cannot get out of her blue shirt quick enough once she has made her 'self-critical' speech. Clearly, one must not forget the point made by Wolfgang Hilbig, that it is ridiculous to condemn a person for simply being a member of a mass youth organization. However, in the publicity pictures, as well as her interview about the young pioneers, Witt seemed to revel in her membership of such institutions and thus, for some, showed herself not to be an 'everyday' member of GDR society, but rather part of the establishment. In commodifying this particular aspect of society, the show consequently seemed to be over-playing the 'normalization' card. Indeed, it actually inverts what I described above as the 'exoticization' of the mundane. Instead, it constructs as everyday behaviour what was for many 'normal' people in actual fact extraordinary. The appearance of Witt in the publicity photographs in an FDJ uniform even saw Günter Nooke try to bring a court action against her for wearing the symbols of an organization damaging to the German constitution. Since the 1950s the FDJ has been banned in the West. In 1991, when it was re-founded in the eastern regions, the law was rescinded, but just in the east. Since the *DDR Show* was filmed in Cologne, Witt was breaking the law by wearing the shirt.

In the *Ostalgie Shows* we see the commodification of the GDR past. This is in itself nothing new, since consumer culture has always been a part of east German identity construction. However, in these programmes we see a number of developments. Most importantly we find this consumer culture enter mainstream television discourse. Furthermore, it goes beyond its use as a reference point for east German self-expression. Instead, it becomes a means whereby 'inner unity' can be evoked through the construction of all Germans as consumers. In these shows the GDR is no longer presented as a 'Stasi state'. Instead, through *Ostalgie*, it is constructed as a world with a curious material culture. Nevertheless, even if the gasps of horror and disapproval of earlier representations of the GDR are replaced now by curiosity and amusement, the *Ostalgie* shows still furnish us with a representation of the east from which the Federal Republic can distance itself. Thus, they reinvent an exotic eastern 'Orient'. This, in turn, allows the programme-makers to reconfirm the FRG as the better German state, but which, for many indignant east Germans at least, still fails to engage honestly and in a differentiated manner with their pre-unification experience.

Notes

1. ZDF *Ostalgie Show*, presented by Andrea Kiewel and Marco Schreyl, first broadcast Sunday 17 August 2003 at 9.45 pm; MDR *Ein Kessel DDR*, presented by Gunther Emmerlich und Franziska Schenk, in six parts, broadcast weekly from Friday 22 August at 9pm; SAT 1 *Meyer und Schulz: Die ultimative Ost-Show*, presented by Ulrich Meyer and Axel Schulz in two parts, broadcast weekly from Saturday 23 August at 8.15 pm; RTL *Die DDR Show*, presented by Oliver Geißen and Katarina Witt in four parts, broadcast weekly from 3 September at 9.15 pm.
2. Figures from the *Tagesspiegel*, 19 August 2003.
3. Figures from *Quotenmeter.de*, www.quotenmeter.de/index. php?newsid=3040, accessed 21 February 2004.
4. Antonia Kränzlin, 'Wie baut man sich seine DDR?', *Der Tagesspiegel*, 21 August 2003.
5. Quoted in Marcus Jauer, 'Seid bereit? Immer bereit!', *Süddeutsche Zeitung*, 22 August 2003.
6. Quoted in Harald Martenstein, 'Schön war die Zeit', *Der Tagesspiegel*, 23 August 2003.
7. Leander Haußmann 'Es kam dicke genug', *Der Spiegel*, 8 September 2003.
8. Thomas Brussig, 'Mrux, die deutsche Einheit', *Der Tagesspiegel*, 31 August 2003.
9. See 'Interview mit Hans-Hermann Tiedje', http://www.mdr.de/mdr-kultur/figaro/890308–hintergrund-894348.html, accessed 23 February 2004.

10. Quoted in Pascale Hugues, 'Auf der Suche nach der verlorenen Heimat', *Tagesspiegel*, 6 September 2003.
11. Harald Martenstein, 'Schön war die Zeit'. Theodor W. Adorno, *Minima Moralia*, Frankfurt/Main: Suhrkamp, 1951.
12. See 'Emnid Poll', www.quotenmeter.de/index.php?newsid=2889, accessed 23 February 2004.
13. Quoted in Torsten Hampel, 'Was wirklich bleibt: Wie Frau Scheibe, Trainerin in Kati Witts Eislaufverein, die DDR als Fernsehshow findet', *Der Tagesspiegel*, 5 September 2003.
14. Hampel, 'Was wirklich bleibt'.
15. See Max Horkheimer and Theodor W. Adorno, *Dialectic of Enlightenment*, trans. by John Cumming, New York: Continuum, 1989, pp. 120–67.
16. Stefan Wolle, *Die heile Welt der Diktatur: Alltag und Herrschaft in der DDR: 1971–1989*, Berlin: Ch. Links Verlag, 1998, pp. 106–10. On the influence of Western consumer goods in the GDR see Phillip J. Bryson, *The Consumer under Socialist Planning: The East German Case*, New York: Praeger, 1984.
17. Andreas Staab 'Testing the West: consumerism and national identity in eastern Germany', *German Politics*, 2(6) (1997), 139–49 (p. 145).
18. Quoted in Thomas Ahbe, 'Der Dammbruch: Anschlag auf den Einheitsgeschmack', *Freitag*, 29 August 2003.
19. Paul Betts, 'The Twilight of the Idols: East German Memory and Material Culture', *The Journal of Modern History* 72 (2000), 731–65 (p. 742–3). For a further more detailed examination of attitudes towards the material culture of the GDR in unified Germany see Martin Blum, 'Remaking the East German Past: Ostalgie, Identity as Material Culture, *The Journal of Popular Culture*, 34 (2000), 229–54.
20. Patricia Hogwood, '"Red is for Love ...": Citizens as Consumers in East Germany', in Grix and Cooke, pp. 41–54 (p. 50).
21. Hogwood, p. 50.
22. See Ahbe.
23. I am grateful to Peter Thomson of the University of Sheffield for suggesting this metaphor to me.
24. Katharina Rieger, '"Wir sind Ostimisten": Die Werbeagentur Fritzsch & Mackat macht spezielle Kampagnen für Ostdeutschland. Denn die Menschen dort sollen hören, dass sie auch etwas geschafft haben', *Die Zeit*, 4 November 1999.
25. Patricia Hogwood, 'After the GDR: Reconstructing Identity in Post-Communist Germany' *Journal of Communist Studies and Transition Politics*, 4(16) (2000), 45–67.
26. Steffi Hugendubel, 'Ostagenturen auf dem Vormarsch', *Werben &*

Verkaufen, 22, http://www.wuv.de/news/archiv/6/a12186/index.html, 1 June 2001.

27. See for example, Ostprodukte.de, www.ostprodukte.de; Ossiladen.de, www.ossiladen.de; *Ostwarenversand*, www.ostwaren-versand.de, Mondos Arts, www.mondosarts.de, Ebay, the biggest internet auction house also has a whole section of its site dedicated to GDR products. See www.ebay.de.

28. See Michael Bartsch, '"Kost the Ost" zahlt sich nicht aus', *taz*, 6 November 2003.

29. Institut für angewandte Marketing- und Kommunikationsforschung, *Eikaufsverhalten im Lebensmitteleinzelhandel/Fokus Neue Bundes-länder 2003*, Erfurt: IMK GmbH, 2003.

30. The one famous exception to this is *Rotkäppchen*, the Freyburg company, which in 2002 acquired, with much public fanfare, the west German sekt company *Mumm*.

31. For further discussion of this phenomenon see Mark Duckenfield and Noel Calhoun, 'Invasion of the *Ampelmännchen*', *German Politics*, 3(6) (1997), 54–69.

32. See *Event und Touring AG*, www.trabisafari.de/.

33. See 'Welcome Back, Lenin!', *Spiegel Online*, www.spiegel.de/wirtschaft/0,1518,238037,00.html, 27 February 2003.

34. 'Welcome Back, Lenin!'

35. Betts, p. 742.

36. Peter J. Humphreys, *Media and Media Policy in Germany: The Press and Broadcasting since 1945*, second edition, Berg: Oxford, 1994, p. 293.

37. Naughton quotes surveys conducted at the time which claim that between 80 per cent and 90 per cent of the population were keen to maintain the GDR's television and radio stations. Naughton, p. 85.

38 John Sandford, 'The German Media', in *The New Germany: Social, Political and Cultural Challenges of Unification*, ed. by Derek Lewis and John R.P McKenzie, Exeter: University of Exeter Press, 1995, pp. 199–219 (p. 204).

39. Humphreys, p. 314.

40. Humphreys, p. 294.

41. Humphreys, p. 331.

42. See Fritz Pleitgen, 'Ich bin ostagisch: WDR-Indendant Fritz Pleitgen über Ost-Shows und Stasi-Überprüfungen im RBB', *Der Tagesspiegel*, 8 September 2003.

43. See Humphreys, p. 303.

44. Holger Briel, 'The media of mass communication: the press, radio and television', *Modern German Culture*, ed. by Eva Kolinsky and

Wilfried van der Will, Cambridge: CUP, 1998, pp. 322–37.

45. Jo Groebel et al. *Bericht zur Lage des Fernsehens*, Gütersloh: Verlag Bertelsmann Stiftung, 1995, p. 13.

46. Werner Früh and Hans-Jörg Stiehler, *Fernsehen in Ostdeutschland: Eine Untersuchung zum Zusammenhang zwischen Programmangebot und Rezeption*, Berlin: Vista Verlag, 2002, p. 12.

47. Früh and Stiehler, p. 22.

48. Manuela Glaab, 'Viewing the "Other": how the east sees the west and how the west sees the east', in Grix and Cooke, pp. 69–88 (p. 76).

49. Werner Früh et al., *Ostdeutschland im Fernsehen*, Munich: KoPäd, 1999, p. 52.

50. John Fiske and John Hartely, *Reading Television*, second edition, London: Routledge, 2003, p. 65.

51. Früh et. al., *Ostdeutschland*, p. 13.

52. See, for example, Jakob Hein, *Mein erstes T-Shirt*, Munich: Piper, 2001, for further discussion of this text, as well as more recent general trends in east German writing see Paul Cooke, 'East German Literature in the Age of Globalization', in *German Literature in the Age of Globalization*, ed. by Stuart Taberner, Birmingham: University of Birmingham Press, 2004, pp. 25 –46.

53. Früh and Stiehler, *Fernsehen*, p. 88.

54. Früh and Stiehler, p. 21.

55. Früh and Stiehler, p. 77.

56. Jens Schneider, 'Kinder, wisst ihr noch', *Süddeutsche Zeitung*, 13 July 2000.

57. See, for example, Bernhard Honnigfort, 'Modern und sparsam- und sämtlichen Kritikern ein Gräuel', *Frankfurter Rundschau*, 15 July 2000.

58. Axel Beyer, 'Showformate- Trends und Veränderungen', in *Unterhaltung und Unterhaltungsrezeption*, Baden Baden: Nomos, 2000, ed. by Gunner Roters, Wlater Klingler, Maria Gerhards, pp. 173–81 (p. 177).

59. For further discussion of the importance of the television audience within German light-entertainment programming see H. Burger 'Diskussion ohne Ritual oder: Der domestiziert Rezipient', in *Redeshows. Fernsehdiskussionen in der Diskussion*, ed. by W. Holly, P. Kühn and U. Püschel, Tübingen, Niemeyer, 1989, pp. 116–41.

60. Andreas Garaventa, *Showmaster, Gäste Publikum: Über das Dialogische in Unterhaltungsshows*, Bern: Peter Lang, 1993, p. 29.

61. Fiske and Hartley, p. 65.

62. Christoph Schutheis, 'Das Kuriositätkabinett', *Berliner Zeitung*, 19 August 2003.

63. Peter Hoff, 'Der ultimative Ost-Zoo', *Neues Deutschland*, 25 August 2003.
64. *Elis und Escher: Die DDR – nur eine Lachnummer?* First broadcast, MDR 15 September 2003.
65. Kränzlin.
66. See Hans-Ulrich Brandt, et al., *Das war unser Kessel Buntes*, Berlin: Kai Homilius Verlag, 2002.
67. Maja von Hohenzollern is the third wife of Prince Ferfried von Hohenzollern. They married in 1999.
68. Glaab, p. 75.
69. Glaab, p. 76.
70. 'Stasi-Killer: Was weiß das Bundeskriminalamt wirklich', *Superillu*, 2, 9 October 2003, p. 14–15; 'Stasi-Schatten über Olympia', *Superillu*, 43, 16 October 2003, p. 10–11.
71. 'Diana und ihr Butler: Verrat oder Huldigung?', *Superillu*, 45, 30 October 2003, p. 98; 'Traumhochzeit mit einer Geschiedenen', *Superillu*, 46, 6 November 2003, pp. 10–11.
72. See *Superillu: Das Offizielle Magazin zur grossen RTL-Show*, Sonderheft 1 (2003).
73. Erika Reimann, *Die Schleife an Stalins Bart*, Hamburg: Hoffmann & Campe, 2002.
74. Marcus Theurer, 'Die Einwicklerin Katarina Witt erinnert sich mit RTL an die alte DDR', *Süddeutsche Zeitung*, 3 September 2003.
75. The publicity surrounding her *Playboy* appearance was, however, subsequently eclipsed by the scandal surrounding the publication of her Stasi file, which suggested that Witt had closely cooperated with the East German Security Service, an accusation that Witt still strenuously denies. See Günther Lachmann and Ralf Georg Reuth, 'Die Stasi-Akten der Katarina Witt', *Die Welt am Sonntag*, 12 May 2002.
76. Martenstein, 'Schön war die Zeit'.
77. Betts, p. 758.
78. The FDJ, or 'Free German Youth', was the GDR's mass organization for teenagers.

–6–

A Postcolonial Culture? Surfing for the GDR in Cyberspace

Since unification, probably the biggest development in the German media and communications landscape, as with the rest of the world, has been the rapidly increasing importance of the Internet, or 'cyberspace'. Although at present the demographic of Internet usage in Germany remain predominantly male, university educated, under forty and western, this is beginning to change. Of these categories, the most rapidly changing seems to be the increasing number of east Germans who are going online. As *Der Spiegel* has put it, 'Slowly but surely the east is catching up digitally.' Based on the findings of the DENIC agency, *Der Spiegel* reported that the number of World Wide Web (WWW) domain names registered in the eastern regions was up by 50 per cent in 2001, whereas elsewhere in Germany the number sank by up to 20 per cent.[1] In 2000 only 9 per cent of east Germans used the Internet. In 2004, research carried out by the Leipzig Institute for Empirical Research (*Leipziger Institut für empirische Forschung*) suggested that this had risen to 45 per cent. Also, the length of time easterners were spending online was on the increase. In 2000 east Germans spent on average approximately 7 hours a week on the Internet. By 2002 this had risen to 7.6 hours.[2]

One of the effects of the increased usage of the Internet by east Germans has been a growing number of Internet sites focusing on east German issues, many of which point to the continued impact of the GDR on the present.[3] As we saw in the previous chapter, in some parts of the mass media attitudes towards this period of history have shifted recently. Specifically, certain types of *Ostalgie* have become part of mainstream culture. This development has itself been controversial, but it does mean that, on the face of it at least, aspects of this nostalgia are now being treated more sympathetically by the media than they had been previously. However, in the press coverage that the recent growth in east German Web sites has attracted, the representation of the GDR has remained a problematic issue. The journalist Henryk M. Broder, for example, in his analysis of east German Web sites, follows a popular conception of the

Internet as a potentially dangerous frontier world, a 'Wild West', often seen to be populated by sexual deviants and political extremists, in which the normal rules of civilization do not apply and from which the vulnerable members of society must be protected.[4] Broder tends towards an image of the Web as having been infiltrated by extremist east German cells looking potentially to overthrow the unified government and reinstate the GDR. He even refers to sites where one can ostensibly re-arm for any coming revolution, buying 'A Kalashnikov for 98 Euros'.[5] Thus, unlike the *Ostalgie* television shows, in such articles on Web use, expressions of east German identity continue to be taken a sign that the project of inner unity still has a good way to go.

In this concluding chapter, I explore the representation of the former East German state on the WWW, using material collected during two surveys, carried out in March 2002 and January to February 2004. In so doing, I question the view of journalists such as Broder, arguing that while one does find some opinions that are more extreme than those aired in other cultural discourses, the majority of representations of the GDR on the Web are far more mundane than he suggests, but at the same time no less culturally significant. What is particularly interesting about the Internet as a communications medium is the relative ease with which individuals can produce cultural texts, compared with the cultural discourses discussed in previous chapters. Consequently, the Web is a particularly useful tool for an exploration of 'grass roots' attitudes perhaps not represented so clearly elsewhere. That said, on the WWW we find many of the themes already examined. In this chapter, therefore, I revisit the now familiar debates on GDR history and the place of east Germans in unified society, examining how Web pages reflect a wide range of issues, from the question of justice for victims of the old regime, to an engagement with 'everyday' GDR culture and *Ostalgie* (of which there is an abundance).

In much of this usage we find evidence of continued mutual resentment between easterners and westerners, but particularly of east German dissatisfaction, underscored by what are perceived to be western colonial attitudes. At the same time, and as we have seen elsewhere, we also find the blurring of geographical boundaries. For example, we find westerners producing 'east German' sites, using aspects of GDR history in order to reflect critically on the nature of life in unified Germany. Yet, co-existing with images that show continuities with previously discussed issues, there are Web sites that use the GDR past in a way that is indistinguishable from the manner that west Germans might represent their personal history, or indeed from the way past experience is often presented on homepages on the Web more generally.

Here, it is possible to identify a strand in the historical appraisal of the GDR that we have not yet examined in any depth, but which some commentators are now beginning to identify as one that is becoming increasingly important. At times, we find that Web authors' experiences of the GDR are simply one marker amongst many through which they construct their identity. In terms of the broader postcolonial framework of the volume, this might be taken as a further echo of Hall's 'productive' hybridity, such as we saw in east German cinema, and to which the *Ostalgie* shows, however unsatisfactorily, were in part a response. But in this forum it is taken to a new level. On Web pages there is often no sense of the centrality of the author's eastern heritage. Instead, the GDR becomes the background for other, and for the individual or group concerned, more important, activities. Consequently, while east German Web use is often portrayed in the press as further proof of the potential 'dangers' of east German distinctiveness, we can, in fact, find even clearer evidence here than in the other cultural discourses examined thus far that there is very little to worry about. Indeed, I suggest that on the Web it might even be possible to identify the east becoming a truly 'post'-colonial culture, where the colonization metaphor is simply no longer relevant because individuals do not now necessarily feel that they must justify the relevance of their biographies, or that they perceive themselves to be second-class citizens in unified Germany. On a good number of sites, it is impossible to find any traces of 'defiance' and the GDR simply becomes one point of reference amongst many that make up a Web author's presentation of him or herself.

Approaches to Studying the Internet

In the 1990s, scholarship on the cultural application of the Internet was dominated by two commentators, Howard Rheingold and Sherry Turkle, both of whom give highly enthusiastic accounts of this new technology. The focus of Rheingold's work is the concept of the 'virtual community'. He argues that the Internet will be the key to a revitalization of the public sphere.[6] Putting forward the reverse side of the Internet as a 'Wild West', Rheingold constructs it as a 'brave new world', a frontier of change that can potentially bring about a technological utopia in which the tyranny of time and space are subordinated to a 'citizen-designed, citizen-controlled worldwide communications network', which will ultimately recreate the sense of community that has been lost in western (post) modern society.[7] Sherry Turkle, too, argues that the Internet can fulfil what she perceives as society's need to recreate a lost sense of community.[8] Specifically, she explores the potential for identity experimentation in a forum where, as one of her interviewees famously declared, 'R[eal] L[ife] itself ... can be 'just one more window''.[9] The notion that the individual can be whoever they wish to be is seen as a further means of reinvigorating society, allowing people to try out roles in 'Virtual Reality' that can potentially liberate them in real life, giving them the opportunity 'to express multiple and often unexplored aspects of the self, to play with their identity and try out new ones'.[10] Identity experimentation is a particularly important element in the work of a number of scholars. Daniel Chandler, for example, in his study of personal home-page construction examines how the Web is used by a range of marginalized groups. Specifically, he looks at some Internet use by gay communities, exploring how the technology can potentially give an individual a means of experimenting with a gay identity before having to risk coming out in the physical world.[11]

Rheingold, Turkle and Chandler adopt what Flis Henwood *et al.* term a 'technologically determinist' approach to the Internet, which sees the very existence of this new medium as *de facto* moving society forward1.[12] However, in recent years such views have been challenged in a number of ways. First, commentators have started to question Rheingold and Turkle's unequivocally positive readings of the Internet. James Slevin, for example, notes:

> the Internet, more than any other medium, is seen by some as eroding 'community' and 'emptying' day-to-day life by allowing individuals and organizations to enter into a virtual time-space which is seen as competing with reality and which clouds whatever they do with a sense of inauthenticity.[13]

Slevin points to an image of cyberspace that has much in common with the popular conceptions propagated by some journalists. He poses a number of questions: Is the Internet not, in fact, undermining notions of community in real life, replacing face-to-face encounters with virtual ones? Furthermore, even if communities are formed, how valid are they if they are full of individuals who are performing identities that potentially bear no resemblance to their offline selves? Here we have a dystopian view of the Internet that radically counters the utopianism of Rheingold and Turkle. Yet, more recently commentators have begun to suggest that both these positions are flawed, since they treat cyberspace as a separate metaphysical realm, which is either reinvigorating or undermining the physical world. Consequently, they ignore the fact that cyberspace is, of course, a product of this physical world. Instead, as Slevin himself later suggests, it is crucial to see the Internet as what he terms 'a modality of cultural transmission' that results from actual human interaction and thus as a medium that is completely embedded in the individual's offline life.[14]

This rejection of earlier views is also central to recent changes in the ways that scholars have approached the question of authenticity on the Internet, a concept central to my analysis of GDR Web pages. Christine Hine, for example, critiques Turkle's notion of the Internet as a realm dedicated to identity experimentation, suggesting that 'the academic (specifically postmodern) preoccupation with the Internet as a sphere of identity play, fragmentation, and virtuality without real referent is not mirrored in the majority of everyday Internet use.'[15] Rather than viewing the Internet as a place for identity experimentation, commentators such as Hine and Judith S. Donath examine how and why Internet users seek to construct authenticity online, as a means of validating their cultural expression, and the extent to which Web authors' strategies to have their sites taken seriously reflect societal positions in the physical world. Donath, for example, looks at how the complexity of a Web site can often be taken as a measure of authenticity, or at least as a measure of the Web author's desire to be read as authentic, making the point that the more effort Web authors puts into a site, the less likely they are simply to cast it away as an experimental game.[16] Hine similarly uses the criterion of complexity as a marker of authenticity, as well as looking at the efforts to which Web authors go to publicize their sites and, thus, make their voices heard.[17] One such measure might be the number of links to other sites that a page includes. The use of links potentially suggests the extent to which Web authors wish to embed their site in a broader network, which in turn points to what he or she sees as the range of their page's points of contact with other sites, and thus the significance of its topic. To these measures, one might also add certain features included on Web pages themselves, designed to validate the information contained on them. These include elements showing that the site has been online for some time and is popular. In this category we find, for example, 'hit counters', which indicate the number of visitors a site has had, or the 'guest book' feature, which highlights both a site's history and its value to visitors. Furthermore, authors often include devices to show that their Web site is up-to-date. This is sometimes indicated by a 'last updated' marker, which, if it has a recent date, might be taken as proof of the contemporary relevance of a site. Chandler also notes the frequent inclusion of the 'under construction' caveat on many individual homepages, which makes a similar claim to the 'last updated' feature, namely that a particular Web page is a dynamic space, subject to constant revision.[18]

All of these elements shape the representations of the GDR on the WWW. Returning specifically to the 'positive' or 'negative' images of the Web that dominated discussions in the 1990s, although there are a number of competing versions of the GDR to be found 'there', many authors themselves tend to perceive cyberspace as a separate world that vacillates between being a utopia and a dystopia. Ultimately, however, these views are to be understood only if the Internet is seen not as a separate realm but as one that is embedded within social praxis. This chapter considers, for example, how a good number of authors (although, as I discuss below, by no means all) see the WWW as a forum that allows them to construct a virtual community and find a sense of authenticity that they feel as being denied them in the physical world, while concurrently viewing their 'exile' to the Internet as further proof of western colonization, and of their continued marginalization within unified Germany.

Who is putting the GDR on the WWW?

The presence of the GDR on the WWW is immense, and is currently on the increase. A search on Google for Deutsche Demokratische Republik at the time of my first survey generated approximately 37,600 hits. By 2004 this number had more than doubled to 77,400. Obviously, this field has to be limited if any form of analysis is to be attempted. The vast majority of hits are links to newspaper articles, museums and other institutions that have connections to the GDR, as well as to sites dedicated to the type of e-commerce discussed in the previous chapter, which have fed into the recent *Ostalgie* craze on television.[19] In order to explore 'grass roots' attitudes, my examination concentrates on the representation of the GDR on the pages of private individuals and groups, the primary focus of which is non-commercial use. As anyone who uses the WWW knows, sites come and go. Consequently, any survey of its content is liable to change and at best can only be a snapshot of its contents at a specific time, in my case the winters of 2002 and 2004. Furthermore, it is not just the moment one picks that influences the picture gained. This is also shaped by the search mechanisms used. All the sites discussed here were found on the search engines Google and Yahoo (two of the largest on the Web), or a number of specialist lists that were found connected to the theme of the GDR. These include the DDR Webring, DDR-im-Web.de, DDR-im-WWW, and DDR-Suche.[20] Clearly, there will be other sites not noticed by these mechanisms. However, following Hine's model, the sites picked up by these search engines and lists tend either to a high degree of complexity, or it is clear that their authors have gone to some effort to make their pages visible. As such, they would seem to be more concerned with the issue of authenticity, or at least of having something worthwhile to say to an audience, than those that have not made this effort. In my first survey through these various search instruments I collected one hundred of the most popular sites (popularity being judged by how often a page occurred across the spectrum of searches I carried out). Whenever possible, the Web authors were approached by e-mail with a number of questions about themselves and their reasons for building the site. Of those emailed, forty-three responded. In my second survey, I repeated this exercise, increasing the sample group to 200 sites. Here the email questionnaire yielded seventy-two responses.

The demographics of the Web authors who responded in the surveys were very close to the national picture of Web use in Germany, suggesting that the 'snap shots' obtained can be taken as reasonably representative. In survey one 83 per cent of respondents were men, 17 per cent women. In survey two, 88 per cent were men, 12 per cent women. In the first survey 87 per cent came from university-educated backgrounds. In the second, the backgrounds of the participants had become slightly more diverse, with 73 per cent now coming from this milieu. In both, the single biggest group of participants consisted of people still in full-time education, although the percentage dropped significantly in the second sample (28 per cent to 18 per cent). The next most popular field was computing, and in particular jobs connected to the Internet (for example, Web-page design or e-commerce: 12 per cent and 16 per cent respectively).

Also, the spread of ages was fairly typical of the national picture, although the sample was slightly older in the second survey. 76 per cent of respondents in the first survey were under forty: Dropping in the second to 66 per cent. In the first survey it was interesting to note that a significant number of respondents were under the age of 20 (17 per cent), a group that, at the most, could have been no more than seven years old at the time of the *Wende*. The significance of this finding is, however, thrown into doubt by the fact that in the second survey this number decreased to 3 per cent. The relationship of this age group to the GDR past, nonetheless, remains an interesting issue, and is one to which I shall return at the end of this chapter. The other main development between the first and second surveys was an increase in the group of Web authors aged between forty-one to fifty and between sixty-one to seventy.

The one difference from the national demographic of Internet use in the first survey was the fact that virtually all the respondents (93 per cent) were east Germans. In the second the number dropped to 70 per cent. Now 21 per cent of respondents came from the west, and 9 per cent came

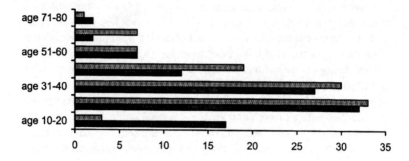

Figure 6.1 Age spread of respondents in per centages (survey one light-coloured bars, survey two dark-coloured bars).

from outside Germany. This broadening of appeal might reflect the shift in interest in the GDR identified in the previous chapter, where we saw aspects of GDR history becoming part of mainstream consumer and television culture. As also mentioned, the WWW has had a role to play in this development. However, in this chapter we shall see that in west German non-commercial GDR Web sites the type of commodification identified as central to shifts in mainstream attitudes is largely rejected by authors. Instead, we find the reassertion of the whole range of orientalist attitudes towards the east discussed throughout this study, that is: of those that attempt to legitimize, as well as those that critique, the Federal Republic.

The GDR and Cyberspace: Images of an Oppressive Regime

In both surveys, Web sites could be roughly divided into two main groups. The smallest of the two was the collection of sites that focused on negative aspects of the GDR regime (26 per cent and 29 per cent). A common denominator of the majority of these Web pages is a wish to provide information that the Web authors feel is not to be found elsewhere. As the Web author of the highly developed site DDR-Geschichte.de (GDR history) put it in response to the question 'why did you decide to build this site?':

> GDR research is still a very new area. A few years ago there was very little information to be found (books, TV programmes, lessons at school, courses at university). In the meantime there has been a boom in research into the GDR, but there is still a massive lack of information. [My site] is important not least due to the rose-tinted presentation [of the GDR] in the *Ostalgie*

craze. This has led to a situation in which children and young people in particular no longer know why the GDR was an *Unrechtsstaat* and why the *Wende* took place.[21]

The author, a twenty-eight year-old student from east Berlin, sees it as her task to provide a corrective to the recent *Ostalgie* craze. The impulse for her site is educational. It is particularly aimed at 'school pupils, students and interested non-experts' and focuses on key moments in the GDR's history of oppression – including the uprising of 17 June 1953 and the building of the Berlin Wall on 13 August 1961.[22] In her attempt to counter what she views as a damaging form of nostalgia, we see a return to the view of the GDR discussed in Chapter 2 and found in the Enquete Commissions' reports. This east German adopts a similar position to some former civil rights activists, where the notion of the state as an *Unrechtsstaat* is of crucial importance. However, she is also aware of the criticisms that have been raised against such a view of the GDR. Her site, she insists, is to be read in conjunction with a second project, DDR-Zeitzeugen.de (GDR eyewitnesses), where she collects first-hand accounts of life in the GDR. This is the impulse behind a number of the Web sites in both surveys, particularly those concerned with presenting more positive aspects of life in the East. In answer to the question 'what sort of image of the GDR do you wish to present?', she responds:

> I want to present an objective and differentiated image of the GDR. The negative, but also the positive aspects of life for GDR citizens living in this socialist totalitarian system should be made understandable and stimulate comparison with the FRG.[22]

Pre-emptively countering the type of criticisms raised to the Enquete commissions' reports, namely that they present a one-sided image of life in the GDR, she insists that it is her intention to give a differentiated picture, which shows the positive as well as the negative aspects of the regime. Nevertheless, it remains clear that the educational focus of her site, like that of the reports, is the legitimization of the FRG through a comparison with the GDR as a totalitarian state. Indeed, this view also permeates the eye-witness site, on which the personal accounts differ markedly from many other memoir Web pages. As we shall see later in this chapter, there are, for example, a number of sites that give accounts of individual experiences in the military. These tend to look back nostalgically at the authors' service days, communicating what they view as the feeling of warmth and companionship between army comrades. The eye-witness site also includes a personal account of army life. However, here the focus is on the dehumanizing aspects of life in the GDR's military. In a detailed statement by a former border guard, we learn that alcohol abuse amongst conscripts was rife, and that theft was endemic. Moreover, the notion of army camaraderie is relativized here. The relationship between a group of soldiers, this eyewitness maintains, 'is always based on stress', with recruits using whatever means at their disposal to jockey for position.[23] Consequently, while the author acknowledges the value of individual testimony in presenting a nuanced image of life in the GDR, the role of such testimony on this site, unlike much of that found elsewhere, is largely to give greater depth to our understanding of the state's dictatorial record.

Interestingly, many of the non-east German Web authors appeared in this group of sites. This suggests, perhaps, that while some discourses may have shifted in the way they present the GDR, and also while many of those responsible for propagating a view of the East as a totalitarian *Unrechstaat* in the state-led processes of historical appraisal came from the GDR, the totalitarian view remains important within popular western opinion. The fifty-nine-year-old mathematics professor from Bavaria who is the author of the satirical site Laputa, a role-playing project in which he has built a 'virtual country' based on the GDR, speaks for a number of respondents when he insists that his intention is to present a 'picture of a dirty tyrannical regime, with a contempt for humanity'. As such, his site stands in radical contrast to the recent *Ostalgie* craze, which for him is 'a terrible thing: myths are being created and the murderous, unjust nature of the dictatorship is being trivialized'.[24]

DDR-Geschichte.de, and Laputa take a thematically broad-ranging approach to the GDR and, in so doing, are rather unusual. More frequently, the Web sites collected in both surveys tended to focus on very narrow aspects of history. In the group that discussed the negative features of the regime, we find sites dedicated to the inner German border, in particular the Berlin Wall, sites about the problems of oppositional activity, escape attempts and the state's treatment of prisoners.[25] However, of this group, the sites that have received the most press attention are those concerned with the activities of the MfS. This is rather unsurprising given the number of column inches dedicated to this organization in the early 1990s, discussed at length in Chapter 3, where I examined responses by writers to the view of the GDR precisely this focus on the Stasi presented. In January 2000, *Der Spiegel* reported a flurry of interest in the Web site nierenspende.de which at the time included a list of the names of 100000 Stasi officers. Within cyberspace there was a return to the type of Stasi fever that was seen throughout the media in the early 1990s.[26] The author of this site also appeared in my survey, although his response provided very little information, other than his name: 'Manfred Willi Lerch ... alias Tom Moak' (information not solicited by my questionnaire), and that he is freelance Internet journalist from east Berlin (confirming the information given in *Der Spiegel*).[27] He did also say that he is now banned from working as a journalist in Germany, although he did not explain why. Lerch was quickly advised by the German Data Protection Agency to remove the list from his site. This he did; nevertheless, nierenspende.de has not stopped its general campaign against former Stasi operatives.[28] Furthermore, Lerch now also uses his site as a means of countering what he views as a dangerous form of censorship by the Federal Government. On the title page of nierenspende.de at the time of my visit, the Web author posed the rhetorical question: 'Who is to protect data from the data protectors?' We are then invited to click on a link to an article that explains how the government is intent upon drastically limiting Web access in Germany: 'Blocks are to make it impossible for *You* to view thousands of Internet sites'.[29]

Nierenspende.de belongs to a small, tightly interlinked, network of sites that deal with the role of the Stasi, as well as the question of justice for its victims and retribution against those who collaborated with it. On sites such as stasiopfer.de (Stasi victim) and H.T.'s Stasi-Infoseite (H.T.'s Stasi Info page), the authors of which are clearly aware of each other's activities, as well as those of Lerch,[30] we similarly find Web pages that publicize apparently ignored Stasi human-rights violations, publishing documents passed to their authors by visitors. Indeed, they also see it as their function to counter what they view as the continued 'virtual' existence of the MfS itself. All the sites make reference, for example, to 'mfs-insider.de', which has been set up and is run by former Stasi officers, and is taken by these anti-Stasi sites as proof that the organization is still operational. Moreover, all these sites support Lerch's view that democracy, and particularly freedom of information, is not guaranteed in unified Germany. As such, while they present a similar image of the past to that found in the Enquete Commissions' reports, the anti-Stasi sites do not use the GDR as a means of legitimizing the FRG. Rather than foregrounding the difference between the two systems, using the GDR as the FRG's abject 'orientalist' other, these sites point to ostensible continuities in the behaviour of the SED regime and the FRG. For example, the author of H.T.'s Stasi-Infoseite, a thirty-one-year-old student from east Berlin, stated in his questionnaire response that one of the reasons for building this site was 'to spread information that would otherwise not be available ... to counter censorship (there have been lots of attempts both by the state and privately to close down this site)'.[31] In a subsequent email, he said that he has, in fact, now had to move his Internet provider from

Germany to Britain in order to ensure that his site remains online.[32] The claim that this type of site is being targeted by the state would also seem to hold for stasioper.de. As reported in *Der Spiegel*, its author, Mario Falcke, a former victim of the Stasi was, like Lerch, threatened with prosecution, but in his case for merely including a link to a site that had a link to the list of Stasi officers already mentioned.[33]

Of course, the impression that these authors are being, to some extent, persecuted must be balanced against the potential of their 'naming and shaming' policy to provoke vigilante attacks against those accused of working for the Stasi, a fact that perhaps makes the state's concern understandable. However, leaving aside the rights and wrongs of their treatment by the authorities, of importance to my discussion is that these sites clearly view the WWW as a forum where marginalized voices can be heard. Nevertheless, they also suggest that such voices are not protected here. For these authors, the democracy of the Web is under threat, because the state is trying to remove even this method of communication from easterners keen to air past grievances. The victims of the former regime continue to be victims in the present. As such, these sites produce highly charged, emotional images of both the GDR and unified Germany. Indeed, at times they exhibit the Internet phenomenon of 'flaming', that is of airing extreme views and of using the type of abusive language that would not be acceptable in other forums. For example, at the time of my visit, the H.T.'s Stasi-Infoseite was set up as a parody of the title page of the SED's daily newspaper *Neues Deutschland*, which evoked on its title banner the Communist Manifesto's call 'workers of the world unite!' Copying *Neues Deutschland's* graphic design, the 'Neue HTseite' demands instead that 'secret services of the world, piss off!' This is a sentiment that clearly highlights the site's belief in continuities between the past and present regimes, of its author's awareness of the ostensible limitations placed on freedom of information in democratic society, and also of his defiance in the face of these limitations.

Ostalgie Revisited: Representing 'Positive' Aspects of the GDR

Although the Stasi sites have attracted a good deal of attention, they make up a very small section of what is itself a small group of sites dealing with negative aspects of the SED regime. By far the largest group in both surveys were sites that included more positive aspects of GDR culture and society (74 per cent/71 per cent), sites that might broadly be defined by the umbrella-term *Ostalgie*, or have at least been presented in such terms when they have been discussed in the press.[34] The dominance of *Ostalgie* in the presentation of the GDR on the Web could be taken to be proof positive of the dominance of Internet use by revisionists who are rejecting the present-day state, a position towards which some journalists tend. As such, it could be viewed as evidence of a trend away from honest appraisals of the GDR as a corrupt dictatorship, towards a more ideologically narrow-minded, or worryingly rose-tinted view that is, in turn, impeding the process of coming to terms with the past, and thus inner-unity. However, as we have seen throughout the discussion of GDR nostalgia in this study, although this is a common perception, it is very rarely found to be the case on closer inspection. Across my two surveys it was possible to identify four sub-groupings within the main *Ostalgie* group:

		Survey One	*Survey Two*
1	Virtual GDRs	17 per cent	13 per cent
2	*Ostalgic* remembrance sites	19 per cent	7 per cent
3	Hobby/collector sites	55 per cent	64 per cent
4	*Ostalgie* as pure by-product	9 per cent	16 per cent

Figure 6.2 Chart to show breakdown of subgroups within the Ostalgie sample.[35]

The first group of sites, which might be seen as the most worrying form of *Ostalgie*, are those that ostensibly wish to refound the GDR – termed 'virtual GDRs' here. At first glance, these appear to give weight to the position of the anti-Stasi sites discussed above, that is they seem to suggest the continued existence of GDR attitudes, and even structures, which sites such as nierenspende.de try to publicize. One of the most often mentioned of these sites is the so-called Offizielles Internetorgan der DDR-Staatsregierung im Exil (The official Internet Organ of the GDR State Government in Exile). This was one of the most complex and popular sites in the first survey, with pages dedicated to a large number of GDR institutions, including the various GDR official bloc parties as well as the Stasi. As a result, it would seem that the authors are particularly concerned with the issue of authenticity. This is then further underlined by the inclusion of a number of authenticity-enhancing features on the pages themselves, such as a hit counter, and a 'last updated' marker. Visitors can interact with the site in a number of ways. They are offered, for example, the opportunity of joining an underground SED. Indeed, it is through these pages that visitors can buy the Kalashnikov that Broder mentions in one of his articles (although it should also be mentioned that it is a replica weapon). The tone of the site is highly combative, with the self-styled 'authorial collective' that runs it, made up of east and west Germans, provocatively claiming to be the representative voice of an oppressed community of GDR citizens under occupation by the FRG.[36] The site portrays itself as the last voice of freedom, fighting a rearguard action against the violent imperialism of the USA and its lackeys, the post-unification German government. The WWW would, thus, appear to be the only place where the Marxist-Leninist values of the GDR can find expression. However, even here their position is not safe. As we are also informed on the first page of the site:

> You are lucky still to be able to read these pages. The self-proclaimed gate-keeper of the GDR on the Internet – www.ddr-im-web.de – has only indexed certain sites. For it, links to condoms are more important than the truth! Other search engines have also refused to list us.[37]

As is the case with the anti-Stasi sites, the Web is initially seen as the last resort for the marginalized voice of truth, in this case as a utopian space where the GDR can continue to exist, free from western oppression. However, this utopia is almost immediately replaced with a dystopian image. Cyberspace, like the east in the physical world, is a realm that has been colonized, and is controlled, by big business, where the 'truth' must fight to be heard even harder than in real life, since sites on the Web appear to be at the mercy of all-powerful and yet arbitrary search mechanisms. Interestingly, the Web authors see their site as even being marginalized within the GDR Web community. Although it is a part of the DDR Webring, they feel that they are being excluded from the more powerful GDR Web space that they claim is protected by DDR-im-Web.de, an apparently impure GDR Web site, blinkered by capitalist values.

In this virtual GDR one finds a sense of community based strongly on the official rhetoric of the SED. Membership of this community is completely ideological. We see a revisitation of the old socialist concept of the GDR as 'the better Germany', and its people as the one-time 'Victors of History'. The authors appear to use the WWW to recreate virtually an imagined past and an idealized socialist community. Now that this GDR community has had its political inheritance stolen from it, its members must fight to reconfigure its utopian dreams in cyberspace. In so doing, however, the citizens of this version of the East German state are instead faced with a dystopian, capitalist wilderness.

On this site we would seem to have a very extreme expression of *Ostalgie*. Its authors would appear to be calling for nothing less than a rebuilding of the Wall. However, as one explores the site further it becomes clear that this is not its rationale. Its purpose is, rather, to use the official rhetoric of the GDR as a leftwing prism through which they attempt to present a satirical critique of present-day capitalist society. As such, it echoes some of the *ostalgic* attitudes of the PDS, discussed in Chapter 2. However, a crucial difference in this site is that it does so with a heavy dose of irony. Moreover, the fact that west Germans are involved in this site is revealing, because it suggests that the site is also influenced by the type of 'orientalism' discussed in connection with *Die Unberührbare* and *Good Bye, Lenin!*, where GDR socialism is nostalgically invoked to recuperate leftwing political and intellectual positions that have ostensibly been lost in both the east and west since unification. This is shown most obviously by the fact that the focus of the site is not wholly the past. Instead, the GDR is used to read present-day issues. At the time of my first visit, these were specifically the events of 11 September 2001 and the so-called 'War on Terror' this has engendered. The GDR view of the USA as an imperialist warmonger is resurrected to question its present-day foreign policy, as well as that of its allies, particularly the FRG (it should be mentioned that my visit to the site took place before the cooling of relations between the USA and Germany in the run up to the war in Iraq. At this point the policies of both countries are considered by the Web authors to be interchangeable.) As the authors put it in their response to my questionnaire, the site's central function is 'to reveal the lies and propaganda of the FRG through exaggeration'.[38] In effect it is not the GDR that is at the centre of this site, but unified Germany and its place in the world.

It is satire, the authors insist, that is at the heart of this Web project. However, because of the site's extremist tone, which often, like the anti-Stasi sites, tends towards 'flaming', it is at times hard to know where satirical exaggeration ends and actual beliefs begin, a fact that may well be behind the large number of violent threats the Web authors claim they receive on a regular basis.[39] A more obviously satirical, and consequently less contentious, tone is struck by the site Honecker.de, another one of the more sophisticated virtual GDR Websites, which appeared in both my surveys. As with the Offizielle Internetorgan site, Honecker.de sees itself defending socialist values, taking the rhetoric of the GDR's official discourse and applying it to the nature of life in unified Germany. The site sets out its stall on its front page, which, like H.T.'s Stasi-Infoseite, is constructed as a parody of the front page of *Neues Deutschland*. While *Neues Deutschland*, during the GDR period, declared itself the 'Organ of the Central Committee of the SED,' Honecker.de is portrayed as the 'Organ of the Central Committee for German Unity'. In a more overt manner than the previous site discussed, Honecker.de does not wish to return to the past or undermine the present system but rather to use the ideological values of the former regime (albeit in an idealized form) to critique present-day German society. In so doing, it hopes finally to achieve what it perceives as a true sense of German unity.

Once again, Honecker.de views cyberspace as a space for a marginalized east German colony, and at the same time also expresses a strong sense of this community continuing to be under threat. In one particularly tongue-in-cheek article, the site announces that this virtual GDR intends, in true Marxist-Leninist fashion, to declare the Internet public property in order to protect it from saboteurs:

> It has just been announced that by the 9 November this year the Internet is expected to be nationalized. This is to be done so that the Central Committee for German Unity can prevent the disruptive manoeuvres of those who would sabotage Honecker.de and ensure open access to its joyfulness and happy nature, its socialist morality and progressive knowledge.[40]

Of significance here are some of the values that Honecker.de claims are at the heart of its socialist project, namely 'joyfulness and [a] happy nature', qualities that need not been seen as specific to GDR socialism, in however an idealized form this may be constructed. This is a tendency that can be found on a number of *Ostalgie* Web sites, which again runs counter to the notion that their authors simply wish to return to the past or that they even reject the fact of unification. Instead, an east German value system is constructed as a way of viewing the world that can be shared by any 'reasonable' person. Thus, Honecker.de universalizes the concept of being an *Ossi*, a tendency inscribed on the site's first page. Again recalling *Neues Deutschland,* the *Communist Manifesto*'s 'workers of the world unite' is replaced on this site by 'confused people of the world unite!' GDR socialism is reconfigured as a value system with which all those who feel marginalized under capitalism can identify, wherever they happen to live. A similar attempt to universalize the notion of being an *Ossi* was also implied in a comment by the west German author of Knobi's *Ostalgie* Seiten (Knobi's *Ostalgie* Pages), another of the virtual GDR sites: 'I don't live in the east, but if they stick to the policies they have now, soon "the east" will be everywhere.'[41] Here we find a further echo of Engler's notion that the east is Germany's 'avant garde'. Rather than the former GDR having eventually to catch up and become like the west, this Web author suggests that the reverse might, in fact, be the case, and that the state of the east is pointing to a dystopian future that might well also be awaiting the west.

As already discussed, the fact that these sites tend to present an idealized ideologically based view of East Germany perhaps makes understandable the reason why we find a mixture of east and west Germans building these sites. As we saw in the Offizielles Internetorgan site the GDR is often used in this group as a nostalgic lens to examine the problems that their authors have with the present trajectory of German society. Thus, as examined in connection with Becker's film *Good Bye, Lenin!*, we see utopian leftwing politics transcends east-west geographical divisions. Nevertheless, it should also be pointed out that a very different picture is often gleaned if we look at the guest books on some of these sites. More often than not, here we find responses by visitors in which geographical background is central, and where the attitudes of easterners towards westerners, and vice versa, continue to be seen almost wholly in terms of the negative mutual stereotyping widespread within discussions of unification in the early 1990s, but which seem to have dissipated more recently in other discourses. On the site Aktion Wiederaufbau der Mauer (Campaign for Re-building the Wall), for example, where visitors are encouraged to sign a petition to reintroduce division (although this is again in the name of satirizing the present-day situation in Germany – as the warning 'Attention Satire' at the head of each page makes clear), the guest book overflows with abusive comments by easterners and westerners providing evidence of their continued mutual loathing.[42]

In many of the virtual GDR sites, authors use the Web as a means of escaping the feelings of marginalization they experience in the physical world and as a place where they can reconstruct a sense of GDR community that they think has been lost since unification. However, in the process, the Web merely appears to highlight further these authors' continued exclusion. Nevertheless, none of the sites, not even Aktion Wiederaufbau der Mauer in reality wishes to undermine German unification. This is made explicit on Honecker.de which, as the 'Organ of the Central Committee for German Unity', sees itself at the vanguard of this very process. Ultimately, then, it would appear that these sites are more concerned with present-day Germany than the GDR past.

In the second group of sites, those termed '*Ostalgic* Remembrance Sites', the GDR does take centre stage. Here authors attempt to find a communal identity and a level of authenticity that, they suggest, is denied to them within other cultural and political forums. In these sites, west German authors played virtually no role. This is understandable because such Web pages tend to present an image of an east German cultural identity predicated not on an ideological and idealized vision of GDR socialism, but rather on a more visceral conception of what it means to be an *Ossi*. A wide range of topics is covered, but the reasons for building these sites, as evident in the questionnaire responses to both surveys, tend to be very similar. First, and most importantly, authors see their Web pages as a useful forum for preserving their own individual past. In answer to the question 'why did you decide to build this site?' responses such as 'it's part of my past', or 'to maintain my own identity' were typical. Second, respondents tended to see themselves as correcting versions of GDR history found in other media, which many respondents see as synonymous with a west German colonialist position. In response to 'what sort of image of the GDR do you wish to present?' respondents said that they wanted to show, for example, 'that not everything was bad in the GDR', that 'the topic has not been discussed enough, or only in a one-sided fashion'.[43] In my second survey, the fifty-year-old Saxon author of the site Der-Jagdflieger.de (The Fighter Pilot) was particularly effusive on this point, speaking for many when he wrote, 'The majority of my life was [spent in the] GDR! I was born there. I worked there. I spent the happiest days of my life there. Why should I keep quiet about it, or forget it?'.[44] In many respects the aims of this group echo the type of *Ostalgie* one finds in Haußmann's *Sonnenallee*. On the one hand, they counter what their authors view as the common claim that it was impossible to have a 'normal' life in the east, while on the other, preserving the specific problems GDR citizens faced. As the forty-year-old Web author of the Digitalen Daten Republik (Digital Data Republic) put it: 'We worked, we served in the army, we were in love with girls, we had friends and relatives, we drank lots of beer' but at the same time this respondent also insists that 'We did our best to run our lives under conditions, for citizens of the West perhaps unimaginable or even unknown.'[45]

One of most developed site amongst this group is the *Zonentalk* project, run by students from the TU in Chemnitz and the Humboldt University. For several years these students have collected reminiscences by individuals about life in the GDR, as well as providing a forum for people who have lost touch to resume contact with each other. As with many east German Web sites, the rationale for *Zonentalk* is the search for a democratic forum of expression.[46] However, here the Web authors suggest that their site can also have a quasi-therapeutic function, recalling both Rheingold's and Chandler's view of the Internet as a space in which marginalized groups, in this case east Germans, can rediscover a sense of community and thus re-enter society. As the Web authors maintain in their introduction to a published book of selected postings from the site:

> Here people who would normally not be given a voice are able to write down and discuss their stories and memories of the GDR. They are able to give up their role as passive recipient and themselves take part in this long overdue discussion in a democratic and interactive manner.[47]

Zonentalk, like DDR-Geschichte.de, is a broad ranging project, and as such is similarly untypical of the majority of Web sites in my surveys. As we have seen, these generally tend to preserve very small aspects of GDR life. If we return to Hine's model of authenticity production, due to the limited scope of many Web pages, they might not appear to be as concerned with the issue of authenticity as other more complex sites. However, on the pages themselves one invariably finds features such as a guest book or a hit counter, which do, perhaps, suggest that their authors wish to present their sites as worth exploring. Within the remembrance group one finds sites dedicated to closed-down GDR firms, such as the Air-travel company Interflug.[48] Or, in one particularly interesting example, a Web author has constructed a highly detailed image of his old firm VEB Eisen- und Hüttenwerke (EHW) Thale (The People's Iron and Smelting Works, Thale) in its heyday, which he identifies as 1986.[49]

As with the first group of nostalgia sites, these could be seen as a dangerous tendency, proof that east German nostalgia is a means of ignoring the truth of SED oppression. However, such views do not take into account that an engagement with ideology is simply not the rationale for these sites. The focus here is almost invariably on everyday life in the east. Other sites in this group include GDR joke pages, sites dedicated to school life in the East, or GDR sport.[50] As such, some of these sites echo the examples of *Ostalgie* discussed in the previous chapter. However, they generally avoid the crass consumerist agenda that we find in the television shows and that so enraged elements of the east German public. That said, they also tend not to exhibit any of the self-reflexive deconstruction of GDR nostalgia discussed in connection with Haußmann's film.

For example, a particularly popular topic for such sites is the military, with Web authors setting up forums to keep in touch with former comrades. This is the rational behind the Digitale Daten Republik and Der-Jagdflieger.de, mentioned above. Both these sites do, it must be said, present a somewhat idealized image of life in the military, pointing to the warmth of friendship between people, which stands in radical contrast to the border-guard account on DDR-Zeitzeugen.de. However, for both these authors the main focus is maintaining contact with friends, rather than promulgating a specific image of the GDR.[51] Nostalgic they may be, and indeed they may also give a forum for the expression of dissatisfaction, but ultimately the majority of these Webpages can be seen as nothing more sinister than east German versions of British and American nostalgia sites such as Friends Reunited, a site that allows individuals to get back in touch with old schoolmates.[52] At the same time, in creating specifically east German Web communities, authors also seek to reclaim their past from what they continue to see as reductive constructions of the GDR that present it as nothing more than a 'Stasi state' that destroyed all 'normal' human interaction. As the author of a site dedicated to GDR radio plays put it (almost seeming to cite the publicity for *Sonnenallee* discussed in Chapter 4) there was a large part of life in the GDR 'that wasn't about the Stasi, the SED and the Wall, but about everyday life'.[53] Feeling that their past experience is being misunderstood, the Web becomes a means of re-establishing an authentic, more 'normal' sense of self.

Throughout the responses of this group of authors (as we saw in the sites that focus on more negative aspects of the regime) there is a strong tendency to assert the objectivity of their site and that they are producing a 'neutral picture, which avoids the view of the media, which only looks at the bad side', as one twenty year-old Web author from Saxony put it (a view that, incidentally, he does not see as having radically altered with the arrival of the GDR nostalgia shows).[54] Crucially, however, these sites also generally insist that they are not trying to bring back the GDR, but to preserve aspects of life within the German historical record. One sixty-one-year-old Web author from Mecklenburg made this point very clearly: 'It's particularly hurtful when people claim ... that we want the GDR back. That's just complete rubbish'.[55] This view does not change across the two surveys. In both there is, therefore, the suggestion that nostalgia for the GDR need not necessarily be seen as a problem. Yet, when in the second survey, respondents were asked directly about the GDR craze of the Summer of 2003, there were very few who had positive comments to make. Indeed, there was very little difference between the authors of sites that criticized the SED regime and those who looked at more positive aspects. Moreover, unlike the newspaper debate about the shows, there was a far clearer sense that this craze was wholly about making money, rather than dealing with the past. One thirty-two-year-old author from Thuringia, for example, saw it a nothing more than the 'commercial exploitation of eastern memories'.[56] A forty-three-year-old author from Saxony confirmed this view, suggesting bluntly (and in the process drawing a similar conclusion to that of Chapter 5) that 'The *Ostalgie* Craze is predominantly a product of the Culture Industry.'[57] However, of particular interest to my study is the fact that this craze is also seen as a further moment of western colonization: 'I don't think very much of this *Ostalgie* Craze', the oldest respondent in the second survey, a seventy-three-year-old Web author from Brandenburg, claimed. 'The east is being treated like a developing state, or a province for colonization. This *Ostalgie* Craze in the media ... is all about people making a name for themselves and for business.'[58] We find here a continued sense that the east and its history is not being treated with respect, and that its citizens remain second-class colonial subjects within contemporary German society.

Between group one and group two, then, we see a shift from an exploitation of GDR ideology for political ends to a more visceral understanding of the relationship between present-day east German identity and the GDR. As we have seen elsewhere, much contemporary *Ostalgie* can similarly be divided into 'ideological' or 'visceral' manifestations of this phenomenon. Moreover, with regard to the Web sites examined here, in both groups there is evidence of the type of dissatisfaction discussed throughout this book, although, neither group would finally seem to wish to return to the past. Rather, their sites are a means of using the Internet to create virtual communities that they feel cannot find expression in the material world.

Interestingly, in the third and fourth groups of Web sites, however, the sense of dissatisfaction described above begins to disappear. Here we find authors who do not necessarily see themselves in any way as the marginalized victims of unification. Instead, the GDR is used as a context for other activities, not explicitly related to the question of dealing with the GDR past at all. Here we return to the issue of hybridity, discussed in connection with east German literature and film. However, rather than Web sites self-consciously evoking hybridity either to critique the influence of western views, as we saw in our discussion of literature, or to show similarities between the east and west, as was the case in *Sonnenallee*, here we see further confirmation of the sentiment shown at the end of Becker's film, namely that these two cultural traditions can live side by side.

The largest group of sites in my surveys were those that dealt with hobbies or the collection of GDR memorabilia. The topics covered here are highly diverse and their authors include collectors of stamps and coins, to GDR motorbikes, and of course, sites built by *Trabant* enthusiasts.[59] To be sure, some of the authors in this group gave responses in their questionnaires that were very similar to those found in group two. Like the '*Ostalgic* Rememberance Sites', some of these Web authors saw their sites as a corrective to other misreadings of GDR history promulgated, it was generally felt, by ignorant westerners. The forty-eight-year-old author of a Web page about east German cars, for example, is one of many to make the claim already discussed in connection with sites in group one and two that 'it wasn't all bad during GDR times ... In west Germany the GDR is usually seen as something to be laughed at, but lots of people in east Germany see it in a different way.'[60] Many of the subjects covered by these sites, as was the case with the remembrance sites, are similar to the topics found in the *Ostalgie* television shows.

However, again as with the Web page discussed above, as well as in this Web author's remark, the tone is very different. Unlike the presentation of the *Trabant* in the *Ostalgie Shows*, or indeed in the tourist industry more generally, on the Web sites we find authors wishing to correct their re-exoticization of East German experience. Instead, there is an insistence on the normality of GDR material culture, in a similar fashion to east German advertising earlier in the 1990s. For example, this particular respondent went on: 'I want to show that, given the conditions then, the *Trabant* car was not as bad as it's now always presented.' For this individual, the *Trabi* is not a 'cute' tourist gimmick, but a valued part of her past heritage and thus no different from an equivalent object in west German cultural history.[61]

Although some of the responses here are similar to those found in group two, there is also a crucial difference. The main focus of these sites is not the GDR *per se*, but the objects under investigation in their own right. This is a particularly pronounced tendency in a number of sites concerned with the GDR's now largely forgotten microcomputer, the 'Z1013'. For example, in response to the question about the image of the GDR the site is to present, one thirty-year-old Saxon, currently living in China, told me:

I don't want to create any picture [of the GDR]. That is not the aim of this site. It is all about my computer. If anyone wants to draw conclusions about the GDR, then that's up to them … This page is just a collection of all the documents I could find on the topic of the Z1013.[62]

On this site we find links to a large number of other sites on the topic of the 'Z1013' (an attempt, perhaps, to point to the importance of this topic for a number of Web users, and so, in turn, of this author's Web site), as well as detailed circuit drawings, downloadable programmes and other technical information. While the Web author admits that the GDR is important to his site, because without it this piece of technology would not have existed, it is the computer, not the East German state, that is its real concern: 'If the Z1013 was not connected with the GDR but with Great Britain (like the BBC Acorn), I would have done exactly the same thing.'[63]

In the final group of Web sites, this tendency to underplay the importance of the GDR in a Web project becomes even more pronounced. Here, any implied nostalgia for the GDR appears to be wholly the by-product of other Web-based activities. In this group, we find the type of personal homepage common throughout the WWW, where an *Ostalgie* section is just one amongst many, the casualness of its inclusion seeming to suggest that it is just there to fill up some space.[64] Or, we find sites about places in the east that might happen to mention life before 1989, but which do not dwell on this topic. A good example of this tendency is a site dedicated to the Rose Garden in Dresden which, its Web author informed me, is the only park in the city to survive intact from the 1930s. This particular author was clearly baffled by the point of my questionnaire, seeing in it no relevance to his site: 'Of course, it's obvious that a site about a rose garden is fundamentally about roses. This was a topic in the GDR as much as it is in the Federal Republic.'[65] This is not, for the author, an 'east German' Web site, and he certainly has no political axe to grind.

Another common response by this group of authors to the question 'why did you decide to build this site?' was that they wanted to practise building Web pages and just needed something to put on them. A forty-two-year-old author of a personal homepage from Saxony, for example, suggested that the reason he built his site 'was just due to a technical interest in computers. The topic suggested itself because I grew up in the GDR.'[66] The key trend in responses by Web authors of this group of sites, as already seen in the Dresden Rose Garden site, is the apolitical nature of their project. Individuals here generally refused to accept that they wanted to produce a specific picture of the GDR, often claiming that the only reason they built their site was 'for fun'.

Some of the most interesting sites amongst this group are the small number that use the GDR as a basis for role-playing games. We have already discussed one of these, Laputa, in connection with those pages that present a negative image of the GDR. However, most of these virtual worlds are far less overtly political. They are mainly centred around the 'Micronation' game site, in which individuals construct a 'cyber society' that they then invite other Web users to enter and play the specific roles they are allotted. One of the most developed of these I found was the world of Kaputistan. The opening page initially seems to echo the virtual GDRs of group one: 'Kaputistan is a pleasant little state in the south of the Internet. Here there still is true communism.' However, it quickly becomes clear that there is very little that is overtly political about this site. As the site's Web author underlined in his response to the questionnaire: 'This site is just for fun, and is really only of any use to people who actively participate in the Micronations project.'[67] Indeed, the main function of this joke world, run by the *Sozialistische Einheitsbrauerei* (Socialist Unity Brewery, a play on the name of the SED), seems to be to provide a space for its Web author to publish his pop art, art that actually gives an interesting insight into the relationship of many of this group's members to their past.

In the one of the site's pages, entitled VEB für Süßwaren (The People's Sweet Company) we see East German cultural references superimposed onto Western brands of chocolate. These might be read as a critique of the westernization of GDR culture. However, for the Web author himself at least, this could not be further from the truth. Here, even more clearly than in the first two groups, the expression of an east German heritage in the form of *Milka* being turned into *Mielke* chocolate and a *Mars* bar being transformed into a *Marx* bar is not the ideological rejection of western capitalism feared by some critics of these Web sites. Rather, it is simply a joke, the importance of the name change in the case of both brands being the pun not the politics. Nevertheless, it also provides a statement of the continuing relevance of the GDR past for an individual who is fully versed in, and indeed accepting of, the values of capitalist consumer culture.

In this last group, then, we can see, perhaps, a new phase in the use of the GDR past in contemporary Germany, where hybridity is no longer the self-reflexive, and at times provocative, stance that it is in much of the rest of this study, through which an individual attempts actively to negotiate his or her place in post-unification society. Rather, we see that although an individual might come from a different historical context to others, this need have very little, or no, bearing on his or her attitude towards present-day society.

Conclusions

Over the last six chapters, I have sought to use a number of postcolonial concepts to help examine perceptions of the GDR as having been 'colonized' by the west. In my discussion of the WWW, we can, at times, continue to use these concepts to highlight the same attitudes and prejudices we have seen throughout the volume. First, we see sites that paint the GDR as a totalitarian *Unrechtsstaat*. In postcolonial terms, this is the type of 'orientalism' we examined in connection with the Enquete Commissions' reports, where the GDR is used as a means of underlining the legitimacy of unification as the expansion of the FRG. Specifically, East Germany becomes the FRG's 'abject' historical other, from which the population has now been redeemed. Second, we find Web authors who wish to counter or, in the language of Chapter 3 to 'write back' against, such 'orientalism', adopting in the process a number of strategies. For example, this is attempted through the reappropriation of an idealized ideological image of east Germanness, a renaissance of the type of GDR identity that the SED attempted, in vain, to instil in the entire population.

As such we find the reverse side of the GDR as an abject 'Orient'. Instead, it becomes an idealized political other, through which both east and west Germans can recuperate leftwing political positions that they feel have been challenged since unification, an event that has brought with it a string of unexpected social and economic reforms, as Germany has been forced to face the challenges of rebuilding the eastern regions, as well as the broader issue of dealing with its changing place in the world. Consequently, it is clear that the majority of such sites, along with most of the manifestations of *Ostalgie* seen across the cultural discourses I have examined here, are not intent upon refounding a separate East German state, as might be concluded from the reporting of them in the press. Rather, they are an attempt, often by means of satire, to examine a western capitalist value system from *within* unified Germany.

In the second group of *Ostalgie* sites we see a shift from an ideological to a visceral understanding of the place of the GDR in contemporary culture. Again, this could perhaps be seen as evidence of a continuing, and worrying, lack of unity between the citizens of the former FRG and GDR. However, as we have also seen throughout this volume, but most obviously in my discussion of literature and film, such nostalgia is hardly a uniquely east German phenomenon. The suggestion that *Ostalgie* need not be viewed as a barrier to inner unification is then further emphasised by the existence of the final two groups of sites. In the representation of the East German past in many of the hobby-based sites in the surveys, or in 'virtual worlds', such as Kaputistan, we see perhaps more clearly than in any of the other areas discussed in the book that the continued existence of GDR cultural markers does not necessarily imply a rejection of the realities of present-day German society. Indeed, in the case of Kaputistan the Web site is, rather, very much a product of them. Here, we find a further example of the expression of a GDR heritage as part of a postcolonial hybrid identity. However, perhaps even more obviously than in our earlier discussions, manifestations of such hybridity on the Web have nothing to do with the much maligned 'identity of defiance'. Instead, they suggest the complete ownership and co-existence of both contemporary western consumer culture and of the GDR past, rather than the latter being seen as a fly in the ointment of the former.

At this point, we might return to the cover of this book and Langhelle's installation, 'DDR®'. The image of the GDR as an advertising logo on one level, of course, might provide a defiant critique of the commercialization of eastern material culture which has brought with it a concomitant trivialization of the record of SED's dictatorial regime, criticisms to which the television's *Ostalgie* shows, in particular, have been subjected. However, conversely, the Alexanderplatz pop art exhibition, like the final group of Web sites discussed in this chapter, might suggest that east German culture need not be viewed as having been subjugated to and marginalized by a western colonial master. Instead, it might be symbolic of the final integration of GDR culture into present-day Germany. As such, can we perhaps see this, like the final group of Web sites, as an example of real 'inner unity', where although individuals might have different biographies, they show that they have a shared understanding of how to approach present-day society. This is a tendency that was also mentioned in the examination of east German advertising in Chapter 5, where we saw that while marketing companies might make a great deal of east German distinctiveness, in terms of actual consumer patterns, where a person is from plays only a very small role.

As discussed at the outset of this volume, in the second decade after unification, clearly the economic situation in Germany remains difficult. While the programme of financial transfers to the east has brought many benefits to the population, they have not yet created the sustained economic growth the eastern regions require, if the population is to be prevented from voting with its feet and moving west. Of course, as I have also suggested, perhaps this growth will never appear, at least not to the extent that many in the east would wish. Nevertheless, with regard to the question of inner unity, as it is reflected in German culture, the situation might not be as critical as it first seemed. This is a finding confirmed in a recent study by Rita Kuczynski. In the interviews she conducted in the eastern regions in 2003, she suggests 'there was no mention of nostalgia, self-pity or the other clichéd characteristics when one thinks of "east Germans"'. Consequently, she concludes 'it is perhaps high time that we let a lot more voices be heard in the song we sing about east Germans'.[68]

Kuczynski's comments were published just prior to the *Ostalgie* craze. Nevertheless, they are not discounted by it. Indeed, at the time of writing this conclusion *Ostalgie* would seem to be going the way of all crazes as its impact lessens. That said, the GDR past clearly still remains an important element within the social consciousness of present-day German society, and as is clear from some of the cultural spheres examined in this volume, the project of working through this aspect of Germany's problematic past has not yet reached completion. However, my examination of 'grass roots' attitudes to the east on Web pages shows that for some authors at least, while their experience of the GDR is part of their biography, it is not necessarily the defining aspect of their identity, and certainly need not be seen as impeding unification. Consequently, in answer to the question posed in Chapter 1 of this study, perhaps we are indeed seeing here the beginnings of a truly 'post'-colonial moment in east German cultural identity, where we can at last begin to move beyond the construction of any hierarchical 'oriental' relationship between the eastern and western regions.

Whether the role of GDR history will remain important to the German social psyche in years to come remains to be seen. In my first survey, it appeared that it would at least continue to be an important issue for the first post-GDR generation, since 17 per cent of the authors of east German sites were under twenty. Other sources, such as the 2002 Shell report on German youth, or the recent spate of autobiographical texts by young east Germans, confirm this view.[69] The findings of my second survey, however, paint a different picture, suggesting that interest in the GDR amongst this age group is not particularly pronounced and, consequently, that its importance might be on the wane. Nevertheless, whatever importance the topic might currently still have, it is also clear that we need not fear east German 'reds under the beds', communicating through cyberspace and trying to undermine the democracy of the Berlin Republic. The GDR continues to be examined and instrumentalized in a variety of ways by a wide range of people in both east and west: from marking political positions to learning how to use computer software. Yet, although the way the GDR is used is still worthy of exploration, the vast majority of this use is generally far more mundane than much of its reporting. As such, perhaps the only conclusion that can finally be made is, as Kuczynski's study implies, that 'inner unity' need not mean homogeneity, or as Hans-Joachim Veen puts it, 'We live in a state of inner unity and diversity. Democracy does not require more unity. Everything else is politics and lies beyond the realm of fundamental questions of state cohesion.'[70] Thus, far from being a threat to social stability, might not the continued existence of certain cultural legacies of the GDR, within a context where the vast majority of the population accept the structures of the unified state, point, in fact, to the existence of a healthy, democratic culture, a vibrant sphere of politics, in Veen's terms, which can support a diverse range of views?

Notes

1. 'Aufholjagd bei De-Domains, *Spiegel Online*, www.spiegel.de/netzwelt/technologie/0,1518,196235,00.html, 15 May 2002.
2. 'Immer mehr Ostdeutsche benutzen das Internet', *heise online* www.heise.de/newsticker/meldung/45426, 18 March 2004. For further discussion of the development of Internet use in the German-speaking world see Inke Arns, *Netzkulturen*, Hamburg: Europäische Verlangsanstalt, 2002.

3. For reasons of space, I confine my discussion in this chapter to the WWW, leaving aside other cyberspace phenomena such as Usenet news groups and Internet Relay Chat.

4. For further discussion of this popular conception of cyberspace see L. Miller, 'Women and children first: Gender and the settling of the electronic frontier', in *Resisting the Virtual Life: The Culture of Politics of Information*, San Francisco: City Lights, 1995, ed. by J. Brook and I.A. Boal, I.A., pp. 49–57 (p. 57)

5. Henryk M. Broder, 'Eine Kalaschnikow für 98 Euro', *Der Spiegel*, 41 (2000), 70.

6. Howard Rheingold, *The Virtual Community: Homesteading on the Electronic Frontier*, Reading: Addison-Wesley, 1993, p. 14.

7. Rheingold, p. 14.

8. Sherry Turkle, *Life on the Screen: Identity in the age of the Internet*, New York: Touchstone, 1995.

9. Turkle, p. 14

10. Turkle, p. 12.

11. Daniel Chandler, 'Personal Home Pages and the Construction of Identities on the Web', www.aber.ac.uk/media/Documents/short/webident.html, accessed 10 January 2001.

12. Flis Henwood et al 'Critical perspectives on technologies, In/equalities and the information society', in *Technology and In/equality: Questioning the information society*, ed. by Sally Wyatt et al., London: Routledge, 2000, pp. 1–18 (p. 8–9).

13. James Slevin, *The Internet and Society*, Cambridge: Polity, 2000, p. 49–50.

14. Slevin, p. 72.

15. Christine Hine, *Virtual Ethnography*, London: Sage, 2000, p. 120.

16. Judith S. Donath, 'Identity and deception in the virtual community', *Communities in Cyberspace*, ed. by Marc A. Smith and Peter Kollock, London: Routledge, 1999, pp. 29–59.

17. Hine, p. 89.

18. Chandler.

19. For a discussion of my first survey see Paul Cooke, 'Ostdeutsche kulturelle Identität und der *Cyberspace*', *Berliner Debatte Initial*, 1 (2003). Some of the Web sites examined here also formed part of my second sample group and consequently have also been included. I initially used as my point of departure the figures on Google for the term 'ddr'. This generated some 2.25 million hits (rising by the time of my second survey to 8 million). However, on closer inspection it became clear that these figures were being swelled by sites dealing with the 'Dance Dance Revolution', a computer-based dance game

which has swept across North America in recent years, the acronym for which is 'DDR'. Consequently, these figures were not a reliable indicator of interest in the GDR on the WWW.

20. DDR Webring, home.germany.net/rageville/de/ddrwebring.html; DDR-im-Web.de, www.ddr-im-web.de/index.asp; DDR-im-WWW, www.ddr-im-www.de/; *DDR-Suche*, www.ddr-suche.de/.
21. DDR-Geschichte.de, www.ddr-geschichte.de/, email, 29 January 2004.
22. Email, 29 January 2004.
23. DDR-Zeitzeugen.de, www.ddr-zeitzeugen.de/NVA/Gruppendynamik/ gruppendynamik.html, accessed 23 February 2004.
24. Laputa, www.laputa.de, email, 1 February 2004.
25. See, for example, Berliner Mauer, userpage.chemie.fu-berlin.de/ BIW/d_mauer.html; Berliner Mauer, www.berliner-mauer.de/; Berliner Mauer online, www.dailysoft.com/berlinwall/archive/ index_de.htm; Grenztruppen.de, www.grenztruppen.de; Grenz-turm.de, www.grenzturm.info; all accessed 21 February 2004 and Knast in der DDR, www.belfalas.de/knast.htm, accessed 14 February 2004.
26. Steffen Winter, 'Jadgfieber im Osten', *Der Spiegel*, 7 (2000), 114.
27. Email, 6 February 2004.
28. *nierenspende.de* www.nierenspende.de, accessed 3 February 2004.
29. 'Internet-Zensur in Deutschland', odem.org/informationsfreiheit, accessed 5 March 2004 (emphasis in original).
30. stasiopfer.de, www.stasiopfer.de; *H.T.'s* Stasi-Infoseite, www.geoci-ties.com/m_bakunin_de, accessed 4 March 2004.
31. Email, 16 February 2004.
32. Email, 8 June 2004.
33. For further discussion of this case see Henryk M. Broder, 'Empfindliche Strafen: Der Berliner Datenschutzbeauftragte interve-niert zu Gunsten ehemaliger Stasi-Mitarbeiter und setzt ein Opfer des DDR-Regimes unter Druck', *Spiegel* 20 (2002), 52.
34. See, for example, 'Sie verlassen jetzt West-Berlin', *Spiegel Online*, www.spiegel.de/netzwelt/netzkultur/0,1518,160479,00.html, 2 Oct-ober 2001. Here I have adjusted the figures I used in my earlier article to remove the group of sites that mainly consisted of lists of Web sites which had no other significant thematic content.
35. Here I have refined the groups I identified in my earlier published analysis of Survey One, in which I treated groups two and three as a single unit.
36. Email, 20 March 2002.
37. Offizielles Internetorgan der DDR-Staatsregierung im Exil, home.t-online.de/home/d_d_r/, accessed 13 March 2002.

38. Email, 20 March 2002.
39. Email, 20 March 2002.
40. Honecker.de, www.honecker.de/start2.html, accessed 28 February 2004.
41. Knobi's Ostalgie Seiten, www.mknobi.de/ostalgie/, accessed 3 March 2002, email, 15 March 2002.
42. Aktion Wiederaufbau Der Mauer, www.liquid2k.com/ddr, accessed 12 March 2002.
43. Emails, 10, 15 March.
44. Der-Jagdflieger.de, home.t-online.de/home/juergen.gruhl/, accessed 23 January 2004, email, 1 February 2004.
45. Digitale Daten Republik, www.tf-home.de, accessed 1 March 2002, email, 15 March 2002.
46. Zonentalk, www.zonentalk.de, acessed 5 January 2002.
47. Felix Mühlberg and Annegret Schmidt, 'Eine Einführung', in *Zonentalk*, ed. by Felix Mühlberg and Annegret Schmidt, Cologne: Böhlau, 2001, pp. 7–9 (p. 9).
48. www.interflug.net, accessed 2 January 2004.
49. VEB Eisen- und Hüttenwerke (EHW) Thale, www.veb-ehw-thale.de.vu/, accessed 23 January 2002.
50. See, for example, Sad Girl, www.mrsunshine.de/sadgirl/ddr.htm; Lutz seine DDR-Homepage, www.old-gdr.de; Die Witzige Seite des Lebens, jokes.notrix.net, all accessed 2 February 2002.
51. Emails, 15 March 2002, 1 February 2004.
52. Friends Reunited, www.friendsreunited.co.uk, accessed 10 November 2001.
53. DDR-Hörspiele.de, www.ddr-hoerspiele.de/hoerspielindex.html, accessed 15 January 2004, email 14 February 2004.
54. Email, 29 January 2004.
55. Email, 20 January 2004.
56. www.ostmetal.aeilke.de, accessed 15 January 2004, email, 5 February 2004.
57. Email, 23 February 2004.
58. Email, 20 February 2004.
59. See, for example, DDR-Münzen, www.ddr-muenzen.de; DDR-Briefmarken, www.ddr-briefmarken.de; Trabant IG Unterfranken, members.aol.com/trabiigunterfr; Trabiseite.de, www.t-lino.de/trabi-fan, all accessed 15 January 2004.
60. Rallyfahrer, home.t-online.de/home/Rallyfahrer/Formel1/rallye.htm; email, 30 January 2004.
61. Email, 30 January 2004.
62. See, for example, KC Club, www.iee.et.tu-dresden.de/~kc-club; Die

ultimative Z1013 Seite, z1013.purespace.de, accessed 15 January 2004.

63. Der Mikrorechnerbausatz Z1013, www.nirvana.informatik.uni-halle.de/~ziermann/DE/z1013.html, email, 7 February 2004.

64. See, for example, Steffen Treptau, home.t-online.de/home/steffen. treptau, accessed 10 January 2004.

65. Rosengarten Dresden, www.rosengarten-dresden.de, accessed 15 February 2004, email, 2 March 2004.

66. Kreutzschmer, people.freenet.de/kreutzschmer, accessed 2 February 2004, email, 8 February 2004.

67. Kaputistan, www.kaputistan.de, accessed 3 February 2002, email, 21 February 2002.

68. Rita Kuczynski, *Im Westen was Neues? Ostdeutsche auf dem Weg in die Normalität*, Berlin: Parthas, 2003, p. 8.

69. Klaus, Hurrelmann, *Jugend 2002. 14. Shell Jugendstudie*, Frankfurt/Main: Fischer, 2002. See, for example, Claudia Rusch, *Meine freie deutsche Jugend*, and Jana Hensel *Zonenkinder*, Reinbek: Rowohlt, 2002.

70. Hans-Joachim Veen, '"Inner Unity" Back to the Community Myth? A Plea for a Basic Consensus', *German Politics*, 3(6) (1997), pp. 1–15 (p. 12).

Bibliography

Adorno, T.W., *Minima Moralia*, Frankfurt/Main: Suhrkamp, 1951.

Ahbe, T., 'Der Dammbruch: Anschlag auf den Einheitsgeschmack', *Freitag*, 9 August 2003.

—— 'Deutsche Eliten und deutsche Umbrüche: Erfolg und Verschwinden verschiedener deutscher Elite-Gruppen und deren Wertepositionen', *Deutschland Archiv*, 2 (2003), pp. 191–206.

Ahmad, A., 'Orientalism and After', in *Colonial Discourse and Post-Colonial Theory: A Reader*, ed. by P. Williams and L. Chrisman, Harlow: Longman, 1993, pp. 162–171.

Ahrends, M., 'General Absolution: Thomas Brussig auf der Suche nach dem großen Wir', *Freitag*, 12 April 1996.

Anz T. (ed.), *'Es geht nicht um Christa Wolf' Der Literaturstreit im vereinten Deutschland*, Frankfurt/Main: Fischer, 1995.

Arendt, H., *The Origins of Totalitarianism* London: Allen & Unwin, 1951.

Arnold-de Simine, S., 'Theme Park GDR? The Aestheticization of Memory in post-*Wende* Museums, Literature and Film', in *Cultural Memory and Historical Consciousness in the German-Speaking World since 1500*, ed. by Christian Emden and David Midgley, Oxford: Peter Lang, 2004, pp. 253–80.

Arns, I., *Netzkulturen*, Hamburg: Europäische Verlangsanstalt, 2002.

Arzheimer, K. and Falter J.W., 'Ist der Osten wirklich rot? Das Wahlverhalten bei der Bundestagswahl 2002 in Ost-West-Perspektive', *Aus Politik und Zeitgeschichte*, B 49–50 (2002), 27–35.

Ashcroft, B., Griffiths G. and Tiffin H. (eds), *The Empire Writes Back: Theory and Practice in Postcolonial Literatures*, London: Routledge, 1989.

—— *The Postcolonial Studies Reader*, London: Routledge, 1995.

Aspekte, first broadcast ZDF 24 March 2000.

Aufholjagd bei De-Domains', *Special Online*, www.spiegel.de/ nettwelt/technologie/0,1518,196235,00.html, 15 May 2002.

Bach, I., *Wir kennen die Fremde nicht*, Berlin: Ullstein, 2000.

Barker, P. (ed.), *The GDR and Its History: Rückblick und Revision Die DDR im Spiegel der Enquete-Kommissionen*, Amsterdam: Rodopi, 2000.

Barker, P. (ed.), *The Party of Democratic Socialism: Modern Post-Communism or Nostalgic Populism?* Amsterdam: Rodopi, 1998.

Bartsch, M., '"Kost the Ost" zahlt sich nicht aus', *taz*, 6 November 2003.

Bathrick, D., *The Powers of Speech: the politics of culture in the GDR*, Lincoln: University of Nebraska Press, 1995.

Beckmann, C. 'Die Auseinandersetzung um den Vergleich von "Drittem Reich" und DDR vor dem Hintergrund der Diskussion um Möglichkeiten und Grenzen vergleichender Geschichtsforschung', *Deutsche Studien*, 38 (2002), pp. 9–26.

Berg, S., Hornig F., Kurbjuweit, D., Martens, H., Reiermann, C., Reke, I., Robel, S., Schimmöller, H., Steingart, G., Winter, S. 'Tabuzone Ost', *Der Spiegel*, 15 (2004), pp. 24–41.

Berghahn, D., *Hollywood behind the Wall: The Cinema of East Germany*, Manchester: Manchester University Press, 2005.

Betts, P., 'The Twilight of the Idols: East German Memory and Material Culture', *The Journal of Modern History*, 72 (2000), pp. 731–65.

Beyer, A., 'Showformate- Trends und Veränderungen', in *Unterhaltung und Unterhaltungsrezeption* ed. by G. Roters, W. Klingler, and M. Gerhards, Baden Baden: Nomos, pp. 173–181.

Bhabha, H. K., *The Location of Culture*, London: Routledge, 1994.

Biermann, W., 'Der Lichtblick im gräßlichen Fatalismus der Geschichte: Rede zur Verleihung des Georg-Büchner- Preises', *Die Zeit*, 25 October 1991.

Biermann, W., *Für meine Genossen*, Berlin: Klaus Wagenbach, 1972.

Bisky, J., 'Beleidigend', *Berliner Zeitung*, 29 January 2000.

Blum, M., 'Remaking the East German Past: Ostalgic, Identity and Material Culture', *The Journal of Popular Culture*, 34 (1000), 229–54.

Bock, P., 'Von der Tribunal-Idee zur Enquete-Kommission des Bundestages "Aufarbeitung von Geschichte und Folgen der SED-Diktatur in Deutschland"', *Deutschland Archiv*, 28 (1995), pp. 1171–83.

Böthig, P., 'Trickbetrüger der Schuld: Heute erscheinen Sascha Andersons Erinnerung, die einfach nur Sascha Anderson heiße', *Der Tagesspiegel*, 2 March 2002.

Böthig, P., and Klaus M. (eds), *MachtSpiele: Literatur und Staats-sicherheit im Fokus Prenzlauer Berg*, Leipzig: Reclam, 1993.

Bradshaw, P., 'Good Bye Lenin! *Ostalgie* ain't what it used to be', *Guardian*, 25 July 2003.

Brandt, H.-U., Kaiser, A., Matt, E., Steinbacher, G., *Das war unser Kessel Buntes*, Berlin: Kai Homilius Verlag, 2002.

Brockmann, S., *Literature and German Reunification*, Cambridge: CUP, 1999.

Broder, H.M., 'Eine Kalaschnikow für 98 Euro', *Der Spiegel*, 41 (2000), p. 70.

—— 'Empfindliche Strafen: Der Berliner Datenschutzbeauftragte interveniert zu Gunsten ehemaliger Stasi-Mitarbeiter und setzt ein Opfer desDDR-Regimes unter Druck', *Der Spiegel*, 20 (2002), p. 52.

Brussig, T., Helden wie wir, Berlin: Verlag Volk & Welt, 1995.

—— Am kürzeren Ende der *Sonnenallee*, Berlin: Volk & Welt, 1999.

—— 'Mrux, die deutscheit', *Der Tegesspiegel*,31 August 2003.

Bryson, P.J., *The Consumer under Socialist Planning: The East German Case*, New York: Praeger, 1984.

Buch, H.C., 'Schönen Gruß von Charlie Chaplin', *Der Tagespiegel*, 9 November 1999.

Burger, H., 'Diskussion ohne Ritual oder: Der domestiziert Rezipient', in *Redeshows. Fernsehdiskussionen in der Diskussion*, ed. by W. Holly, P. Kühn and U. Puschel, Tübingen: Niemeyer, 1989, pp. 116–41.

Burmeister, B., *Unter dem Namen Norma*, Stuttgart: Klett-Cotta, 1994.

Burns, R. (ed.), *German Cultural Studies: an introduction*, Oxford: OUP, 1995.

Cafferty, H., '*Sonnenallee*: Taking Comedy Seriously in Unified Germany', in *Textual Responses to German Unification: Processing Historical and Social Change in Literature and Film*, ed. by C. A. Costabile-Heming, R. J. Halverson and K. A. Foell, Berlin: Walter de Gruyter Verlag, 2001, pp. 253–71.

Chakrabarty, D., *Provincializing Europe: Postcolonial Thought and Historical Difference*, Princeton: Princeton University Press, 2000.

Chandler, D. 'Personal Home Pages and the Construction of Identities on the Web', www.aber.ac.uk/media/Documents/short/webident.html.

Childs, D. and Popplewell R., *The Stasi. The East German Intelligence and Security Service, 1917–89* Basingstoke: Macmillan, 1996

Chioni Moore, D., 'Is the Post- in Postcolonial the Post- in Post-Soviet? Towards a Global Postcolonial Critique', *PMLA*, 1(116) (2001), pp. 111–28.

Cooke, P. *Speaking the Taboo: a study of the Work of Wolfgang Hilbig*, Amsterdam: Rodopi, 2000.

—— 'Ostdeutsche kulturelle Identität und der Cyberspace', *Berliner Debatte Initial*, 1 (2003), pp. 15–26.

Cooke, P., and Plowman, A. (eds) *German Writers and the Politics of Culture: Dealing with the Stasi*, Basingstoke: Palgrave, 2003.

Cooke, P., and Grix, J. (eds) *East Germany Continuity and Change*, Amsterdam: Rodopi, 2000.

Cooke, P., and Hubble, N. 'Die volkseigene Opposition? The Stasi and Alternative Culture in the GDR', *German Politics*, 6 (2) (1997), pp. 117–38.

Corino, K., 'Deckname Lyrik: Die Verfolgung eines Dichters', *Stuttgarter Zeitung*, 15 December 1990.

—— 'Es ist unglaublich viel gelogen worden: Ein Gespräch mit dem Schriftsteller Reiner Kunze über seine Stasi-Akte', *Frankfurter Rundschau*, 16 January 1991.

Cornils, I., 'Long Memories: The German Student Movement in Recent Fiction', *GLL*, 56 (2003), pp. 89–101.

Dahn, D., *Westwärts und nicht vergessen: vom Unbehagen in der Einheit*, Berlin: Rowohlt, 1996.

Davidson, J. E. 'Overcoming Germany's Past(s) in Film since the *Wende*', *Seminar*, 4(33) (1997), pp. 307–21.

—— *Deterritorializing the New German Cinema*, Minneapolis: University of Minnesota Press, 1999.

Decker, G., 'Vielfalt statt Einfalt: Zum Ost-West-Kinoerfolg von *Good Bye, Lenin!*', *Neues Deutschland*, 3 August 2003.

Delius, F.C., *Die Birnen von Ribbeck*, Reinbek: Rowohlt, 1991.

Dennis, M., 'Perceptions of GDR Society and its Transformation: East German Identity Ten Years after Unity', in *The New Germany in the East: Policy Agendas and Social Developments since Unification*, ed. by C. Flockton, E. Kolinsky and R. Pritchard, London: Frank Cass, 2000, pp. 87–105.

—— *The Stasi Myth and Reality*, London: Longman, 2003.

Detjen, C., *Die anderen Deutschen: Wie der Osten die Republik verändert*, Bonn: Bouvier, 1999.

Deutscher Bundestag, *Materialien der Enquete-Kommission 'Aufarbeitung von Geschichte und Folgen der SED-Diktatur in Deutschland'*, Baden-Baden: Nomos Verlag; Frankfurt am Main: Suhrkamp, 1995.

—— *Materialien der Enquete-Kommission 'Überwindung der Folgen der SED-Diktatur im Prozeß der deutschen Einheit'*, Baden-Baden: Nomos Verlag; Frankfurt am Main: Suhrkamp, 1999.

'Diana und ihr Butler Verratoder Huldigung?', *Superillu* 45 (30 October 2003), p. 98.

Donath, J.S., 'Identity and deception in the virtual community', *Communities in Cyberspace*, ed. by M.A. Smith and P. Kollock, London: Routledge, 1999.

Drilo, C., 'Das RAF-Mode-Phantom' http://www.salonrouge.de/raf-hype2.htm.

Duckenfield, M., and N. Calhoun, 'Invasion of the Ampelmännchen', *German Politics*, 3(6) (1997), pp. 54–69.

Dümcke, W., and Vilmar F. (eds), *Kolonialisierung der DDR: Kritische Analysen und Alternativen des Einigungsprozesses*, Münster: Agenda Verlag, 1996.

Eckert, R., 'Straßenumbenennung und Revolution in Deutschland', in *Vergangenheitsbewältigung*, ed. by E. Jesse and K. Löw, Berlin: Duncker & Humblot, 1997, pp. 45–52.

Elis und Escher: Die DDR – nur eine Lachnummer? first broadcast, MDR 15 September 2003.

Elsaesser, T., *Fassbinder's Germany: History Identity Subject*, Amsterdam: Amsterdam University Press, 1996.

Elsner, G., *Die Riesenzwerge*, Hamburg: Rotbuch, 1964.

Elster, J., Offe C. and K. Preuss U.K., *Institutional Design in Postcommunist Societies*, Cambridge: CUP, 1998.

Emmerich, W., *Kleine Literaturgeschichte der DDR: Erweiterte Neuausgabe*, Leipzig: Gustav Kiepenheuer, 1996.

Endler, A., 'Gelächter im Akten-Whirlpool', in *Das Vergängliche überlisten. Selbstbefragungen deutscher Autoren*, ed. by I. Czechowski, Leipzig: Reclam, 1996, p. 149.

Endlich, L., *NeuLand: Ganz einfache Geschichten*, Frankfurt/Main: Fischer, 2001.

Engler, W., *Die Ostdeutschen als Avantgarde*, Berlin: Aufbau, 2002.

Eppelmann, R., *Fremd im eigenen Haus- Mein Leben im anderen Deutschland*, Cologne: Kiepenheuer & Witsch, 1993.

Faktor, J., 'Hilbigs »Ich«: Das Rätsel des Buches blieb von der Kritik unberührt', *Wolfgang Hilbig*, ed. by H.L. Arnold, Munich: Text & Kritik, 1994, pp. 75–79.

Fischer, A., Fritzsche, Y., Fuchs-Heinnchs, W., Manchmeider, R., *ugend 2000 13. Shell Jugendstudie*, Opladen, Leske+Budrich, 2000.

Fiske, J., and Hartely J., *Reading Television*, 2nd edition, London: Routledge, 2003.

Fricke, K.W., *MfS intern*, Cologne: Verlag Wissenschaft und Politik, 1991.

Friedrichmeyer, S., Lennox S. and Zantop S. (eds), *The Imperialist Imagination: German Colonialism and its Legacy*, Michigan: University of Michigan, 1998.

Fritze, L., *Die Gegenwart des Vergangenen: Über das Weiterleben der DDR nach ihrem Ende*, Weimar: Böhlau, 1997.

Früh, W., and Stiehler, H.J. *Fernsehen in Ostdeutschland: Eine Unter-*

suchung zum Zusammenhang zwischen Programmangebot und Rezeption, Berlin: Vista Verlag, 2002.

Früh, W.,Hasebrink, U., Krottz, F., Kuhlmann, C., Stiehler, H. J. *Ostdeutschland im Fernsehen*, Munich: KoPäd, 1999.

Fulbrook, M., *Anatomy of a Dictatorship: Inside the GDR 1949–1989*, Oxford: OUP, 1995.

—— 'Heroes, Victims, and Villains in the History of the German Democratic Republic', in *Rewriting the German Past: History and Identity in the New Germany*, New Jersey: Humanities, 1997, p. 175–96.

—— *German National Identity after the Holocaust*, Cambridge: Polity, 1999.

Funck, G., 'Im Auge des Sturms: Wird ein Autor entdeckt: Bernd Lichtenbergs *Good Bye, Lenin!*', *FAZ*, 15 February 2003.

Funder, A., *Stasiland: Stories from Behind the Berlin Wall*, London: Granta, 2003.

Gansera, R., 'Das Leben ist ja kein Genre: Wolfgang Becker über alte Kameraregeln, junge Ganzkörperschauspieler und seinen Film "*Good Bye, Lenin!*"', *Süddeutsche Zeitung*, 13 March. 2003.

Garaventa, A., *Showmaster, Gäste Publikum: Über das Dialogische in Unterhaltungsshows*, Bern: Peter Lang, 1993.

Garton Ash, T., *The File: A Personal History*, London: Flamingo, 1997.

Gauck, J., 'Von der Würde der Unterdrücktn', in *Aktenkundig*, ed. by H.J. Schädlich, Reinbek: Rowoht, 1993, pp. 256–75.

Gaus, G., *Wo Deutschland liegt*, Hamburg: Campe, 1983.

Geizenhanslüke, R., 'Hefe oder Kristall, das ist hier die Frage!: Leander Haußmann und Sven Regener unterhalten sich über Herrn Lehmann, die Vorzüge des Flaschenbiers und die 80er-Jahre', *Der Tagespiegel*, 1 October 2003.

Glaesser, G.-J. (ed.), *Germany after Unification*, Amsterdam: Rodopi, 1996.

Glees, A., *The Stasi Files: East Germany's Secret Operations Against Britain*, London: Free Press, 2003.

'*Good Bye, Lenin!* Big Winner at German "Oscars"', *Guardian*, 9 June 2003.

Göttler, F., 'Der Renner: Auferstanden aus Ruinen- Kinokult um "*Good Bye, Lenin!*"', *Süddeutscher Zeitung*, 27 February 2003.

Grass, G., *Ein weites Feld*, Gottingen: Steidl, 1995.

—— 'Kurze Rede eines vaterlosen Gesellschaft', in *Günter Grass: Essays und Reden III 1980–997*, ed. by D. Hermes, Göttinghen, Steidl, 1997, pp. 230–4.

Greiffenhagen, M., and Greiffenhagen S., 'Zwei politische Kulturen', in

Deutschland Ost- Deutschland West: Eine Bilanz, ed. by H.G. Wehling, Opladen: Leske & Budrich, 2002, pp. 11–34.

Greiner, U., 'Die deutsche Gesinnungsästhetik. Noch einmal: Christa Wolf und der deutsche Literaturstreit. Eine Zwischenbilanz', *Die Zeit*, 2 November 1990.

Grix, J., 'East German Political Attitudes: Socialist Legacies v. Situational Factors: A False Antithesis', *German Politics*, 2(9) (2000)' 109–24.

——— *The Role of the Masses in the Collapse of the GDR*, Basingstoke: Macmillan, 2000.

Grix, J., and Cooke P., *East German Distinctiveness in a Unified Germany*, Birmingham: University of Birmingham Press, 2002.

Groebel, J. *Bericht zur Lage des Fernsehens*, Gütersloh: Verlag Bertelsmann Stiftung, 1995.

Grunenberg, A., *Antifaschismus – ein deutscher Mythos*, Reinbek: Rowohlt, 1993.

Haase, M., *Eine Frage der Aufklärung: Literatur und Staatssicherheit* in Romanen von Fritz Rudolf Fries, *Günter Grass und Wolfgang Hilbig*, Frankfurt/Main: Peter Lang, 2001.

Habermas, J., *A Berlin Republic: Writings on Germany*, trans. by S. Rendall, Cambridge: Polity, 1998.

Hake, S., *German National Cinema*, London: Routledge, 2002

Hall, S., 'Cultural Identity and Diaspora', in *Contemporary Postcolonial Theory: a Reader*, ed. P. Mongia, London: Arnold, 1997, pp. 110–21.

Hampel, T., 'Was wirklich bleibt: Wie Frau Scheibe, Trainerin in Kati Witts Eislaufverein, die DDR als Fernsehshow findet', *Der Tagesspiegel*, 5 September 2003.

Hanenberg, P., '»Ich«', *Die Politische Meinung*, 288 (1993), 90–1.

Harwig, I., 'Krankenhaus und Weltgeschichte: Die Anwendung des Ich auf die DDR: Wo Christa Wolf und Sascha Anderson sich treffen', *Frankfurter Rundsachau*, 15 June 2002.

Haußmann, L. (ed.), *Sonnenallee: Das Buch zum Farbfilm*, Berlin: Quadriga, 1999.

Haußmann, L., 'Es kam dicke genug', *Der Spiegel*, 8 September 2003.

Hensel, J., *Zonenkinder*, Reinbek: Rowohlt, 2002.

Henwood, F., Wyatt, S., Miller, N. and Senker, P., 'Critical perspectives on technologies, In/equalities and the information society', in *Technology and In/equality: Questioning the information society*, ed. S. Wyatt , F. Henwood, N Miller and P. Senker, London: Routledge, 2000, pp. 1–18.

Herf, J., Divided Memory: The Nazi Past in the Two Germanys Cambridge: Harvard, 1997.

Hilbig, W., *»Ich«*, Frankfurt/Main: S. Fischer, 1993.

——— *Abriß der Kritik*, Frankfurt/Main: S. Fischer, 1995.

——— *Preis- und Dankreden*, Rheinsberg: Kurt Tucholsky Gedankenstätte, 1996.

Hine, C., *Virtual Ethnography*, London: Sage, 2000.

Hoff, P., 'Der ultimative Ost-Zoo', *Neues Deutschland*, 25 August 2003.

Hogwood, P., 'After the GDR: Reconstructing Identity in Post-Communist Germany', *Journal of Communist Studies and Transition Politics*, 4(16) (2000), 45–67.

——— 'Identity in the former GDR: statements of "Ostalgia" and "*Ossi*" Pride in united Germany', *Globalization and National Identities: Crisis or Opportunity?*, ed. by C.J. Danks and P. Kennedy, Basingstoke: Macmillan, 2000, pp. 48–59.

Holmes, L., *Post-Communism: an Introduction*, Cambridge: Polity, 1997.

Hölscher, J., and Hochberg A. (eds.), *East Germany's Economic Development since Unification*, London: Macmillan, 1998.

Honnigfort, B., 'Modern und sparsam- und sämtlichen Kritikern ein Gräuel', *Frankfurter Rundschau*, 15 July 2000.

Horkheimer, M., and Adorno T.W., *Dialectic of Enlightenment*, trans. by John Cumming, New York: Continuum, 1989.

Hough, D., *The Fall and Rise of the PDS*, Birmingham: University of Birmingham Press, 2002.

Howard, M., 'An East German Ethnicity? Understanding the New Division of United Germany', *German Politics and Society*, 4(13) (1995), pp. 49–70.

Hugendubel, S., 'Ostagenturen auf dem Vormarsch', *Werben & Verkaufen*, 22, http://www.wuv.de/news/archiv/6/a12186/index.html, 1 June 2001.

Hugues, P., 'Auf der Suche nach der verlorenen Heimat', *Tagesspiegel*, 6 September 2003.

Humphreys, P. J., *Media and Media Policy in Germany: The Press and Broadcasting since 1945*, 2nd edition, Berg: Oxford, 1994.

Hurrelmann, K., *Jugend 2002. 14. Shell Jugendstudie*, Frankfurt/Main: Fischer, 2002.

'Immer mehr Ostdeutsche benutzen das Internet', *Heise Online*, www.heise.de/newsticker/meldung/ 45426, 18 March 2004.

Institut für angewandte Marketing- und Kommunikationsforschung, *Eikaufsverhalten im Lebensmitteleinzelhandel/Fokus Neue Bundesländer 2003*, Erfurt: IMK GmbH, 2003.

'Internet-Zensur in Deutschland', www.odem.org/informationsfreiheit.

'Interviencmit Hans-Hermann Tiedje', www.mdr.de/mdr-beultur/figaro/890308-hintergrund-894348.html.

Jäger, M., 'Das Loch in der Wand Objekt Autor', *Deutsches Allgemeines Sonntagsblatt*, 8 February 1991.

Jarausch, K.H., and Geyer, M., *The Shattered Past*, Princeton: Princeton University Press, 2002.

Jauer, M., 'Seid bereit? Immer bereit!', *Süddeutsche Zeitung*, 22 August 2003.

Jones, A., *The New Germany: A Human Geography*, Chichester: John Wiley, 1994.

Kane, M. (ed.), *Legacies and Identity: East and West German Literary Responses to Unification*, Oxford: Peter Lang, 2002.

Kane, M., 'Writing as Precarious Salvation: The Work of Wolfgang Hilbig', in *Contemporary German Writers, their Aesthetics and their Language*, ed. by A. Williams, S. Parkes and J. Preece, Bern: Peter Lang, 1996, pp. 71–82.

Kässens, W., and Tötenberg, M., 'Gizela Elsner', *KLG*, 2(1992), 1–12.

Kaufman, L., Gunn, J., Corman, R., *All I Need to Know About Filmmaking I Learned from the Toxic Avenger: The Shocking True Story of Troma Studios*, New York: Boulevard, 1998.

Keller, D., and Kirchner, M.,(eds), *Zwischen den Stühlen: Pro und Kontra SED*, Berlin: Dietz, 1993.

Klötzer, S., '(Sub)kultur und Staatssicherheit: Rainer Schedlinski', in *Im Widerstand/ Im Mißverständnis: Zur Literatur und Kunst des Prenzlauer Bergs*, ed. by C. Consetino and W. Müller, New York: Peter Lang, 1995, pp. 51–74.

Kolbe, U., *Hineingeboren: Gedichte 1975–1979*, Frankfurt/Main: Suhrkamp, 1982.

Kolinky, E. and Van der Will, W. (eds), *The Cambridge Companion to Modern German Culture*, Cambridge: CUP, 1998.

Kraft, T., 'An der Charmegrenze der Provokation – Thomas Brussigs Realsatire über 20 Jahre DDR-Geschichte: Helden wie wir', *Freitag*, 13 October 1995.

Kränzlin, A., 'Wie baut man sich seine DDR?', *Der Tagesspiegel*, 21 August 2003.

Küchenmeister, D., 'Linkssozialistisch oder ostdeutch? Die PDS am Scheideweg', *Deutschland Archiv*, 6 (2002), pp. 926–930.

Kuczynski, R., *Die Rache der Ostdeutschen*, Berlin: Parthas, 2002.

—— *Im Westen was Neues? Ostdeutsche auf dem Weg in die Normalitat*, Berlin: Parthas, 2003.

Kulick, H., 'Der Dorfpolizist von Prenzlauer Berg', Horch und Guck, 28 (1999), 1–39.

Kunze, R., *Deckname »Lyrik«: Eine Dokumentation*, Frankfurt/Main: S. Fischer, 1990.

—— *Wo Freiheit ist ... Gespräche 1977–1993*, Frankfurt/Main: S. Fischer, 1994.

218 • *Bibliography*

Kutter, A., 'Geschichtspolitische Ausgrenzungen in der Vereinigungspolitik. Das Beispiel der Enquete-Kommission', in *Die DDR war anders: eine kritische Würdigung ihrer sozialkulturellen Einrichtungen*, ed. by S. Bollinger and F. Vilmar, Berlin: Verlag Das Neue Berlin, 2002, pp. 25–59.

Lachmann, G., and Reuth, G.R., 'Die Stasi-Akten der Katarina Witt', *Die Welt am Sonntag*, 12 May 2002.

Landtag Mecklenburg-Vorpommern (ed.), *Leben in der DDR, Leben nach 1989*, Schwerin: Stiller & Balewski, 1995–8.

Leeder, K., *Breaking boundaries: a new generation of poets in the GDR*, Oxford: Clarendon, 1996.

Lejeune, P., *Le pacte autobiographique*, Paris: Seuil, 1975.

Lemke, C., *Die Ursachen des Umbruchs 1989: Politische Sozialization in der ehemaligen DDR*, Darmstadt: Opladen, 1991.

Lenin, V.I., *Imperialism, the Highest Stage of Capitalism*, Moscow: Foreign Languages Publishing House, 1947.

Lewis, A., 'Reading and Writing the Stasi File: On the Uses and Abuses of the File as (Auto)biography', *GLL*, 56 (2002), pp. 377–97.

——— *Die Kunst des Verrats: Der Prenzlauer Berg unddie Staatssicherheit*, Würzburg: Königshausen & Neumann, 2003.

Lischke-McNabe, U. and Hanson, K.S., 'Introduction: Recent German Film', *Seminar*, 4(33) (1997), pp. 283–9.

Lochte, J., and Schulz, W., *Schlingensief! Notruf für Deutschland: über die Mission, das Theater und die Welt des Christoph Schlingensief*, Hamburg: Rotbuch, 1996.

Loest, E., *Die Stasi war mein Eckermann*, Göttingen: Steidl Verlag, 1991.

Loomba, A., *Colonialism/Postcolonialism*, London: Routledge, 1998.

Maass, E., 'Und das ist geschehn: ein Betroffener über die Stasi-Mitarbeit von Sascha Anderson: Es war mehr als Freunesverrat', *Berliner Zeitung*, 25 July 2002.

Maaz, H.J., *Das gestürzte Volk*, Berlin: Argon Press, 1991.

Maaz, H.J., *Die Entrüstung: Deutschland Deutschland Stasi Schuld und Sündenbock*, Berlin: Argon, 1992.

Mangold, I., 'Ich ist ein Anerdson: Hinter mir gibt es kein Mysterium, es stehlt alles in den Akten: Wie Sascha A. in seiner Autobiografie verschwindet', *Süddeutsche Zeitung*, 2 March 2002.

Maron, M., *Pawels Briefe. Eine Familiengeschichte*, Frankfurt/Main: S. Fischer, 1999.

Martenstein, H., 'Schön war die Zeit', *Der Tagesspiegel*, 23 August 2003.

McAdams, A.J., *Judging the Past in Unified Germany*, Cambridge: CUP, 2001.

McFalls, L., 'Eastern Germany Transformed: From Postcommunist to Late Capitalist Political Culture', *German Politics and Society*, 2(17) (1999), pp. 1–24.

McLuhan, M., and Fiore, Q., *The Medium is the Message: An Inventory of Effects*, Harmondsworth: Penguin, 1967.

Meckel, M., 'Demokratische Selbstbestimmung als Prozeß: Die Aufgabe der Politik bei der Aufarbeitung der DDR-Vergangenheit', in *Die Partei hatte immer recht – Aufarbeitung von Geschichte und Folgen der SED-Diktatur*, ed. by B. Faulenbach, M. Meckel and H. Weber, Essen: Klartext, 1994, pp. 250–78.

Meier, C.S., *Dissolution: The Crisis of Communism and the End of East Germany*, Princeton: Princeton University Press, 1997.

Meinhardt, B., 'Dich muss man rütteln und schütteln! Katrin Saß in 'Good Bye Lenin!', und das unverhoffte Glück in einem Leben, das schon fast zu Ende war', *Süddeutscher Zeitung*, 12 April 2003.

Merkel, I., 'Sex and Gender in the Divided Germany: Approaches to History from a Cultural Point of View', in *The Divided Past: Rewriting Post-War German History*, ed. by C. Kleßmann, Oxford: Berg, 2001, pp. 91–104.

Mielke, A., 'Der Bundestag ist auch nur ein Mensch', *Die Welt*, 4 April 2003.

Miller, L., 'Women and children first: Gender and the settling of the electronic frontier', in *Resisting the Virtual Life: The Culture of Politics of Information*, ed. by J. Brook and I.A. Boal, San Francisco: City Lights, 1995, pp. 49–57.

Minkenberg, M., 'The Wall after the Wall', *Comparative Politics*, 26 (1993), pp. 81–103.

Mittenzwei, W., *Die Intellektuellen: Literatur und Politik in Ostdeutschland 1945–2000*, Berlin: Aufbau, 2003.

Modrow, H., Keller, D. and Wolf, H. (eds), *Ansichten zur Geschichte der DDR*, I–IV, Bonn/Berlin: PDS/Linke Liste im Bundestag, 1993–4.

Moles Kaupp, C., *Good Bye, Lenin! Film-Heft*, Berlin: Bundeszentrale für politische Bildung, 2003.

Moore-Gilbert, B., *Postcolonial Theory: Contexts, Practices, Politics*, London: Verso, 1997.

Mühlberg, F. and Schmidt, A. (eds), *Zonentalk*, Cologne: Böhlau, 2001.

Naughton, L., 'Wiedervereinigung als Siegergeschichte: Beobachtungen einer Australierin', in *Apropos: Film 2000*, Berlin: DEFA Stiftung, 2000, pp. 242–53.

—— *That Was the Wild East: Film Culture, Unification, and the 'New' Germany*, Ann Arbor: University of Michigan, 2002.

Negt, O. (ed.) *Der Fall Fonty: 'Ein weites Feld' von Günter Grass im Spiegel der Kritik*, Göttingen: Steidl, 1996.

Niven, B., 'The *Wende* and Self-Exclusion Theory', in *1949/ 1989 Cultural Perspectives on Division and Unity in East and West*, ed. by C. Flanagan and S. Taberner, Amerstdam: Rodopi, 2000, pp. 87–99.

——— *Facing the Nazi Past: United German and the Legacy of the Third Reich*, London: Routledge, 2002.

Noelle-Neumann, E., 'Eine Nation zu werden ist schwer', *FAZ*, 10 August 1994.

Noelle-Neumann, E. and Köcher, R., *Allensbacher Jahrbuch der Demoskopie*, Munich: K.G. Sauer, 2002.

Nolte, E., 'Die Vergangenheit, die nicht vergehen will', in *Historikerstreit: Die Dokumentation der Kontroverse um die Einzigartigkeit der nationalsozialistischen Judenvernichtung*, Piper: Munich, 1987, pp. 39–47.

Ó Dochartaigh, P., *Germany since 1945*, Basingstoke: Palgrave, 2004.

Osang, A., *Die Nachrichten*, Frankfurt/Main: S. Fischer, 2002.

Owen Smith, E., *The German Economy*, London: Routledge, 1994.

Pleitgen, F., 'Ich bin ostagisch: WDR-Indendant Fritz Pleitgen über Ost-Shows und Stasi-Überprüfungen im RBB', *Der Tagesspiegel*, 8 September 2003.

Plenschinski, H., *Ostsucht: eine Jugend im deutsch-deutschen Grenzland*, Munich: C.H. Beck, 1993.

Plowman, A., '"Westalgie" Nostalgia for the "Old" Federal Republic in Recent German Prose', *Seminar Special Issue: Beyond Ostalgie East and West German Identity in Contemporary German Culture*, ed. by D. Clarke and B. Niven, 40 (2004), pp. 249–61.

Pollack, D., 'Ostdeutsche Identität- ein multidimensionales Phänomen', in *Werte und nationale Identität im vereinten Deutschland: Erklärungsansätze der Umfrageforschung*, ed. by Heiner Meulemann, Opladen: Leske & Budrich, 1998, pp. 301–19.

Reid, J.H., *Writing without Taboos: The New East German Literature*, New York: Berg, 1990.

Reimann, E., *Die Schleife an Stalins Bart*, Hamburg: Hoffmann & Campe, 2002.

Rentschler, E. 'From New German Cinema to the Post-Wall Cinema of Consensus', in *Cinema and Nation*, ed. by M. Hjort and S. Mackenzie, London: Routledge, 2000, pp. 260–77.

Rheingold, H., *The Virtual Community: Homesteading on the Electronic Frontier*, Reading: Addison-Wesley, 1993.

Richter, W., 'Kolonialisierung der DDR', in *Mut zur Utopie*, ed. by F.

Vilmar, K.J. Scherer and U.C. Wasmuht, Münster, Agenda Verlag, 1994, pp. 98–100.

Rieger, K., '"Wir sind Ostimisten": Die Werbeagentur Fritzsch und Mackat macht spezielle Kampagnen für Ostdeutschland. Denn die Menschen dort sollen hören, dass sie auch etwas geschafft haben', *Die Zeit*, 4 November 1999.

Rinke, A., 'From Models to Misfits: Women in DEFA Films of the 1970s and 1980s', in *DEFA: East German Cinema, 1946–1992*, ed. by S.A. and J. Sandford, New York: Berghahn, 1999, pp. 183–203.

Röhler, O., 'Die übergroße Sehnsucht', *Die Tageszeitung*, 2 August 2001.

—— 'Ein freies Strömen der Gedanken', in *Die Unberührbare: Das Original Drehbuch*, Cologne: Kiepenheuer & Witsch, 2002, pp. 13–22.

Ross, C., *The East German Dictatorship: Problems and Perspectives in the Interpretation of the GDR*, London: Arnold, 2002.

Rotberg, R.I., and Thompson, D., *Truth v. Justice: The Morality of Truth Commissions*, Princeton: Princton University Press, 2000.

Roth, D., and Jung, M., 'Ablösung der Regierung vertagt: Eine Analyse der Bundestagswahl 2002', *Aus Politik und Zeitgeschichte*, B 49–50 (2002), 3–17.

Rusch, C., *Meine freie deutsche Jugend*, Frankfurt/Main: S. Fischer, 2003.

Said, E.W., *Orientalism: Western Conceptions of the Orient*, Harmondsworth: Penguin, 1991.

Sandford, J., 'The German Media', in *The New Germany: Social, Political and Cultural Challenges of Unification*, ed. by D. Lewis and J.R.P McKenzie, Exeter: University of Exeter Press, 1995, pp. 199–219.

Schädlich, H.J., *Tallhover*, Reinbek: Rowohlt, 1986.

—— (ed.) *Aktenkundig*, Berlin: Rowohlt, 1993.

Scheer, U., 'Die Maske hinter dem Gesicht', *Rheinischer Merkur*, 8 March 2002.

Scherstjanoi, V., *Operative Personenkontrolle »Futurist«*, first transmitted by SDR, 30 December 1996.

Schirrmacher, F., 'Abschied von der Literatur der Bundesrepublik', *FAZ*, 2 October 1990.

Schneider, J., 'Kinder, wisst ihr noch', *Süddeutsche Zeitung*, 13 July 2000.

Schneider, P., *Der Mauerspringer*, Reinbek: Rowholt, 1982.

Schönherr, A., *Ein Volk am Pranger?* Berlin: Aufbau, 1992.

Schulz-Ojala, J., 'Eins, zwei, drei', *Tagesspiegel*, 20 February 2003.

Schutheis, C. 'Das Kuriositätkabinett', *Berliner Zeitung*, 19 August 2003.

Schwartz, C. 'Das wahre Leben im falschen: GBL- Wolfgang Beckers komischer Wendefilm', *Neue Züricher Zeitung*, 17 March 2003.

—— 'Nachgetragene Liebe', *Neue Züricher Zeitung*, 29 December 2003.

Schwilk, H., 'Ensetzter Blick in den Spiegel. Aus den Akten des Staatsfeinds', *Rheinischer Merkur*, 4 January 1991.

Sharp, I., 'Male Privilege and Female Virtue: Gendered Representations of the Two Germanies', *New German Studies*, 1(18) (1995), pp. 87–106

Shohat, E., 'Notes on the "Post-Colonial"', *Social Text*, 10(2–3) (1992), pp. 99–113.

'Sie verlassen jetzt West-Berlin', *Spiegel Online*, www.spiegel.der/netzwelt/netzkutur/0,1518,160479,00.html, 2 October 2001.

Slevin, J., *The Internet and Society*, Cambridge: Polity, 2000.

Smith, G., *The Post-Soviet States: Mapping the Politics of Transition*, London: Arnold, 1999.

'SPD kannsich Koalitionspartner aussuchen', *Süddeutsche Zeitung*, 19 September 2004.

Staab, A., 'Testing the West: consumerism and national identity in eastern Germany', *German Politics*, 2(6) (1997), pp. 139–49.

—— *National Identity in Eastern Germany: Inner Unification or Continued Separation*, Westport: Praeger, 1998.

'Stasi-Killer Was weiß das Bundeskriminalamt wirklick', *Superillu*, 2 (9 October 2003), pp. 14–15.

'Stasi-Schatten uber Olympia', *Superillu*, 43, 16 October 2003, pp. 10–11.

Stecher, T., 'Sexy DDR', *Die Weltwoche*, 18 November 1999.

Superillu: Das Offizielle Magazin zur grossen RTL-Show, Sonderheft 1 (2003).

Taberner, S., 'Das Versprechen (The Promise)', in *European Cinema: an Introduction*, ed. by J. Forbes and S. Street, Basingstoke: Palgrave, 2000, pp. 157–68.

—— (ed.) *German Literature in the Age of Globalization*, Birmingham: University of Birmingham Press, 2004.

—— *German Literature of the 1990s and Beyond: Normalization and the Berlin Republic*, Rochester: Camden House, 2005.

Theurer, M., 'Die Einwicklerin Katarina Witt erinnert sich mit RTL an die alte DDR', *Süddeutsche Zeitung*, 3 September 2003.

Thierse, W., Spittmann-Rühle, I., Kuppe, J.L. (eds), *Zehn Jahre Deutsche Einheit: Eine Bilanz*, Opladen: Leske & Budrich, 2000.

Toteberg, M. (ed.), *Good Bye, Lenin! Ein Film von Wolfgang Becker*, Berlin: Schwarzkopf & Schwarzkopf, 2003, pp. 148–5.

'Traumhochzeit mit einer Geschiedenen', *Superillu*, 46, 6 November 2003, pp. 10–11.

Turkle, S., *Life on the Screen: Identity in the age of the Internet*, New York: Touchstone, 1995.

Veen, H.-J., '"Inner Unity" Back to the Community Myth? A Plea for a Basic Consensus', *German Politics*, 3(6) (1997), pp. 1–15.

—— 'Einheit, Einheit über alles: Das Gerede vom nötigen Zusammenwachsen Ost- und Westdeutschlands führt in die Irre', *Die Zeit*, 13 July 2001.

Venn, C., *Occidentalism Modernity and Subjectivity*, London: Sage, 2000.

Vinke, H. (ed.), *Akteneinsicht Christa Wolf: Zerspiegel und Dialog*, Hamburg: Luchterhand, 1993.

Von Becker, P., 'Hier riecht es nach Lysol', *Der Tagesspiegel*, 9 November 1999.

Von Plato, A., 'Eine zweite "Entnazifizierung": Zur Verarbeitung politischer Umwälzungen in Deutschland 1945 und 1989', in *Wendezeiten-Zeitenwände zur 'Entnazifizierung' und 'Entstalinisierung'*, ed. by R. Eckert, A. von Plato and J. Schütrumpf, Hamburg: Ergebnisse, 1991, pp. 7–31.

Walther, J., *Sicherungsbereich Literatur: Schriftsteller und Staatssicherheit in der Deutschen Demokratischen Republik*, Berlin: Ulstein, 1996.

'Welcome Back, Lenin!', *Spiegel Online*. www.spiegel.de/wirtschaft/0,1518,238037,00.html, 27 February 2003.

Wengierer, R., 'Vertracktes Leben', *Die Welt*, 21 December 1999.

Winter, S., 'Jadgfieber im Osten', *Der Spiegel*, 7 (2000), 114.

Wolf, C., *Was bleibt*, Frankfurt/Main: Luchterhand, 1990.

Wolle, S., *Die heile Welt der Diktatur: Alltag und Herrschaft in der DDR: 1971–1989*, Berlin: Ch. Links Verlag, 1998.

Yoder, J.A., 'Truth without Reconciliation: An Appraisal of the Enquete Commission on the SED Dictatorship in Germany', *German Politics*, 3(8) (1999), pp. 59–80.

Zeller, R., 'Hannelore Elsner: Die Wahnsinns-Frau', *Eurogay*, www.eurogay.de/artikel/0300/promi_elsner.html, 15 March 2000.

Zielcke, A., 'Die Kälteschock des Rechtsstaates', *FAZ*, 9 November 1991.

Filmography

Becker, Wolfgang, *Das Leben ist eine Baustelle* (1996).

—— *Good Bye, Lenin!* (2002).

Buck, Detlev, *Wir können auch anders* (1993).

Büld, Wolfgang and Reinhard Klooss, *Das war der wilde Osten* (1992).

Carow, Heiner, *Die Legende von Paul und Paula* (1973).

Dresen, Andreas, *Halbe Treppe* (2002).

—— *Nachtgestalten* (1999).

Fassbinder, Rainer Werner, *Die Sehnsucht der Veronika Voss* (1982).

—— *In einem Jahr mit 13 Monden* (1978).

Haußmann, Leander, *Herr Lehmann* (2003).

—— *Sonnenallee* (1999).

Kleinert, Andreas, *Verlorene Landschaft* (1992).

—— *Wege in die Nacht* (1999).

Kluge, Alexander Brustellin A., Cloos, H., Fassbinder, R.W., Mainka-Jellinghaus, B., Reitz, E., Rupe, K., Schloendorft, V., Schubert, P., Sinkel, B, *Deutschland im Herbst* (1978).

Mucha, Stanislaw, *Die Mitte* (2004).

O'Donnell, Damien, *East Is East* (1999)

Peterson, Sebastian, *Helden wie wir* (1999).

Roddam, Franc, *Quadrophenia* (1979).

Roehler, Oskar, *Die Unberührbare* (2000).

Schlingensief, Christoph, *100 Jahre Adolf Hitler* (1989).

—— *Das deutsche Kettensägermassaker* (1990).

—— *Terror 2000* (1992).

Schlöndorff, Volker, *Die Stille nach dem Schuß* (2000)

Thomas, Betty, *The Brady Bunch Movie* (1995).

Timm, Peter, *Go Trabi Go* (1991).

Tykwer, Tom, *Lola Rennt* (1998).

Von Trotta, Margarethe, *Das Versprechen* (1995).

Wenders, Wim, *Im Lauf der Zeit* (1976).
Wilder, Billy, *Sunset Boulevard* (1950).
Wortmann, Sönke, *Allein unter Frauen* (1991).
—— *Der bewegte Mann* (1994).

Select WWW Resources

Included here is a selection of Web sites referred to in this book, as well as some general WWW resources. References to specific Web articles are included in the main bibliography.

Aktion Wiederaufbau der Mauer, www.liquid2k.com/ddr
Berliner Mauer online, www.dailysoft.com/berlinwall/archive/index_de.htm
Berliner Mauer, userpage.chemie.fu-berlin.de/BIW/d_mauer.html
Berliner Mauer, www.berliner-mauer.de/
Das Interflug.net im WWW, www.interflug.net
DDR-Briefmarken, www.ddr-briefmarken.de
DDR-Geschichte.de, www.ddr-geschichte.de/
DDR-im-Web.de, www.ddr-im-web.de/index.asp
DDR-im-WWW, www.ddr-im-www.de/
DDR-Hörspiele.de, www.ddr-hoerspiele.de/hoerspielindex.html
DDR-Münzen, www.ddr-muenzen.de
DDR-Suche, www.ddr-suche.de/
DDR Webring, home.germany.net/rageville/de/ddrwebring.html
DDR-Zeitzeugen.de, www.ddr-zeitzeugen.de/NVA/Gruppendynamik/gruppendynamik.html
Der Mikrorechnerbausatz Z1013, www.nirvana.informatik.uni-halle.de/~ziermann/DE/z1013.html
Der-Jagdflieger.de, home.t-online.de/home/juergen.gruhl/
Die ultimative Z1013 Seite, z1013.purespace.de:
Die Witzige Seite des Lebens, jokes.notrix.net
Digitale Daten Republik, www.tf-home.de
Ebay, www.ebay.de.
Event und Touring AG, www.trabisafari.de
Friends Reunited, www.friendsreunited.co.uk

German Filmförderungsanstalt, www.ffa.de
Grenztruppen.de, www.grenztruppen.de
Grenzturm.de, www.grenzturm.info
Honecker.de, www.honecker.de/start2.html
H.T.'s Stasi-Infoseite, www.geocities.com/m_bakunin_de
Kaputistan.de, www.kaputistan.de
KC Club, www.iee.et.tu-dresden.de/~kc-club;
Knast in der DDR, www.belfalas.de/knast.htm
Knobi's Ostalgie Seiten, www.mknobi.de/ostalgie/
Kreutzschmer, people.freenet.de/kreutzschmer
Laputa, www.laputa.de
Lutz seine DDR-Homepage, www.old-gdr.de
Mondos Arts, www.mondosarts.de
Nierenspende.de, www.nierenspende.de
Offizielles Internetorgan der DDR-Staatsregierung im Exil, home.
    tonline.de/home/d_d_r/
Ossiladen.de, www.ossiladen.de
Ossi-Versand, www.ossiversand.de
Ostmetal, www.ostmetal.aeilke.de
Ostprodukte.de, www.ostprodukte.de
Ostwarenversand, www.ostwarenversand.de
Quotenmeter.de, www.quotenmeter.de/index.php?newsid=3040.
Rallyfahrer, home.t-online.de/home/Rallyfahrer/Formel1/rallye.htm
Rosengarten Dresden, www.rosengarten-dresden.de
Sad Girl, www.mrsunshine.de/sadgirl/ddr.htm;
Sonnenallee, www.sonnenallee.de
Stasiopfer.de, www.stasiopfer.de
Steffen Treptau, home.t-online.de/home/steffen.treptau
Trabant IG Unterfranken, members.aol.com/trabiigunterfr
Trabiseite.de, www.t-lino.de/trabifan
VEB Eisen- und Hüttenwerke (EHW) Thale, www.veb-ehw-thale.de.vu/
Zonentalk, www.zonentalk.de

Index